JOURNEY TO THE MOTHERLAND

OBSERVATIONS, STORIES, POETRY, TRAVEL GUIDE AND COLOR PHOTO GALLERY

JOHN WATUSI BRANCH

Power Of The Word Publishing Co.
(Jamaica, New York, 1999)

Cover Design by John Watusi Branch
Cover Layout by Venture Graphics

Photos by John Watusi Branch

Photos of Benin by Teddy Wilson

Other miscellaneous photos from various sources

Printed in the United States of America
S&S Graphics - New York, NY

Published and distributed by
Power of The Word Publishing Co.
a division of
Watusi Enterprise Unlimited
176-03 Jamaica Ave.
Jamaica, NY 11432-5503
Tel: (718) 523-3312 - Fax: (718) 523-1054
E-mail: Jwatusi@aol.com - Jwatusi@concentric.net
Visit the Afrikan Poetry Theatre Website:
http://www.afrikapoetrytheatre.com

Books by John Watusi Branch

"Getting' Down" *(1974)*

"A Story of Kwanza" *(1977)*

"Inner Voices" *(1982)*
Anthology of Poets of The Afrikan Poetry Theatre

"Christianity and African Traditional Beliefs" *(1991)*
Edited this series of lectures by Oseadeeyo Addo Dankwa III
Omanhene (Paramount Chief/King of Akuapem Traditional area of
Ghana), wrote the introduction, and published.

Recording

"Kuulula I Azania" *(1985)*
(Free South Africa)
With The Afrikan Poetry Theatre Ensemble

"Shaka Zulu Live" *(1987)*
With The Afrikan Poetry Theatre Ensemble

Videos

"Journey To The Motherland" *(1997)*

"Coming Full Circle" *1999*

To obtain copies of this and other books, videos, recordings, and to
book tours to Africa for individuals and groups, send all inquiries
and correspondence to:

Watusi Enterprise Unlimited
176-03 Jamaica Avenue
Jamaica, NY 11432-5505
E-mail: Jwatusi@aol.com – Jwatusi@concentric.net
or Call: (718) 523-3312 and Fax: (718) 523-1054

contents

Dedication: This book is dedicated to the Africans of the great ancient civilizations that gave birth and humanity to the world. To the millions of Africans that lost their lives and freedom in the East African Arab slave trade, the millions that perished in the middle passage of the European Atlantic African Holocaust and to those who struggled against all odds on the plantations of North, Central, South America, and the Caribbean. Finally this book is dedicated to the Africans of the twentieth century who struggled for independence and liberation in Africa and the Diaspora.

Acknowledgements:

Special Thanks to:

My wife Safiya, for allowing me the freedom of time and mind to travel and create. Asante Sana, Jeri jef, and Medase to my friends and extended family members on the African continent, Moustapha, Awa, Fallou, Balla, Kofi, Nafisatu, Kwabena, Emmanuel, Kojo, Hannah, Solo, Jabril, Omar Diallo and his family. Nana Boakeywe, Nana Dankwa, Victor and his sons, Garba Nying and his family, and to those countless Africans from the United States and the Caribbean who traveled with me over the years and shared in these 'Journeys'

"May We
as an African people
stand firm as a rock
grow tall as a tree
and blossom
like the flowers in Spring"

Foreword

Often we talk of culture as a way of life, a certain way of walk, a special kind of talk, smells, sounds, rhythms, variations of spices to universal foods, and sometimes new and different foods. Each culture becomes distinct in varying degrees, it is like putting on your own stamp, your own design, your own way of recognizing a people.

Africa for the most part has many vibrant and different expressions of life, the level of these various rhythms are deep and embedded in the life of the people. And we are talking about the vast majority of the people, not the few elite, western influenced and educated individuals one might meet in America and Europe, or perhaps when visiting African cities as tourists or business people.

When meeting these individuals that because of the difficult reality of African life becomes a hustler, devoid of or expressing low levels of African ethics. Or those that have acquired European cultural views and tries to emulate them, raises them to levels of worship in some cases. I am not talking about them. I am talking about the masses of Africans in the villages, towns and cities, who have carried on centuries of African culture and tradition for the most part, while adapting to the world's changing technology, yet not consuming all of the western culture that comes with it.

Sometimes we get certain impressions of African life from various sources of western media, and other times when we visit Africa. The masses in most cases in African countries have maintained their culture. One example of false impressions from the media and from those who visit Senegal, West Africa is that, 'Senegal is a French speaking country', in fact the official language of Senegal is French, and most of the people tourist or business people from the West might encounter speak French. But the reality is that only approximately 10% of the people of Senegal speak French!

The vast majority of the people of Senegal speak various regional languages with the Wolof language being the most widely spoken. But because these 10% who speak French come in contact with westerners in some form or fashion, it is perceived that this is a French speaking country, it fact the people of Senegal say so themselves. What we are saying here is that, to understand the true culture of Senegal or Africa as a whole is to experience the ways of the people. To begin to recognize these ways and expressions of life so that one can truly understand this exciting rhythmic and vibrant continent from another perspective. To began to analyze and recognize the uniqueness of continental African culture, at the same time viewing the world through western eyes. American views and values are not entirely bad, of course American culture is rapidly becoming the world wide model of a desired way of life, mainly because of the comfort and viability of technology and the advanced media that exposes it to the world.

It has been said by some French speaking continental Africans, that the French do not like Americans. This is probably mainly due to the competition of American culture and its attractiveness to modernity, compared to the suave and chic manifestations of French culture that has dominated the world's cultures. It has become a model of what has been projected as an example of Western civilization, with its art, literature, foods, fashion and language as a desired form of European civilization.

The United States of America is somewhat of a cultural stepchild in the eyes of French and British age old culture, and Italian and European Spanish culture to a lesser degree.

The things that really make Africa interesting to most visitors is its cultures, its history and its diversity. It is these diverse cultures that attract almost entirely all African American visitors to this continent, and the history that emerge out of these cultures.

Some Europeans also find great interest in the study and exploration of these varying cultures. However there is a very large number of Europeans who visit Africa not so much for its cultural diversity, but to soak up its always vibrant sun, enjoy its beaches, observe its organized wild life, in the form of Safari's, and unfortunately due to poverty encourage and engage in prostitution.

The poems, prose, stories and expressions in 'Journey To The Motherland' reflect on more than 30 years of this author's feeling the spirit of my ancestors, reading about Africa, meeting Africans, visiting Africa approximately 50 times and interacting with its people on different levels in varying degrees. Being able to analyze these experiences honestly with an understanding of Kawaida, the cultural philosophy of views and values, tradition and reason introduced to the African American community by Dr. Maulana Karenga and the organization Us in 1965. It is through Kawaida that I feel I have been able to develop my cultural Nationalism that I acquired in the 1960's, to an honest, comprehensive and productive level. I have been able to observe African culture from a fad, a fashion, a sometimes occasion to a way of life, meshed with where I am and might be in the 21st century.

I also feel that Africa is my mother and historically we know that she is the mother of all civilization. All human offspring have this attachment or love for their mother. It is a natural thing to love your mother, no matter if your mother may not have the same education as you do, understanding that education is measured today in appreciation of Western culture. No matter if your mother has not acquired the material wealth that you might have, or whether she is ill, not as strong as she used to be, you love her for what she is, your mother. For the African American person, Africa is our root, our source of ethics and values that systematically have been taken from us all along the middle passage and through centuries of slavery and oppression in this land many of us proudly call America, or the nations of the Caribbean.

It is my intention to encourage people in general, and African communities in the western world in particular, to get to know Africa in a broader way. Historically (a prerequisite), get to know its religions, its politics, educational systems, chieftaincy systems, its economic and business areas, its total culture.

We must understand the past very clearly, and study the contemporary and current state of affairs in the above mentioned areas. Visit Africa, open your eyes not only to its history but to all those previously mentioned areas, particularly to business. So that we can begin to look at how we are going to lift our mother up, make her strong again, so that all her offspring will be powerful and influential in the world's affairs.

The Blues came out of the spirituals, the slave songs, that feeling that clutches at your stomach and fills your heart, that feeling that touches your soul, you know that deep hurt and that longing.

The Africans then who were slaves, their souls cried out to God to save them from the horrible, the terrible, inhumane system that started at places like Goree Island, Elmina and Cape Coast Dungeons, and continued on the middle passage, and the plantation, the organized system of chattel slavery.

In the evenings, in their shanties, all tired and sore from working long hard hours in the blistering sun, some of them sore from the open infested wounds on their backs from the whip lash. Huddled in their shanties crying out for their motherland, where their lives made sense, had meaning, the difficulties, but the accomplishments, the joys and tribulations as is said, but now this madness, this terror, this torture.

They longed for their motherland, the first generation and continuing generations until today. That feeling that longing remains in the souls of many Africans who live in the western world. With some it lay dormant, others it was always there and at the forefront of their lives.

The idea is to go the full cycle, the total 360 degrees, go to Africa and bring your more than 400 years of developmental experiences with you. Did you not play a dominant part in building the most affluent society in the world? Go and build up your motherland, make her strong so that Africa and her people can step back on the stage of human history as a free, proud and productive people. Go to Africa, not with a chauvinistic American attitude that you are superior to all other nations and cultures, that everything must be viewed and measured by the standards that have been projected as ideal "Americanism". This is also directed to those Afro-centric African Americans who discover how American they really are when they find themselves in various countries in the world. Go with an open mind, and go Black people in South America, the Caribbean, Canada and elsewhere outside of Africa. Go with the reality of reconnecting to a land base, history and the many cultures of Africa. And finally go with the respect in mind that Africa is not only the mother of her sons and daughters of darker hue in the Diaspora, but in fact she is the mother of all civilization.

I welcome you to 'Journey To The Motherland' through these pages and in reality to plan to visit Africa in the near future.

For the uninspired, it will be one of the most exciting and rewarding times in your life, and your most memorable vacation.

For those who feel they cannot afford to go, plan and it will not take long.

- **John Watusi Branch**
March 9, 1996

Part 1
"Pre-Africa....Or In the Spirit"

With the fact of mankind starting in Africa, we must understand that this continent is a very special place. No matter the origin of its name, it never really had a name, there were many names of many places, nation states and empires. There were words to describe the land or the people, Alkebuland "Land of the Blacks" Nubia, etc. This continent is called the "cradle of Civilization" that is to say that this continent gave birth to human kind, gave rise to its development, with the introduction of consolidation, philosophy, ethics, science, writing, mathematics, medicine, etc.

It is where simple forms were developed into civilized empires and were introduced to the world. Africa has a special place in the history of the world's major religions, which for the most part have their mythology and legends in the history and stories of Africa. And that her mineral riches, her gold, platinum, diamonds, her rubber, her cocoa, her oil and countless other minerals and natural resources have advanced Europe over the centuries, while Africa was retarded.

Of course we realize that the world's leader, the richest and most powerful country in the world, the United States of America is so because of 250 years of free labor and extracting the genius, brilliant ideas and cultural contributions from millions of Africa's sons and daughters. This is so significant that it can not be easily erased.

There is a special energy, a special rhythm, a constant beat, sometimes faltering, sometimes strong, sometimes very faint, but a constant beat that was always there through extremely difficult times. The slave dungeons, castles and slave making houses of West Africa, the incredibly horrible great odds against survival middle passage; the cold, hard and systematic slave plantation organizations which were the center of the making of America.

With cruelty and inhumanity as a lesson in the study of not a short burst of genocide of a madman, but almost four centuries (400 hundred years!!) of the destruction of countless African cultures and the creation of a slave

1

class, a class designed to serve white masters. Creating a society of thoughts, ideas and practices that always made it clear that Black people were less than human, not quite civilized. Black people were put in a category between animals and white people. This attitude of course still prevail today, which is the basis for the lack of advancement of Black people, which given its natural evolution would have created another African empire in North America. But an ethical empire, an empire guided by values that produces morality. For thousands of years this was the world's reality, the last 500 years of course going another way.

In spite of all this oppressive history, the rhythm, the beat continues through the veins of many African people in the west. Africa's soul was always in the drum beat, a constant reminder to several of us that we are African, and that it is great being African, wonderful, that you could have peace with the creator that you were not without sin, but had not ravaged the world. It is this soul that is in all African people that sometimes has to be cultivated in most, with others it is a spiritual awakening. It awoke in the African revolutionaries in the slave plantation system, Denmark Vesey, Gabriel Prosser, Nat Turner, Harriet Tubman, Sojourner Truth, Martin Delaney, Frederick Douglas and countless other brothers and sisters, martyrs who resisted! Who fought, organized, plotted and planned a way to freedom! It was in Garvey, this rhythm, this beat this pulsating soul of Africa that opened his eyes and his voice demanded to know "Where is the Black mans government? Where is his army and navy and men and women of important affairs?"

This rhythm, this beat, this African soul spirit told Garvey "At one time you were great, what has happened? There was a scene in Alex Haley's controversial "Roots", where Kunta Kinte encounters a reluctance of most of his fellow Africans enslaved on the plantations over a few generations, to discuss escape and a return to Africa. He asks a fellow enslaved and conscious African "What has happened to our people? What has happened to them?"

This rhythm, this beat has entered many of Africa's sons and daughters, the Honorable Elijah Muhammad, Malcolm X, Fanny Lou Hamer, Ida B. Wells, Martin Luther King Jr., Mary McCloud Bethune, Dr. Maulana Karenga, Min. Louis Farrakhan, Kwame Ture, Dr. John Henrik Clarke, Dr. Yosef-ben Jochannan and many others.

This rhythm, this beat, this African spirit has been the center of my being for more than 35 conscious years, and before that in the unconscious years it was there waiting to be nurtured. Didn't Aunt Lillie say "That boy is going to be a preacher or somethin" It was no more than my African soul

2

beginning to stir.

My grandfather, better known to the community of Charleston, South Carolina during that period of time as "Papa Fritz" Fritz Branch came from the Island of Barbados bringing with him the genius of thousands of years of high African civilization.

He began to make an impact on Charleston with his fishing boat the "Maude" and other businesses, he became a man of great influence.

It was said by one of my uncles that only the Mayor of Charleston and Papa Fritz, owned one of the hot automobile items at that time "The Pierce Arrow". The generation of business men and influential people in the African American community of Charleston my father's age, told me years ago of how Papa Fritz had helped them, had guided them. Politicians, businesses owners, and ministers, told of how he had encouraged them.

You see I come from that stock, that African who was dropped off in Barbados, grew and developed in America, and helped in the restoration of African people. That stubborn and mean West Indian, that strong and determined African.

As the chains of slavery were broken for Africans in the West, our chain and link to Mother Africa must never be broken.

Randy Weston, the great African American Jazz pianist and griot, at a tribute the Afrikan Poetry Theatre had for him in January of 1999, said of Africa, "Africa the beautiful continent, that I love so much"

Images

If You white, You right
If you yellow, you mellow
If you brown, stick around
If You Black, stay back, way back

Back in the memories of my young mind
shy little Black boy uncertain of his image
because images of Tarzan and white folks
in power positions and television images of
lily whites and buffoonery Blacks
swing before his young eyes
They say he had a walk on him
a deacon or preacher's walk

3

That, I own the whole damn block walk
but those images of Tarzan
and Amos and Andy
and brutal white cops
and Klu Klux Klan terrorism
would clash with those rapidly rising
visions of African royalty and greatness
those Nana's and Oba's and Calipha's
Yes, the cultural and political battle was on Jack!
and out of the 60's the fight became intensified
Kujichagulia came forth with a ferocity
with Garvey's voice bellowing in our ears
"Up You mighty people
you can accomplish what you will"
Malcolm X became the war counselor of the
 Chaplains and we gathered our information
removed the cobwebs from our minds
and organized ourselves and our approaches
to the struggle for restoration of our
traditional dignity and power, and to up the
ante on African life and the struggle against
"If you Black stay back, way back

The 1960's we often hear of as being an explosive period, it was. Many important things were happening to African people in the United States, Africa and the Caribbean during the 60's.

Major changes were taking place and if your African soul was starting to grow and develop, then the energy of the times would make it explode! Its development certainly excelled through the 60's. The African soul during this period had an opportunity to implant itself firmly in me and settled itself down to began the slow but steady climb up the ladder to hopefully reach where African people were at one time in the history of the world.

As Dr. Maulana Karenga states in the 5th principle of the Nguzo saba 'Nia' "To make as our collective vocation the building and developing of our communities in order to restore our people to their traditional greatness" What is this traditional greatness that we should return to? It is a time in history when African people were looked upon with great respect.

Dr. Maulana Karenga is professor and chair of the Department of Black Studies at California State University, Long Beach and the Chair of the Organization Us and the National Association of Kawaida Organizations (NAKO). He is the creator of Kwanzaa and The Nguzo Saba (The Seven Principles) and author of numerous books including, *Selections from the Husia: Sacred Wisdom of Ancient Egypt, Kwanzaa: A Celebration of Family Community and Culture, and Odu' Ifa': The Ethical Teachings*

Dr. Maulana Karenga

People from other cultures, nations and races came to study at our universities and temples, did research in our libraries, traded and connived for our rich spices and cloth, benefited from our knowledge of medicine and marveled at our understanding of the universe, the stars and the planets. They listened and took notes on our explanations of love, war, peace, death, marriage, family and god. What has happened to that respect that African/Black folks are now looked down upon by so many people? Europeans (white people) as a result of slavery and colonization of the African continent have created an image of African people as intellectually inferior, unable to organize and manage governments, companies, and structure. Other races have picked this up also. We are looked at as niggers, which means nothing, what is being said is African people are a nothing people, niggers! nobody cares about a nigger!

The return to greatness means that African people must control and develop our businesses, our institutions, build powerful and productive systems and become leaders of ourselves.

The poet Askia Toure suggested a decline of the African race in his book titled "From The Pyramids To The Projects" and we must begin the climb back to the Pyramids.

This vision is very difficult for most to see unless your African soul /spirit has been awakened.

We awoke and started moving on the path to restoration, This path after more than 20 years would lead me back to my mother, Africa. It was a perilous path, one with many dangers, but a one way path, an ascending path on my 'Journey To The Motherland.

The Rise And Fall Of The Fort Green Chaplins

Lolly Lolly Ding Dong!
We are the Chaplins!
The Mighty Chaplins!
Lolly Lolly Ding Dong!
We are the Chaplins
The Mighty Chaplins
Lolly Lolly Ding Dong!

In Nineteen hundred and fifty five
When the Mighty chaplins
had just arrived
On the corner drinking their wine
Kicking down doors
Poppin' those girls
And calling them whores
Lolly Lolly Ding Dong !
We are the Chaplins !
The Mighty Chaplins!
Lolly Lolly Ding Dong

I mean we were like cooooooooooooooool man!
You dig ?
Baaaaaaaaaaaaaaaaaad Jack!
Ya know ?
Rich warm brotherhood was our base
for collective might
Why when we rolled on Coney
we were dressed down in Black 'n' White
Black caps throwing dark shadows
on starched white China boy shirts
tucked into pressed Black
belt in the back chinos
resting on top freshly polished white bucks
Man we were quick of lip
and hip of gait
we carried mean sharp razors
and called them 'straits'

we were players
dressed in the best
tailor made suits
Wing tips
Split Toes/Kangaroos
and our hair processed
we were cool cats
nobody messed with us
I mean we were like a tribe
a nation!
We had our leaders/our laws
we were blind and ignorant
but to us we had a cause
believe in the Chaplins empire
defend its honor
and fight for its principles
we protected the community
the turf
hey jack!
If you messed with somebody's momma's bag!
Molested a brothers sister!
Jack you would have an army on your ass!
Rolling all the way cross town
armed to the teeth!
Sawed off shot guns/knives
Zip guns/razors & car antennas
going down!
Lolly Lolly Ding Dong!
we are the Chaplins!
the Mighty Chaplins!
Chaplins like a motherfucker Jim!!
The Chaplins are here motherfuckers!!!
If you didn't belong and had some sense
you'd stay out of our turf
the Fort Greene projects
where the Chaplins gave birth
we didn't break into nobody's house
we were like Robin Hood
stole from the rich

and sold to the poor
and we were entertainers
we sang those coooool smooth
Rhythm 'N' Blues
they called it Rock 'N' Roll
but it was really the urban bop
and it wasn't until years later
that we heard of Do-wop
"The closer you are" Ooohooooooooohoooooooo
"The brighter the stars in the skyyyyyayayay"
and then from the wine
to the nickel bag
to the scagg
sinking into a world of
bottomless weight
nose running
head swelling
getting heavier
eyes/lips
absorbing the intimacy
of time and space
slipping from the rat race
sinking deeper into the mire
that was designed to be produced
sinking and sliding
down waves pounding
your eardrums
drowning out relevant sounds
trying to throw you a lifeline
slipping deeper
not hearing Malcolm's voice
as it spits fire!
hot tongue lashes of Black consciousness
screaming out to you!
to raise yourself up
but you slip deeper & deeper & deeper & deeper
& deeper not hearing his words
deeper into a Doogie dream
as your lips laboriously form the words

Lolly Lolly Ding Dong
we are the Chaplins
the Mighty Chaplins
Lolly Lolly Ding Dong.............

(1981)

The 1970's brought more involvement with cultural institutions for me
and I became more rooted in manifestations of African culture.
I became involved with cultural institutions such as The East, various literary organizations and institutions (Poet-tential Unlimited Poetry Theatre,
and Afrikan Functional Theatre) and subsequently the founding of The
Center For Culture, The Afrikan Poetry Theatre in 1976.

Creativity/Kuumba (Swahili language)

Create create create
what you wannna create?
create a language
a slave dialect
as you toil in the sun
as day turns to night
as night turns into painful
and pleasurable screams
the agony of watching
create a dance
you know ya'll can dance
as the wind rips through your bodysoul
whispering the rhythms of ancient Africa
create, sing
create the wail of a sister in trouble
the regrets of a do wrong man
and the sorrows of a people
a whip lashed down trodden people
create the blues
create the styles
select the colors
you know ya'll a colorful people

create a system
a philosophy
a play
a machine
a feeling
a love for self
create a baby
never stop
never fail
never end creation
because creation is the beginning
so let's begin to create
create
create
create
create
create
our souls are overflowing
about to burst with new ideas
feelings, thoughts and actions
so let's give of ourselves
let's give ourselves to each other
to ourselves
that we may know of each other
that we may know of ourselves
create
create
create
Kuumba, create, Kuumba, create

-1971

Part 2
The Maiden Voyage

The Journey To The Motherland was drawing nearer, the drum was calling me home. The preparation however was not complete, the time had not yet arrived. In either late 1980 or early 1981, Sonny Carson, long time Brooklyn activist had asked myself and many other Black activists and community leaders to travel to Liberia. Sonny was invited by the Liberian government and Sergeant Samuel Doe, who overthrew the Tubman government in a coup d' etat to come to Liberia and bring Africans in the Diaspora with him to see how they could contribute to the development of Liberia. Unfortunately I was unable to travel at that time and would not get another opportunity to do so until 1984.

The preparation for my first trip to Africa started out pretty mundane, practical planning, trying to scrape up the money, documents and such. It was not until the time was drawing nearer to departure that the realization that I was preparing to go to Africa really hit me. My Africa, the Africa that I wrote so passionately about as a poet and short story writer in two previously published books, "Gettin Down" an anthology of poems published by The East Publishing company in 1974 and "A Story Of Kwanzaa" in 1977. My Africa that I sang and blew powerful words and descriptions of with my Jazz and poetry band, an Africa I never saw, but an Africa that burned in my soul. I was going home.

The flight across the Atlantic was long, 3,812 air miles, but the excitement was high. We ate and slept and drank and talked, and the time approximately 7 hours had elapsed. Senegal, the closest point in Africa to North America, it is why Goree Island, the slave making and transport dungeon became strategic in the infamous, terrible, horror filled slave trade/holocaust. Senegal is called the gateway to West Africa, it is most often the first stop when visiting West Africa. When the big DC 10 Air Afrique jet wheels touched the tarmac, touched Africa, the applause was strong, an applause for some for a safe landing, and for others a safe return home.

SENEGAL

Located in Western Africa, bordering the North Atlantic Ocean, between Guinea-Bissau and Mauritania.

Area; 196,190 sq Km - slightly smaller than South Dakota

Climate: tropical; hot, humid; rainy season (May to November) dry season (December to April) low rolling plains to rising foothills in the Southeast.

Population: 9,500,000 -(July 1997 est.)

Ethnic groups: Wolof 36%, Fulani 17%, Serer 17%, Toucouleur 9%, Diola 9%, Mandinka 9%, European and Lebanese 1%, other 2%
Languages: French (official), Wolof, Pulaar, Diola, Mandinka

Independence: April 4, 1960
Exports: Fish, ground nuts (peanuts), petroleum products, cotton.

Currency: CFA, value is approximately 615cfa = $1

-Internet and other sources (print materials)

Teranga (Welcome)

Senegal is a land of variation with dry Savannah in the northern part and dense forest in the southern Casamace area. In the northern part the city of Saint-Louis was the capital of the French colonial empire in West Africa. In 1907 Dakar became the new capital of the French colonial administration. Senegal is a very interesting country, it has three main component populations, the African being the vast majority, but it also has a sizable French and Lebanese population that has a distinctly different lifestyle, and socio-economic political views and structures. The African population however is my main focus and concern in these observations and we will primarily report on them with any observations of French and Lebanese as they relate to the indigenous people of this and all countries that are subjects of this report. 92% of the African population of Senegal are Muslim, their religion is Islam, but their culture is African. They have not put their religion in the closet, but their culture is at the center of their lives. 6% are practicing their traditional beliefs and are called Anamists, and the remaining 2% are Christian.

Senegal is home to the late great scientist, Egyptologist and historian Cheikh Anta Diop. Cheikh Anta Diop was born in the town of Diourbel, in western Senegal. He was of a Muslim peasant family and attended Koranic schools. He was of the Brotherhood of the Mouride sect founded by the great Muslim leader and anti-colonialist Cheikh Ahmadou Bamba Mbacke.

Diop completed his bachelor's degree in Senegal and then went on to Paris in 1946 to do his graduate studies. To earn his doctorate, he presented a lengthy and closely argued dissertation on ancient Egyptian history. The main lines of his thesis may be summarized and simplified thus: That Egypt was the node and center of a vast web linking the strands of Africa's main cultures and languages; that the light that crystallized at the center of this early world, had been energized by the cultural electricity streaming from the heartland of Africa; that the creators of classical Egyptian civilization, therefore were not the brown Mediterranean Caucasoids, nor the the equally mythical Hamites, nor the Asiatic nomads and invaders, but indigenous, black skinned, wooly-haired Africans. Diop's thesis was not entirely new, others had stated this before. What was new was the formidable competency in many disciplines that he brought to bear to establish this thesis on solid, scientific foundations. Although it was rejected by the University of Paris, it was published in 1955 under the title of *"Black*

Nations and Culture", earning its author international recognition. It took him Ten years and two more doctoral dissertations, both of which were revolutionary in perspective, before he was granted the doctorate.

These dissertations were published as *"The Cultural Unity of Africa"* (1959) and *"Pre-Colonial Black Africa"* (1960)

He became one of the very few Africans with access to the most advanced body of scientific knowledge, at a time when only a handful of people in the world understood Einstein's relativity Theory, Diop translated a major portion of it into Wolof, the language of his people. His greatest strength, perhaps lay in linguistics. Assisted by the Congolese Egyptologist and linguist Theophile Obenga, Diop established at the UNESCO conference on "The Peopling of Ancient Egypt" (January 1974) that the Egyptian language was African and that it was genetically related to a family of African languages, including his own native Wolof .

Cheikh Anta Diop however , was not merely fighting battles on the intellectual front. He realized that his new conception of history could provide a ground for unity and continuity on the African continent, forging new and powerful political forces to transcend the instability and fragmentation, the lack of real pride and faith and a sense of a collective destiny in modern Africa. Diop was deeply disturbed by this grave instability of modern Africa, he became politically active and founded the *Block of the Masses of Senegal,* a militant political party in 1960. The party was banned and he was arrested and imprisoned. He founded a second political party in 1964, *The Senegalese National Front.* This was declared illegal and he was again arrested. He founded a third political party, the *National Democratic Rally,* in 1976.

Diop was no armchair theorist. He worked furiously to build the Radiocarbon laboratory at IFAN in Dakar. This was established in 1966 for the purpose of low energy radioactivity research and carbon - 14 dating. He led the struggle for the formation of an African technology consortium.

The African Origin of Civilization: Myth or Reality? Was another one of his great works, and his last monumental work was *Civilization or Barbarism: An Authentic Anthropology.* This was translated into English by Yaa Lenghi Ngemi from Zaire/Congo.

(From "Great African Thinkers" edited by Ivan Van Sertima, co-editor Larry Williams - Journal of African Civilizations 1986)

Cheikh Anta Diop

I was deeply impressed by this African giant, this model of African intellectualism, of African genius. Here was an African that was confident, able to stand up to the best of European minds and declare through scientific proof and grounding that the African gave birth to civilization and human development. This same African that is looked down upon today, that is spat upon, treated as niggers, and considered as inherently inferior. And yes he fought the political battle and the cultural battle in Senegal for the control of the African's land and mind. He argued and struggled with Leopold Senghor the first president of Senegal, over the political direction of the country immediately after independence from the French. Senghor, the poet and one of the articulators of 'Negritude' was a strong supporter of the Francophone West African structure.

One major argument was over what would be the official and national language of Senegal. Senghor opted for French the language of the former colonial masters, Diop wanted Wolof to be the national language. During Diop's involvement with his political party and his run for political office he campaigned on radio, speaking in the Wolof language, in which he was able to reach the masses of the Senegalese people. Understanding that the masses of the people were able to understand him, whereas only a small minority spoke French. Diop was banned from speaking on the radio after this. According to Saido Diallo and other young lions of the remnants of his political party, Diop was very popular with the masses, but lost some of his popularity because of his marriage to a white woman. I have to seriously question this relationship, particularly when it involves a person who has dedicated his life to revealing the truth of the origin of race, and who has fought to restore the African to his rightful place in history. One who has researched and analyzed the barbaric beginnings of the European, and has revealed the 'law of percentage', where he talks about the European becoming hostile when the numbers of the population of Blacks within his midst reaches a certain percentage.

There often seems to be this contradiction among the educated African elite, who have struggled for independence from the European colonialists, this marrying of their women. However in spite of this seemingly contradiction Cheikh Anta Diop remains in my mind and in the minds of most Africans, a giant of the twentieth century.

My most proudest moment in Senegal was on my first visit in 1984 when I was able to meet this great man. I was part of a group, along with my traveling partner Bill Dyer led by Tshaka Tonge and his wife. Tshaka arranged for a two hour meeting with the great scientist, where we would meet in his laboratory at IFAN, located at the University of Dakar (since renamed Cheik Anta Diop University) This was a most memorable occasion that will live with me forever. We were all impressed with all of the test tubes and artifacts, and the aura of this icon and this fascinating laboratory. We had an interesting discussion with Diop, while he does speak English, he asked that he be allowed to speak in French so that he could be as articulate as possible in this important visit with his brothers and sisters from America. We had an excellent young Senegalese student, a friend of Tshaka and his family to translate the words of Diop into English for us, and to translate our questions and his answers during this discussion. During our visit Diop showed us some specimens where he had encased some evidence of the racial origin of some mummies, where he had scraped some 'skin' from a mummy to test the melanin content to establish the racial identity. He also told us that there was an African American woman working with him, doing some research, and that her name was Rhkty Wimbly, who would become one of the leading teachers of the ancient Khemitic language called Medu Neter, in the U.S.

Being in the presence of this great man in this historical and important place was a very special occasion for all of us 17 proud Africans from the west.

Cheikh Anta Diop
and
John Watusi Branch

16

Dakar is the capital of Senegal, some what northerly and is a seaport with one of the world's finest harbors, most people in this area and to the far north are Muslim, in the south which is on the other side of The Gambia, is the Casamace area of Senegal. This area is primarily Anamist, the traditional African beliefs, this is where you find African culture in its purest form. The life style, the language, the ability to master discipline exhibited in their acrobatics, combined with dance and drums, and their flutes and percussion.

The Casamace area has The Gambia between itself and the rest of Senegal, this separation has caused much unrest in the south due to few services and resources and less support from the more affluent central government based in Dakar, the capital. This division was caused by the Europeans, and how they divided Africa during the colonial period. The British wanted a certain area of SeneGambia for their own exploitative reasons, mainly the access to the waterways, and colonized a small part that cuts into Senegal like a knife. This caused friction and confusion between the north and south of Senegal and The Gambia, which speaks English and Senegal speaking French. Of course with their indigenous languages such as Wolof, Mandinka, and several others, the culture did not completely change, in fact many people in Senegal and The Gambia are related, particularly the Wolof. However rivalries and hostilities developed between The Gambia and Senegal and between the southern area of Senegal, the Casamace, and the northerly area of Senegal. Both Gambian and Senegalese complain of each other being thieves and not to be trusted. This division of the African family, the Wolof, Sierra, Mandinka, Diola, Fulani and others is directly caused by the colonization of these places. The Europeans caused many fundamental problems in the culture of African people.

However there is hope, because in spite of the European languages, its versions of religions, the SeneGambia culture has been strong enough to hold the people close enough to its base, its roots, its soul and its strength. They have their distinct way of expressing themselves, their caftans and grand buba's and lovely flowing garments have a special and distinct flair. Their women are blue/black regal stepping, smooth skin, intricate braids and exotic beauty. Their men are grand buba down, tall strong handsome cats. Their children sliver sharp, deep shades of Black smiling faces in a sea of happiness. The children in the towns and villages are seemingly always happy, always warm, and so likable.

The children in the cities are very sharp, survival is at the center of their activities from sun up to sun down when the lorries began to load up and leave the city. Every minute is involved in making money to share with their families. But that is life in Dakar, every one is selling something, there is a vibrant hustle in the air, in the heart of the city where commerce is everywhere. However on close examination it becomes clear that the stores and shops, the boutiques, the clearly established and apparently prosperous businesses are owned not by the Senegalese, the Africans, but are owned by French and Lebanese people, who exploit the African.

The Africans, custodians of the land, who is all you see in the crowded sea of shoppers, a colorful sea of African cloth and urban African rhythm, on the other hand is in the open market, on the street, in stalls and make shift cubicles.

The visitor to Senegal find these marketplaces exciting, and they are, but why can't we see the African in the store more often, this is an African country.

This is of course evidence of the neo-colonialism that still remain in Senegal and most of Africa. The economics are like the period of colonialism when there was total domination of the African's country, they didn't control their own economics then and don't now. This situation is at least surprising when so many African people in the Diaspora think of Africa as a place where Black people have their own country and are visibly running their governments.

Dakar is considered a cosmopolitan fast paced city with a lot of game, a lot of hustle, with numerous con games, sly pickpockets and overly aggressive sellers. When walking the streets a Senegalese brother might walk up to you and say. "You look just like my sister or brother, welcome to Senegal, you black like me" In most cases this can be a genuine expression of friendship, at other times be careful because it could be a con artist or pick pocket setting you up. One line that is often used is "I want to give you a present as a token of friendship" and gives you a brass bracelet or a leather type necklace that is sometimes mentioned as something that will protect you from all harm. Of course the next thing that happens is that the person is asking you to give something in return to show your friendship.

Not knowing what to give it is suggested that perhaps you can give the person your watch as a symbol of friendship, or perhaps $5 or $10 dollars. In actuality what you have done is buy the item that they have given you under the pretense of a gift, or you have given up a real valuable item of yours for a very inexpensive item. This behavior is not typical of Senegalese, most Senegalese that you meet are friendly and helpful and sincere about being happy to see you and share their country with you.

However Dakar is just another New York, Chicago, L.A. and other big Black urban madness, but it moves with an African rhythm, a Nubian flair. Of course Dakar is not all of Senegal the rest of the country's population is 15 times that of Dakar, with Dakar being approximately 600,000. We will visit a few other areas in Senegal in the continuation of our journey.

Dakar

Dakar, your air filled with residue of decay
clouds of pollution from your open sewers
& uncollected garbage
and your ebony Black super smooth
elegantly dressed women
and your beautiful, bright eyed
sliver sharp children
Dakar, African metropolis
dying in French cultural decadence
denying your own preservation
and will to survive
you bleed and hustle and break the hearts of your
brothers and sisters
you must see the reflection of your ways
Dakar, holder of our history
Goree Island
the middle passage
a memorial etched in our blood
a symbol of a never ending will to always be
masters of ourselves
you are a bridge, a link of past and present
a griots' song
a elders' tale
thousands of hands outstretched with open palms
of needs and wants
strong hands, Ebony smooth Blue/Black hands, gnarled and
broken & cripple & twisted hands
surround you & pull at you & tug you & follow you
and is always there

and Ms Africa be steppin', struttin' very regally
emanating rays of rich warm sun people rainbow colors
brothers be bad be super cool be big chill be the king
& me be Grand Buba down be an Oba a master of
yourself be a scientist & reach for the stars
Dakar, with your echoes of Marley
and your Afro beat/Latin funky kind of thing
you be jammin' to and even your chic more French than the
French including Mercedes & Benson & Hedges
type of Africans
your market place be hummin
your pool lounge luxurious hotels filled with
still yet more tourists
more money/more hustle/more bargaining/more
purchasing/more spreading the wealth/more full
little Black bellies/ more survival
"Too big" "Very Small" "Last price" "Merci"
"Jeri-Jef"
The language, the soul of a people!
You gotta get down, You gotta rap the rap
you gotta communicate with the people
Dakar the future is yours & ours and the hour is here

(1984)

Dakar skyline

ArIal view of Dakar, and Presidential Palace

Independence Square, Dakar

Sandpainting demonstration

Presidential Palace

Streets of Dakar

Approaching Goree Island

Houses on Goree Island

View from the mountains of Goree Island

Goree Island

Goree Island off the coast of Senegal was first taken by the Portuguese in 1444, and was used as a fort. From the beginning of the infamous Western slave trade of tens of millions of Africans, and as some historians charge over 100 million African human beings in the 1600's to its end in the mid 1800's. Goree was one of the pivotal points of the trade in Black people between Africa, the Caribbean and North America. Even though Goree Island changed hands from Portuguese to Dutch to English to French hands, (European hands) the reason for its use remained the same, it was a strategic point of departure for the slave trade because of its close proximity to the West. It was from Goree that the European expansion and settlement of the rest of Senegal began.

The ferry ride from Dakar to Goree Island is approximately twenty minutes.

Every time I visit the slave house on Goree Island I cry, I have visited this place countless times, and every time I cry. I get filled up with emotion, I can feel the spirit of the Africans who were chained to the walls, the children, the women and the men. Many might think that a person would get used to this place after several visits, that it would not continue to affect you in the same way. It is because the spirits of the African ancestors are very strong here and you feel it with full passion every time you visit, you feel hurt and sorrowful, angry and bitter, and their pain comes through you and through your tears. Some of us Black people, Africans from the West, feel this bond with our African brothers and sisters. We feel and realize that this is one of the places of departure that our ancestors left, this place and through the door of "No Return" where they were forced through, never to be seen again by the Africans on that side. That we are the off spring of these people and that we have come full circle, 360 degrees to the point of departure, to belie this saying in regards to this door of "No Return", and say that here we are, we have returned! The reality of this observation hits home, not only for those who might not have had the strongest connections to the people on the continent of Africa, and perhaps came to Africa out of curiosity. But also to those Afrocentric members from the African Diaspora, those Nationalists and Pan Africanists, and Muslims, the sobering reality and clarity was that in analyzing the history of our people's lives, understanding that this was one of the places where this all started! This holocaust of cnslavement, this 400 years of the most horrible organized system that almost eliminated a people. Physically for the millions who died on the slave ships, in the ocean, on the plantations, hanging from the poplar trees and shot in the back. Culturally, for we were lost, cut off from our way of life, our language, our council, our moral and human development, to adopt the culture of the very ones who captured and enslaved us, or to adopt an un-councilled subculture. And finally the elimination of a people economically, to continually work in the interest of making Europeans/white people rich and having very little for ourselves.

At its worst during the chattel slave trade to the Americas, where we worked for nothing, to the state laws that held us back, and the Klu Klux Klan terrorism, and the colonizing of Africa, and the neo-colonism, to integration in America.

A people cannot grow economically under these conditions, and if it does not change African people will be eliminated.

It all hits home on Goree, at this infamous slave house, where emotions flow. The irony of it all though is that this little island with its hideous history could be so beautiful, so sunny and calm. Goree Island aside from the slave house is a garden of red brick topped houses, courtyards, trees and mountains, where they still have the cannons overlooking the Atlantic that was used when the "Guns of Navarone" was filmed. Goree Island, Senegal.

The mountains of Goree are very interesting on the way to the top, you will find shops and interesting brothers who live with their families there in the mountains. They are called Baay Falls who inhabit this area of Goree. They are interesting because of their colorful patch like clothing and their locks, locks like the Rastafarians.

On the low lands of the island the little cobblestone streets are picturesque and quaint. It is a lovely sunny island with charming restaurants that serve tantalizing fish and other delicious food.

It softens to some degree the sadness of the island and its history of inhumanity. As the ferry leaves the harbor young boys climb up to and hang onto the rail of the deck, and when the boat moves further away they jump off and swim back to the shore. If some of the tourists throw coins in the water you will see them dive down and retrieve the coins.

As the ferry boat moves further away from Goree heading to Dakar, the slave house and its fort becomes smaller and smaller, but the memory and visions of the dungeons looms large in our minds and heavy in our hearts.

"Door of No Return" in
Goree Island

Entrance to slave house

Remember Goree Island

As our group of 17 African Americans stand with hands clasped
heads bowed in a semi -circle
amidst the sand, rock walls and stairs of the former slave quarters
we offer words of inspiration on this 17th day of August
to the Honorable Marcus Mosiah Garvey
and to the more than 100 million African
men/women/ and children   ‑
who left Africa in chains
we vowed to always remember Goree
remember the small cramped rooms where children
were chained to walls in preparation for the long un-promised

26

middle passage the holes where they stuffed the rebels
the vision of twisting bodies writhing
in the stench and pain of their chains
sharp long wails of screams pierce the membranes of minds
and you stare long and hard at the long narrow passageway
that leads to a sliver of light
at the end is the beginning of the vast Atlantic
as powerful waves crash ferociously against black rocks
the passageway, the light, the ocean and visions
of glistening Black resistant bodies
being pushed and whipped down the dark narrow passage
to that sliver of light at the end is the beginning of the vast Atlantic
that has become a tomb We must always remember Goree
let it be the basis for our philosophy and religion
the source of our prayers
and the purpose for our will to be free !
Remember Goree !   1984-

Slave chains

Slave house at Goree

The Pink Lake

The Pink Lake in Senegal is one of several fascinating places that tourist visit.

When I speak of places that tourist visit I am not talking about superficial places all the time or places that are designed just for visitors, I am talking about places that are interesting, historical, cultural, exciting, different and enjoyable. Pink Lake is one of these places, it is a natural phenomenon. The water is a rose color and the deepness of its color depends on the intensity of the sun, in other words on a cloudy day the water is not so pink, however on a bright sunny day the brilliance of the pink water is like a beautiful oil painting. In addition to the unusual and lovely color of the water, it is rumored to have healing and medicinal properties. Many have said that after putting the water on their skin it helped to heal very quickly, abrasions, rashes and other topical disorders. Also those who have swam in the lake (or floated) said the water was very relaxing.

I mentioned floating because you cannot sink in this water, you just float, much like the Dead Sea. I always get a kick out of photographing individuals in positions with both legs and arms raised and just floating still and serene, sometimes reading the newspapers.

Some of the reasons for the pink color of the water it is said is due to the algae or vegetation that grow on the bottom of the lake, and when the sun hits the water, it causes this coloration. It is also said that the claims of relaxation that the water brings, is most probably due to the heavy concentration of salt in the water.

The Pink Lake is also a salt mining operation at some points, as your land rover or bus travels alongside the lake's coast, you can see the numerous mounds of raw unrefined salt. There are literally hundreds of small white hills of this salt that is deposited there by the Senegalese salt mine workers. You can see the men as they are returning in their deep bottom boats (Perots or large canoe types) piled high with salt. The men go more in the center of the lake where the salt deposits are abundant, collect the salt in buckets, dump it in the boats then return to the shore. Here the workers began to empty out the boats by filling their buckets with the salt, placing it on their heads, then dumping it in small hill piles near the shore.

This is very tedious work, but it is an industry and it provides a livelihood for the workers. The salt that is collected is used mainly in the industrial sector, is raw and has to be processed. Due to the heavy salt content there is of course no fish or living things in the Pink Lake. It is a very popular tourist attraction with its rose colored waters and varied craft market that line certain areas, you can also take a very adventurous and exciting drive along the shore, up and over the sand dunes in open top land rovers or safari type vehicles. Going up and down the sand dunes remind you of being on a roller coaster!

Mounds of raw salt

Bags of raw salt

After floating in the pink waters, strolling amidst the salt hills and surviving an exciting ride in the land rovers, one is ready for the comforting shade of the restaurant/Canteen's artistically designed bamboo roof from the scorching African sun. Here is where you can relax and listen to the

Senegalese musicians as they drum and sing songs, telling the stories of the area as you await your fish and rice and other delicious Senegalese food. As you collect your seashells and fill your bottles with the water from the Pink Lake, to take back home to heal your skin irritations, you savor your most interesting visit to this quite unusual place.

Fulani Village, Senegal

Close to the Pink Lake area, there is a village that reminds you of villages that you have seen in magazines and films, with people that also seem very familiar to you. These people are Fulani. The Fulani people or Fula for short as some refer to them are a truly West African people. They are considered a nomadic people in that you can find them in several West African countries, whereas you might find different ethnic groups that are indigenous to certain areas of Africa, you will find the Fulani amongst many different people in several countries in West Africa. The Fulani are mostly cattle herders, they are nomadic and their settlements are very mobile. Cattle are very central to the Fulani as they regard cattle as their wealth, their worth, their currency. Cattle is a status symbol with them, and they measure their importance by how large a herd they have. The Fulani are diligent herdsmen, and life revolves around the herd. The breeding of cattle to them is a lifestyle, a culture, not a business or a commodity. In fact they do not breed the cattle for market, they also do not eat them. They raise them and herd them and give them for bride price and are incorporated in various aspects of the Fulani culture.

The Fulani village of Niaga - Peulh in Senegal however is somewhat different in that they are not nomadic, they have settled the land, have become farmers and have permanent houses in addition to the mud and straw thatched houses. (I use houses to describe these dwellings the same as we describe the structures where other people live anywhere in the world, instead of the diminishing term "hut"). These rural type houses have features that adopt to the natural environment. For instance it never ceases to amaze visitors to this village that is situated in a sub-Sahalien region, where the sun can be brutally hot and blistering, especially in July and August, to enter these dwellings and find a natural coolness, a natural air controlled quality, a natural air conditioning. To step out of the hot sun into this mud and straw house and feel cool is like coming out of the sun in the heart of a city in America in the middle of sizzling August into an air conditioned office building. The comparison is startling. A visitor might also be surprised to find a sizable living space, including beds, sometimes linoleum floor covering, and other home life items.

The village of Niaga -Peulh has a population of 120 people which consists of 9 families, and is headed by a chief. The chief of Niaga - Peulh has two wives and the visitors are welcomed by the chief and his wives. This is a Muslim village as is most of the people of Senegal as we stated earlier. Polygamy is practiced here as is allowed in the religion of Islam, as is also practiced in several traditional African cultures.

The visitors are greeted by the chief and his family, and are allowed to visit the houses of the people and see how the Fulani live.

After, they all gather under the huge tree for shade from the hot sun. The young women of the village adorn their traditional welcoming outfits, the percussionists gather (usually with light drums and varied light percussive instruments) and the young maidens then begin to dance and sing and chant the Fulani welcoming and praise songs. The girls eventually invite the visitors to join in the dance and everyone experiences the culture and warm hospitality of the village. The Fulani have a very subtle and quiet air about them, they also are a predominately "Brown" people with Ethiopian and Somalian features. They have distinct facial and other features different from the more indigenous people of Senegal such as the Wolof, Diola, Serer, Mandinka, Serahule, and others. After the dancing and drumming, the visitors present their gifts and presents to the people in the community baskets, so that these items can be distributed to the children such as pens and pencils, composition books, other educational items, games and toys, sweet stuff and clothing. And for the ladies, nail polish, lipstick, perfume, oils, T-shirts and other related items for the men.

It is a warm gathering that leaves many memorable moments in the minds and hearts of the visitors as they board the buses for the return to the city, as the children and adults thank them for their gifts and wave their goodbyes.

As the dust gathers caused by the wheels of the tour bus the memory lingers of the quiet warmth of the Fulani people.

The Holy City Of Touba

The religion of Islam had already been mentioned in this 'Journey' To Senegal, but in my opinion Islam manifests itself in what I have seen and experienced in the United States, and through various media views of what is called the Middle East, as an Arab cultural, and religious expression. This is derived from my understanding, and henceforth what I have offered in the beginning of this journey as my interpretation of culture, its dress, language, etc.

The African, wherever we are, have always expressed our root culture, as we discussed earlier, through whatever the dominant culture might be or through whatever religion may have been introduced into our culture. Our natural way of doing things will always manage to rise out of whatever the dominant culture is or whatever religion that does not come out of the indigenous culture happens to be at that time, as we shall see in other places as this journey unfolds.

The indigenous ways and customs of the people of Senegal take center stage. The religion of Islam does not take a back seat, but is integrated into the dominant culture, it is peppered in the language, it finds its way to attention during the various celebrations like Rahmadan, Ede, Toubasci, and such. It some times to a degree accents the attire, but it is the Senegalese rhythm that the people move to, the Djembe, the Bata, the rich and vibrant colors, which says that this is African, not Arab, or European or any other culture.

The religion is Islam, and yes they are Muslim, but most definitely they are African.

I say all this to lay the groundwork for the introduction to this most unique place, Touba, Senegal, West Africa.

To further emphasize my point I wish to point out the cultural manifestations of the Black or African American converts to Islam in the United States, excluded from this observation at this time is the Nation of Islam. These Black converts to what is referred to as 'Orthodox' Islam, have taken on lock, stock, and barrel the total culture of the Arab Muslims, the dress, mannerisms, the tonal and language inflections, moving to another rhythm, the drum is not there, the hard rhythm,

The village drumbeat is gone, the central beat of the funk is not there, what has happened? I understand the problem, I know that we have lost a lot in the break of a continuum, of a way of life. I know that many of us search for our past, and understand that Euro-American Christian ethics is all that we have been offered and some of us reject it. But we must be rooted in our cultural past, rooted in the continuum of the ancestral realities we must face.

In our search we must carry this ancestral rootedness and question whether this rootedness is being compromised, but of course there is an opinion that this allegiance to our African past is not important. This is unusual for a people, most people band together because of their sameness, their familiarity and comfort with their culture. But because Black converts to Islam in the West are searching, they have moved too far away from their base.

In Senegal the African Muslims are rooted in their culture, Islam has found a place there but it is part of the whole. The culture is strong, the rhythm is distinctly Senegalese and clearly African. If we can began to understand that point, agree or not then we might be better able to understand Touba.

Touba is an African Islamic city 193 km south of the Senegalese capital of Dakar. It has a population that is hard to determine, because several mil-

Cheikh Ahmadou Bamba   Cheikh Ibrima Fall

lion others are connected to Touba spiritually, support it financially, and
some have homes there and in other cities. Of the nine and a half million
Muslims in Senegal, four million are Mouride. Touba is the headquarters of
Mouridism, an African Brotherhood which is one of few such Islamic organizations in Senegal, some of the others being Tidjane, Laynne, Quadria, and
have spiritual and inspirational leaders that are called Marabouts. The
founder and spiritual leader of the Mouride brotherhood philosophy is
Cheikh Ahmadou Bamba , MBacke is the family name, Cheikh Bamba's
name is also Khadim Mbacke. He was born in 1850 at Mbacke, in Senegal.
After his first education in his father's Koranic school (Daara), he traveled
to Mauritania to learn more about theology and Islamic philosophy. At an
early age his father realized that the destiny of his son was to be one of the
top spiritual leaders in West Africa. The way he studied the Koran, his
knowledge and spiritual powers at a young age convinced his father to be
one of his first disciples. He told him: "I am no longer your teacher, but your
student" Bamba it is said communicated with Allah and acquired great wisdom as a child, there is a book in the vast library in Touba that is said was
written by Bamba at the age of nine. The library in Touba contains thousands
of volumes and according to the Marabouts the vast majority of them were
written by Bamba, books on philosophy, religion, Islam, poetry, astrology,

astronomy, geography, economics and many other topics related to the physical and spiritual aspects of mankind.

Entrance to Library

Mouridism began in 1886, in 1895 Cheikh Ahmadou Bamba was exiled to a penal colony in the West African country of Gabon by the French who colonized Senegal, because Bamba had too much influence over the Muslims in Senegal, particularly the Mouride sect that was growing rapidly. The French found out that they had made Bamba a martyr and his following and influence grew even more, and so did the legend of Cheikh Ahamadou Bamba. Legend says that on his deportation to Gabon the French wanted to break his spirit and would not let him make Salat (prayer) on the ship, the story goes that Bamba put his prayer cloth on the sea and prayed. Another famous story is that the French put a couple of hungry lions alone with Bamba and the lions were soon at the feet of Bamba in the position of prayer, making Salat. Still another is that the French summoned Bamba to appear before them to face certain charges. When he appeared before them, they were seated at a tribunal type table and Bamba was expected to stand before them in humiliation.

His aide got down on all fours and made his body into a chair so that Bamba would be seated and on the same level as the colonial masters.

Around the turn of the century there was a terrible drought in Touba. There was very little water, it had not rained in quite some time, and the people were desperate, it is said that Bamba pointed to a spot that when the people started to dig, water sprang in abundance and the fountain has been flow-

Holy Water monument

ing ever since.

Today there is a monument to this spring that has spickets where the pilgrims can get holy water.

Cheikh Ahmadou Bamba returned from captivity in 1903 and settled in Djourbel, near Touba and built the first large mosque. Touba after the death of Bamba would become a great center, continued by his sons.

The name Touba came about according to legend, Cheikh Ahmadou Bamba received a revelation in Touba, because of a single Baobab tree surrounded by desert, with Bamba's blessing, an oasis would grow.

Cheikh Ahmadou Bamba's most devoted convert was a believer named Cheikh Ibrima Fall, Ibrima Fall was a constant companion of Bamba and a fierce believer, he was also a strong personality.

He was known to have worn Black attire and had his hair in dread locks, using the hairstyles of the ancient Africans.

Not much information is available on Cheikh Ibrima Fall. But he also has left his legacy in Senegal, and has left a following of Mourides that are called Baay-Fall. They wear dread locks and colorful patchwork clothing, and are found in the hills of Goree' Island, in the holy city of Touba and on the streets of Dakar devoutly raising money to continue building the great mosque city of Touba.

The Mouride Brotherhood grew rapidly after the release of Bamba, in fact the anniversary of his release from captivity became a cause to celebrate and an annual celebration, to give thanks for his return to the people, and is called the Magal. Every year pilgrims come from all over Africa, Europe and America to be a part of this celebration, approximately 2 million people come for this festival.

Touba would soon become a very powerful place, mainly due to Bamba's spiritual teachings of praising God, being righteous, and hard work. The people were devoted to the "Saint" and gave selflessly and helped to bring prosperity to Touba.

In addition as a result of the Senegalese men joining the French army to help fight in World War I with Bamba's blessings, a relationship was established with France, and Touba designated a holy city was free from colonial rule and taxes. This of course allowed Touba to not only become a commercial hub, but gave them the opportunity to express their African personality. It is said that Bamba Africanized Islam through the Mouride Brotherhood.

This drew criticism and continues to draw criticism from Arab Muslims and those African and African American Muslims that are influenced by, or belong to a school of Islam that is centered in, or influenced by an Arab nation or Arab culture.

Several observations distinguishes Mouridism, as an African spiritual expression, just by the very essence of the atmosphere if one visits the holy city of Touba it has the rhythm of Africa, the members of the Brotherhood carry themselves in this manner in their dress and in their style. The mausoleums that contain the remains of Bamba and his sons, there are five tombs/mausoleums (Bamba and four sons) remind one of the tombs and mausoleums of the Pharaohs of ancient Egypt, and the valley of the Kings. It appears that it is keeping in the tradition of the ancient Africans.

Tomb of Bamba's first
son Moustapha

Inside of Bamba 's
' second son
Fallou's tomb

Tomb of
another son

Minarets of Touba
rising in the sky

The Mouride Brotherhood has grown tremendously since the death in 1927 of Cheikh Ahmadou Bamba. The second son of Bamba Fallou Mbacke the supreme Khalifa and spiritual leader from 1945 to his death in 1968, this son of Ahmadou Bamba started building the grand mosque and other structures of the mosque complex. The other sons that followed, continued this development, including the present Khalifa and son of Cheikh Ahmadou Bamba, Serigne Saliou Mbacke.

The mosque complex which is the core of the holy city is a spectacle to behold, it is magnificent, a wonder to witness, the largest mosque and most beautiful complex in West Africa. It is a magnificent sight as your vehicle approaches the entrance to the city, the vehicle stops at a check point to give to the security, cigarettes that visitors might have, smoking and drinking alcohol is not allowed in the holy city. Women must cover their heads and should not wear pants, men should not wear shorts. As you approach the city the spirals of the minaret looms out of the sky, majestic, colorful and large.

I started visiting the holy city in the mid 1980's and have continued to do so once or twice a year. Each time that I visit I see new development, a continual building process, additions of new structures, since my visits they have added 2 new mausoleums each for a son that had previously passed. I come, and I bring people, because I am awed by its serene splendor, its strong aura of African spirituality. When you enter the mausoleum of Cheikh Ahmadou Bamba you will be captured by the chants and prayers of the disciples that you will find sitting on the thick Persian rugs that ring the inner entrance to the tomb of Bamba. The inner sanctuary is where the remains of Bamba rest and is only open to the follow-ers of Mouridism or to Muslims of other schools of thoughts. I am allowed to enter as a long time supporter of Mouridism and having been given the name Khadim Mbacke which is the name of the founder and revered spiritual leader. I am endeared to this movement because of its anti-colonial history and its African centered Islam.

John Watusi Branch
(Khadim Mbacke)
in Grand Buba

39

The mausoleum is a rich and beautiful temple, with marble walls and ceilings beautifully designed. The crypt/tomb of the founder is surrounded by a solid gold grail outer fence, where the disciples pray around the circular tomb on thick carpets, and coins are tossed inside to fulfill the wishes of the disciples.

In the tomb of Fallou Mbacke, the deceased popular leader who started the massive building of the mosque complex, one will find many of the disciples and Marabouts delivering intensive songs and praises to Bamba and Fallou, the intensity and fervor is incredible, the flavor and accent is uniquely Senegalese.

Entering the tomb of Cheikh Ahmadou Bamba

Disciples chanting in the tomb of Fallou MBacke

Main entrance to the grand mosque

Inside grand mosque

Inside grand mosque

The immediate grounds and out door areas where during mass visits such as the main holiday/holy day Magal, the disciples gather, is made of marble and tile, with colorful minarets, and towers. Entering the main mosque you must enter through a huge hand carved wooden door, inscribed with Arabic writings and designs. Directly inside is the holy water fountain, beautifully and artistically designed is where the converts and disciples drink from the fountain that many believe will make their dreams and aspirations come true. The interior of this grand mosque is an unforgettable sight. With its massive size and numerous thick Persian rugs, its ceilings, walls and huge columns artistically designed in expensive Italian marble, with a tremendous solid gold chandelier as its centerpiece with gold grails surrounding the area where the Marabout addresses the congregation. As you look at the promenade of columns, feel the richness of the gold and marble, and as the serene spirituality embraces you, one can truly appreciate the royalty and majesty of this African spiritual movement.

Another incredible revelation about Touba is the palace, which very few people are privy to. The last time that I was able to see the interior of the palace was in 1992, prior to that I was able to visit the palace several times due to my relationship with a member of the family who was a special guide for my group and myself.

I have never been in quarters so plush, so opulent in any place in the States. The palace had several sitting rooms (living rooms), some with expensive and imported wood finish, wood ceilings and floors, other rooms with plush carpet, all white carpet and white stuffed furniture, it had several dining rooms, bathrooms with solid gold fixtures, a richness certainly reserved for royalty. However some question the richness of the palace and the mosque complex compared to the surrounding houses of some of the common people. One might answer that with an explanation for the surrounding areas of other spiritual and splendorous edifices such as The Vatican, cathedrals, and huge churches.

Palace sitting room (Pape' and Fallou Mboup)

Palace sitting rooms

The Holy City of Touba supplies the people with certain vital services such as fresh water, electricity and other services that sometimes some major cities in West Africa do not provide.

The people however have no complaints, in fact they love to contribute so that the complex can grow. Touba has many contributors, some very wealthy people and some who are very poor, some who are powerful politicians and business people. Many from other African countries, some from Europe and the United States, the little people, the taxi drivers, and farmers, they all give to advance the philosophy of Mouridism.

The Mouride Brotherhood stretches from Senegal, then throughout French West Africa, to France itself, extending to Italy, Spain, Saudi Arabia, South Africa and most recently, New York.

As you stroll through the labyrinths of this grand mosque city, you will gain insight and understanding of this faith and the history of a powerful anti-colonial movement, in addition to a beautiful example of the second principle of the Nguzo Saba (7 principles) Kujichagulia, "To define ourselves".

43

I leave you with one other thought on Touba and its great founder and spiritual leader Cheikh Ahmadou Bamba Mbacke. During my many interviews, and question and answer periods with various guides and keepers of the mosque facilities. I once asked "did Bamba ever make Hajj" (pilgrimage to Mecca that each Muslim should make in his life time, if possible) I was told that no Bamba did not make Hajj, had not gone to Mecca, and I asked why had he not? and was told that Bamba said that had he gone to Mecca, the Prophet Mohammad would have risen from his grave and that the world would end.

Another answer to my question at a different time I was told that Bamba was under a kind of house arrest and was not allowed to travel outside of Senegal as a condition of his release from the penal colony in Gabon.

A full story of Bamba would take volumes, however the reader can research this fascinating person, visit Senegal and find out about this icon in Senegalese history, the spiritual saint wrapped in a simple white sheet, the only image ever shown of Cheik Ahmadou Bamba.

Photo of Bamba, Babacar Saar & myself

44

Spirrrrrrrtual, loving rays of sun shining
On my faceless passionate dream nipple
Of life
Spirrrrrrrtual, feeling sooooooo good
Feeling sooooooo nice
Spirrrrrrrtual, slipping, sliding, gracefully
Down avenues of irridescent glass houses
Of life
Spirrrrrrrtual, I got you
What took you so long?
Spirrrrrrrtual, rocking waving rhythms of
hip superfly slick nigger
Hear me oh lord!
Spirrrrrrrtual, echoes of Kawaida and
Damballah Kareena, Kareena, oh mighty
Shango of Buddah's
lipless love!
Spirrrrrrrtual, 360 degrees of timeless
Ageless loving Black embryos of
future nationhood
Spirrrrrrrtual, militant envoys of peace
Marching with stuff pockets of gold
mounted machine guns full of Umoja
Spirrrrrrrtual, beginning again

legendary Historical empires of powerful
Black nations
                    Spirrrrrrrrtual
                    Spirrrrrrrrtua
                    Spirrrrrrrrtual

The Casamace

"The other Senegal" The southern part of Senegal is called the Casamace, it is situated on the opposite side of the Gambia.

The Gambia, cuts right into Senegal like a knife, this is a direct result of colonialism. The British wanting that particular part of what was SeneGambia, for their own greedy and selfish reasons, and the French taking the rest of the land. A long strip of land approximately 24 miles wide, Casamace extends well over a hundred miles from west to east. This physical cut off from the main part of Senegal has not been very good for the people of the Casamace,

they do not get the services and resources from the government, which has led to decades of discontent, political and social strife. There has been bloody conflict with the people of the south and the central government, and a constant call from the south for autonomy and independence. Another very important factor in the adversarial relationship between the two is that the north is predominately Muslim and in the south there are many who practice the traditional ways and are called "Anamist". The south is an oasis, the green part of Senegal, where as the northern part of Senegal is a dry flatland, the Casamace is a Savanna bush, majestic forests, coconut palm grooves, bending with the wind from the ocean breeze, it is dense and tropical. The Casamace is home to a traditional group called the Diolas, who are the majority and the Mandjakes and Balantes. They live in a very rich area of deep forest where they perform their initiation ceremonies in what is called the "sacred forest" They enjoy the village life and the ability to practice their traditional African cultural beliefs, that some Westerners might call religion. Even though the religion of Islam is practiced by some in this southern region, the majority of people practice the traditional beliefs.

It is the Casamace region that most of the truly strong ritual and performance dances come from, the more energetic forms, the more agile forms, where the energy is at its peak.

In 1992 I led a group of approximately 19 African Americans to southern Senegal. We took a ship called the "Joola" down the coast heading for Ziguinchor, the capitol of the southern region.

It takes approximately 12 hours to make the journey, we left around 10pm, and was expected to arrive in Ziguinchor around 10am the next morning. It was quite an African experience, the cabins that we slept in were very nice, comfortable beds, a clean and efficient bathroom, TV and air-conditioning. The excitement however was on the decks, the ship was overloaded with Senegalese, there was not enough room for them in the passenger sitting rooms and they were sleeping on the floor of the deck. A few of us almost stepped on some of them coming out of our cabins to see the stars in the clear African sky. It was quite an experience with the ship hitting some turbulence in the powerful rolling sea, and sleeping bodies shifting and rolling against our feet. The lounge area was a hot spot, Senegalese music playing and people sitting, eating and drinking and enjoying the sounds of Youssou N' Dour, Baaba Maal and others, coming out of a huge boom box.

After having breakfast and relaxing a bit, our guide Fallou told us that we would be getting off the ship, load into a pirogue, (long boat) and go to an island where we would visit the inhabitants and have lunch. Then we would continue to Ziguinchor by pirogue, which Fallou said would take about 30 minutes. Getting off the ship and dropping down into the long boat was very exciting, the Senegalese deck hands lowering the group into the boat, the group groping for hands and firm footing. Fortunately it was only a short distance to the shore, the boat hit the bank with a bang. After some time trying to get one woman out of the boat because of her fear that she would slip into the water between the shore and the bow of the boat, we ventured into the interior of the island. The name of the island was Karbane, a quiet place where we visited the village and settled down to a nice lunch and fun time dancing in the canteen to popular Senegalese music, taking pictures and frolicking with the locals. After saying our good-byes we all loaded into the boat to begin what we thought was a short boat ride to Ziguinchor, we were soon to find out that the estimated time was more than a gross exaggeration.

The ride in fact took about 3 1/2 hours. A ride that started with everyone in pretty high spirits, and feeling a sense of adventure, even those two or three people who professed that they could not swim. The spirits were so high that everyone laughed when they realized that the young man at the end of the boat was there with a pail in his hand, to bail out the water that was coming into the boat from holes in the bottom. We sang songs, led by our popular Senegalese guide Fallou Mboup (Fallou is one of the most popular, knowledgeable, sociable, guides in all of Senegal, many people in the United States speak very highly of him). But after an hour and a half on the open sea even Fallou could not cheer up those concerned faces, as the young man continued to bail out the water and eyes were locked in front and to the sides trying to spot some land. There was one older guy who talked real militant and tough who had both of his hands on the side of the boat locked in a death grip. After we had reached the second hour on the sea, there was great concern, worried voices constantly asked Fallou, "are we there?" "How much longer?" as bladders began to strain and heart-beats grew faster and louder, and concerns about the possibility of rain were raised.

After about another 11/2 hours sweet land was finally sighted, the air from the sighs of relief almost blew the boat closer to the shore. When the boat hit the shore everyone was relieved, but the older guy who was hold-ing onto the side of the boat for dear life actually got down on his knees and kissed the ground! We however were all happy to see our tour bus waiting for us on the road at the top of the incline.

We continued on to spend two days and a night and enjoy the richness, the history and traditional culture of the Casamace. The visit was a peace-ful one, the motion and pace of the people coincides with the tropical tran-quility of the region.

The Casamace is truly an African tropical and cultural paradise.

African dancers

My experiences have been many and varied in Senegal. Fellow group members and myself have over the years come to know Senegal in several ways. Not only have we visited the many interesting sites, sampled the delicious rice and fish, watched the traditional dances, but we have also experienced the popular culture of Senegal.

The popular culture is a vibrant one, the rhythm, and dance, the fun and excitement of the Soiree' (the all night dance parties and performances by the popular artists of Dakar) has made it a place where the hip folks from Europe, and African Americans from the urban cities of America find comfort in the upbeat pop culture. Dakar is a place of many restaurants which serve exotic French and African cuisine, entertainment spots, live band performances, where participants not only watch but also dance to Mbalax, Yele, Reggae, Latin and funk. Even though Islam is the dominant religion in Senegal, the people are known to party and dance their popular dances with excitement and amazing dexterity. African Americans who are known in the United States to be very agile, find that they have to get it together to move to these Senegalese knee and leg bending movements.

Concerts are popular, crowds pour out to see the mega stars like Youssou N' Dour, Baaba Maal, Kine Lam, Omar Pene, Ismail Lo, Funk master, James Brown and Stevie Wonder inspired Pape Njie, the blind R & B popular drummer and band leader, and Vye McFaye, the popular Jazz guitarist.

There are yearly visitors to Dakar that come with the Black History Month trip during the month of February. This is a trip that is more centered in Dakar and involves concerts, clubs, and parties, in addition to the visit to Goree' Island, marketplaces, and the villages. This program was started in 1995 and since that time there are more African Americans visiting Senegal during February, than all of the rest of the months of the year combined.

What has added to the excitement in Dakar during this time is FESTAM, an international festival of music and art that was started In 1994 by M.Moustapha Diop, owner of Heritage Tours Senegal, and myself. What we had attempted to do was to bring the artists of the African Diaspora, and Senegalese artist together for a festival of music concerts, art exhibits, and symposiums. We also brought tourists on these trips to bring together members of the African family from the United States, the Islands of the Caribbean and the Senegalese family to share and enjoy multi-faceted African creativity. We organized a series of concerts in clubs, hotels, and in a 20,000-25,000 seat stadium. We planned and executed exhibits in galleries, restaurants and hotels, and organized informative symposiums and lectures. In 1994 we launched an ambitious program that included Randy Weston and his band African Rhythms, Bill Saxton Quintet, visual artists and painters Leroy Campbell, and the works of Verna Hart, represented by her sister. Also photographer Cheryl Miller, with her fantastic action photos of some of the icons of Jazz. Filling out the bill from the African American side was Leonard Gaston, master bassist, who at this time delivered a paper on the "Roots of Jazz and the Blues"

Leonard Gaston is an archivist who has much of the history of Jazz in photographs, newspaper clipping, and on film and video. We were pleasantly surprised to discover, thanks to my partner Moustapha Diop who was responsible for organizing things on that side, that there was a Jazz preservation society in Dakar by the name of the Dizzy Gillespie Foundation, who's mission was to teach students the history of Jazz, instrumentation, and maintain an archive. My job was to organize the artists coming from the West. We had an interesting panel discussion with translators of both French and English. We planned elegant poolside concerts, hotel and club jams and attempted to fill the Demba Diop soccer stadium, which holds approximately 20,000-25,000 people. The Demba Diop stadium is the second largest stadium in Dakar, the other larger A'mite holds 60,000.

It was a great coming together of the best of Senegal's musicians and artists including the world famous Togolese artist who resides in Senegal Felicite' Codjo, Samba Laye and other Senegalese painters.

The FESTAM festival of 1995 included an incredible entourage from the States of Larry Ridley and the Jazz Legacy Ensemble, and Reggae superstar Sister Carol and her exciting band that literally rocked Dakar. Also included were the Gladiators, who were wrestlers from the U.S. that were to meet the famous Senegalese wrestlers in combat. The concerts that took place in Dakar were awesome, particularly Sister Carol and her Reggae band.

Reggae is very popular in Senegal, and several Reggae bands appeared in a concert in Independence Square in the heart of Dakar that was attended by several thousand people. Sister Carol rocked the city, everywhere we went people were waving and calling out her name, in the streets, from the buses and lorries. The Mayor of Dakar presented the key to the city to her and several of us. One of the incredible stories involving the Jazz concerts I always like to tell, is because in the States Jazz has for a few decades now is no longer part of the popular culture, it is relegated to a minority of fine art lovers. However at a concert in the 25,000 seat Demba Diop Stadium Larry Ridley and his band were about to play. We were concerned that perhaps this was not the place for straight ahead Jazz. The clubs and hotels were fine, where the elite, the Minister of culture, the Mayor, politicians, business people and intellectuals gathered, but this was a large mostly very young crowd, because Senegalese Super Pop star Youssou N' Dour was also on the bill. However when the group started to play, the audience was surprisingly quiet and attentive. The most amazing thing was when Larry took his bass solo (upright acoustic bass) the young audience was hanging on to every pluck of his strings, gave low audible sounds when he really got down, and roared at the conclusion of his solo. When they left the stage the young people almost mobbed Larry, wanting to touch him and to touch his bass. This must have been a very exhilarating feeling for him, as in the States the youth would probably have been bored with his presentation, and would have been making noises, drowning out the intensity of his solo.

This festival was the center of attention for Senegalese television, radio and the newspapers, there were interviews, and clips of performances that were the focus of the national media. The United States Embassy was involved, hosting the opening reception for both years of 1994, and 1995.

Unfortunately we could not continue with these concerts as the very small amount of money that we received from the U.S.I.A. (United States Information Agency) to help with the expenses in 1995 had dried up. The first festival in 1994 we produced without funding and took quite a financial beating. I discovered that the reason that there were so few Jazz musicians performing in Africa was because it was practically impossible to make your expenses back in promoting these concerts and festivals. This is why the musicians who have performed in Africa, for the most part have done so under the auspices of the U.S. State Department. The main reason that it is so difficult to promote concerts that are financially successful, that involves artist from the United States, is the currency exchange. The CFAF (Community of French African Franc) commonly called CFA (See-Fa) is 615 cfa to $1. In the case of The concert at the Demba Diop stadium with a 20,000-25,000 capacity the most we could charge for the first year was 1,000cfa which is approximately $2 for the young people, which is quite a bit for families that have a monthly income from $30-$50. There were about 10, 000 young people outside the stadium walls that were pushing against the gates so much that eventually the security had to let several thousand of them in. We had perhaps 12,000 paying customers. However even if the entire stadium had paid we would have only raised about $ 40,000-$50,000, that would have barley paid for the expenses of the stadium security, publicity, the Senegalese superstars, and the substantial expenses of the musicians from the States that required airfare, hotels, meals, and their performing fees. The other venues (hotels and clubs) attracted much smaller audiences of from 100-400 persons at a maximum charge of perhaps $15 for these elite affairs.

These festivals must be subsidized either by the U.S. government, corporations and foundations, and the large business conglomerates in Senegal.

The FESTAM International Festival of Music and Art was suspended for the years 1996 and 1997. In 1998 we decided to incorporate FESTAM in the rapidly growing Black History Month discounted trips to Senegal in February, which was attracting record numbers of tourists. We no longer had much of a budget and was not able to pay for any performance fees, and picked up most of the expenses of the visiting musicians that had been reduced to individuals rather than groups. With this new arrangement we were able to bring Jazz saxophonist Harold Ousley to Dakar, where he played with some of the great Senegalese musicians, which brought even more emphasis to the concept of uniting the African American and Senegalese people, in performance and discussion. We also opened up new avenues by bringing a Rap artist with us, a very good artist, a positive and soulful artist, Makeba Mooncycle, who took Dakar by storm, we discovered that Rap was as popular in Senegal as it was in the U.S. with the masses of young people.

We realized that there were many more Rap groups than one that was a part of one of our concerts in 1995 'Positive Black Soul'. We were treated to a variety of Rap artists, rapping in Wolof, Fulani, Mandinka, and French.

We also discovered that the lyrics were hugely popular, I heard Rap praises to spiritual leader Cheikh Ahmadou Bamba and stories of the people of Senegal. Makeba Mooncycle became the darling of the Rap community of Dakar, appearing on television, radio and in the daily press. Makeba and Harold were everywhere.

Atiba Wilson, a noted musician, poet and storyteller, came as a member of the tour group, but soon he was on the stage performing with Harold Ousley, the Senegalese musicians and Makeba Mooncylcle. Atiba was seen playing drums and flute with many of the local street musicians, on Goree' Island, in the marketplaces, and the villages.

In February 1999 we again brought Harold Ousley and his wife, who also brought several ladies from the organization 'Key People' that organized a chapter of the organization among the prominent women of Senegal.

Atiba Wilson also returned, this time as a featured artist, and gospel singer Gwen Phillip, who sang with gospel groups!, yes gospel groups in Senegal, a predominately Muslim country, which has a small Christian population. Gwen also sang the blues with Harold, Atiba and the Senegalese Blues and Jazz musicians.

Many visitors to Dakar, Senegal have experienced the excitement of the marketplaces, and villages by day, and have also discovered 'Dakar by Night'

Randy Weston & Jazz & African musicians & Artists

Larry Ridley & Jazz Legacy

Sister Carol & Baba Maal

Funk master Pape' Njie

Senegalese superstar Youssou N'Dour, Moustapha Diop and myself

Part 3

The Gambia

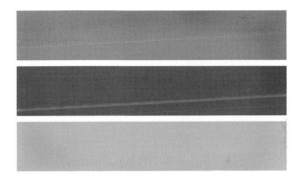

The smallest of African countries, its smallness though gives it an intimacy that is not found in many African countries, and it is in contrast to its larger neighbor and sister country Senegal. One can find solace in its limited borders, and comfort in its slow pace.

The Gambia is 10, 600 sq. kilometers, it is 50km (30 mi.) wide at its widest point, slightly more than twice the size of Delaware. It borders the Atlantic Ocean and the country of Senegal, in fact it appears to cut right into Senegal, as if it was a knife with Senegal on three sides, and the Atlantic Ocean at its feet.

The Gambia has a population of 1,204.984 (July 1996), the ethnic divisions are Mandinka 42%, Fula 18%, Wolof 16%, Diola 10%, Serahuli 9%, other 4% , non Gambian 1%. The major religion in The Gambia is Islam at 90%, Christian 9%, indigenous beliefs 1% .

English is the official language.

The Gambia gained its independence from the United Kingdom, Great Britain in 1965, on December 12, 1981 it signed an agreement with Senegal to form a loose confederation known as Senegambia, that lasted until September 30, 1989 when it was dissolved. The first president was Dawda K. Jawara who was overthrown in a bloodless coup by young soldiers on July 22, 1994, in which they formed the Armed Forces Provisional Ruling Council, led by Capt. Yahya A. J. J. Jammeh, and Capt. Edward Singhateh.

In the presidential elections of 1996, Yahya A. J. J. Jammeh has been elected President of the Republic of The Gambia.

(From Internet sources and travelogues)

New Archway in Banjul, The Gambia

My first visit to The Gambia was in 1984, we had traveled by road to The Gambia, a long and difficult journey marked with a very bad road filled with potholes that had to be carefully navigated, and rest stops with unsanitary toilets or interesting but real 'bush' stops. We had an additional interesting experience in that we took a 'bush' taxi to The Gambia, three years later with the beginning of my planned and organized tours we would have our own bus and driver. However at this time my traveling partner Bill and I and a few other people from our group took one of the local transportation. It was quite an experience, first of all we had to wait quite some time because the vehicle had to be full before we actually took off. That meant waiting for 5 additional persons. It was a station wagon type of vehicle, packed with 11 of us including the driver. Our small pieces of luggage along with sacks of rice, and other parcels of our fellow travelers were tied to the luggage carrier on top of the vehicle. We then shoved off for our trip to The Gambia.

The smells and aromas that emanated from the vehicle were varied, from the funk of non-deodorized arm pits to the sweet and pleasant aromas of Senegalese incense that is burned in dirt and charcoal filled pots that carry through the average Senegalese house and is absorbed into the clothing. The conversation that was carried on was interesting, some did not speak English at all, others speaking in halting English carried on a conversation with us. We made a few stops for personal needs, a few snacks and to let a couple of people off that were going only to Kaolack, one of the larger Senegalese cities, a hub of commerce and a stop off point for those traveling to The Gambia by road. After relieving our selves, grabbing a quick snack and talking with some of the locals we continued along the road to the border. Border crossing is an experience in patience and customs bureaucracy. It also gives a sense of the confusion of colonialism that has affected the people of SeneGambia. Before reaching the border between Senegal and The Gambia, you encounter a language communication of mainly Wolof, and French, after all the formalities, you drive a few yards to the customs office of The Gambia, and here the communication changes to Wolof and English. You begin to see that the people are the same, they look the same, except if they speak Fula, Serra, or some other local language, they still speak Wolof, the only difference is they speak either French or English. This seems like a small difference, but it is a very big social/cultural difference that has been influenced by the Western colonial powers of England and France.

The people of Senegal and The Gambia have picked up the age old rivalry between the British and the French as to who is more civilized, who's culture is higher and more important than the other. The Senegalese who have suffered under the cultural imperialism of the French feel that the Gambians are not as good as they are, less sophisticated, and of course this false concept can sometimes be re-enforced by the fact that Senegal being a much larger country, with more resources can have a superior attitude to The Gambia, a very poor country with little exportable natural resources, an experimental and opportunist entity created by the British for their own selfish benefits, as is the entire division of Africa by the Europeans for their interests, ignoring the boundaries, ethnicity's and cultures of the indigenous peoples of the various regions. And on the other hand the Gambians who's interpretations of the Senegalese are those of thieves, not to be trusted, and imitation French people is one that we are familiar with in the United States, of a Anglo Saxon chauvinism that holds itself above all other cultures and races. It is an example of what Franz Fanon describes in his book "Black Skin, White Masks" of the colonized African, looking to the European as a model of civilization.

We continued on from the border to Barrow, a town that is located at the ferry crossing to Banjul, the capital of The Gambia. Driving to Barrow, you begin to see the difference in the landscape of The Gambia compared to Senegal, which is a dry, arid flatland for the most part, except for a few green areas, such as the Casamace which is actually located south of The Gambia. The Gambia by comparison is green. The changing landscape becomes obvious, you began to see monkeys and baboons in the bushes and trees and sometimes crossing the road. Driving the half hour to Barrow, I reflect on the day before in making plans for this trip.

Our group at this time in 1984 consisted of approximately 17 people, our basic itinerary consisted of a few tours which included, a visit to Goree Island, a tour of the city of Dakar and a visit with Dr. Cheikh Anta Diop. We had plenty of free time as our trip was for 14 days, so we decided to visit The Gambia individually, most of the group would visit The Gambia also, but at different times and by different modes of transportation.

While in Dakar we met a young Gambian student who was visiting Senegal with his uncle. His name was Ebrima Nying, he said to call him Garba, which was the name he was called in Banjul, we talked for several hours and we told him that when we visited The Gambia on this trip that we would visit him and his family. We made arrangements to stay in The Atlantic hotel and that he would meet us there in the evening the day of our arrival. Three sisters that were a part of the group had also made arrangements to visit the Gambia and the village of a brother they met at the hotel. His name if I recall correctly was Lamptey, a very nice person who offered the hospitality of his home and family to the sisters. He said that they could stay there free of charge while they were visiting the Gambia. He also asked Bill and myself if we wanted to stay, but we told him that we had rooms reserved at The Atlantic hotel and that someone was meeting us there, but we would visit his village before going on to the hotel. As we reached the town of Barrow at the ferry crossing, we were met by several brothers with briefcases full of Gambian currency called Dalasis that we exchanged for U.S. dollars, the currency exchange at that time was approximately 8 dalaisi to one U.S. dollar, the current rate is 9..5 dalasis to one U.S. dollar. We waited some time for the ferry, as it runs every 2 hours. The only way that you can reach the capital of Banjul is by ferry from the town of Barrow, the other way is by land from the southern part of Senegal, the Casamance using the back door of the Gambia. The ferry is an interesting experience, there are usually many people at each crossing, traders returning to the capital, buses, cars and other vehicles, people with bags of rice, produce, live chickens, goats, and vendors selling drinks and nuts. It takes about 30 minutes to reach Banjul in regular tide, much longer if the tide is low. The Banjul ferry gives you an introduction to the marketplace women of The Gambia, they are on each side of ferry as it crosses either from

Barrow going to Banjul or vice versa. They are there with their wares, dresses, material, men's up and down print and tie and dye outfits, wood-carvings, etc. Here you will get a sample of the aggressive and exciting bartering that is legend in the marketplaces of The Gambia. From "first price to last price" you will quickly learn this way of life of a people, especially the women, this ability to survive in an environment that is practically penniless compared to the wealth of America and Europe.

Banjul Ferry

This place that was raped of millions of its people. Some hand picked, some thrown to the wind, this place that was colonized and sucked of its god given minerals, this place drained of its finest minds, scattered in the West, groping and fattening the pockets of those that oppress them with the fruits of their labor. And you think to yourself, I'm concerned about Africa, I'm worried about tomorrows for Africa, but I have Imani, I have faith that African people, Black people will return to the source, that they will complete the circle, I have ultimate faith. And it is not just The Gambia, or Africa, that has been seriously underdeveloped, it is also in America, in the Black communities, where slavery, lynching, capitalism, racism, and White supremacy have damaged a people.

In the mist of wealth, poverty, larceny, cheating, drugs, lying and murder they have prevailed. Too many though have succumbed to devastating subcultures. The poet, Askia Toure entitled his award winning book of poetry "From the Pyramids to the projects" is a testimony to the decline of Black civilization. But I have hope, as my mind returns to the moment in Banjul, a small dusty town, many unpaved streets, open sewers emanating unpleasant odors, as you see in most West African cities that I am familiar with. It's not that I am being negative about The Gambia, quite the contrary, it is a beautiful very peaceful place, reminds you of the South, being small everyone knows each other, giving that large family feeling, a place to raise

60

children, a civilized place. I'm not being negative, I love Africa, she is my mother. I always kid my friend Garba, saying that you don't need a taxi to get around the capital, you can walk from one end to the other. But the reality of the situation is that Africa must become strong, become a part of the 21st century, take control of its resources and make a better life for its people. It's in their hands, as Adam Clayton Powell Jr asked "What's in your hand?, and Africans from all over the world must understand this and look at our mother and see what can be done to make her strong and powerful once again, not weak and disrespected.

When we drove off the ferry, we did not go to Banjul, we instead got on the road and drove deeper into the bush, we drove deeper where we saw monkeys and people farming, gut stuck in the mud and continued on until we reached Lamptey's village.

The well outside in front of the village was a center of activity as the young children were fetching water the last time for the day, as the dusk quickly began to envelop the village. It was a nice village, people were very friendly, the ladies waving to us, the children gathering and giggling, and the men nodding their approval. Bill, myself and the three sisters that were going to spend the night, reached Lamptey's compound where we were greeted by several of his family members. We had a great time, talking, eating and enjoying each others company.

After some time Bill and I looked at the time and realized that the two hours were up that we had told the taxi driver to be back in. Lamptey was telling the sisters where they would sleep, and pointed to a thin pallet on the floor with a mosquito net over it as one of the places where they would sleep, you should have seen the look of concern on the sisters' face, one of sisters was pretty large, she was sweating profusely, she said she had to go to the bathroom and Lamptey pointed out in the dark, and said that one of the women in the compound would take her out there, you talk about dark, it's serious in the bush in Africa at night. I mean this really worked on the sisters.

We heard the horn of the taxi driver and said that our driver was here and we had to go. One of the ladies, said "you're leaving?" we said "yes we had told the driver to come back and pick us up and the hotel room was reserved." The look on the sisters' face were expressions of distress, they were trapped, they promised the brother they would stay, he was very hospitable, it would have been an insult if they changed their minds now. We quickly got out of there and into our taxi after saying our good-byes and the sisters giving us unbelieving looks and a few dagger stares. The next day around noon the sisters came to the hotel, their obligation over, they had spent their night. Of course they got on us, how could we leave them like that, and look where we slept, looking around the Atlantic hotel, a very nice hotel in 1984, it had been refurbished in the mid nineties. But the sisters were cool.

We visited several places in the Gambia starting with the museum which has very interesting exhibits on the ancient history of Africa and SeneGambia. The museum also chronicles the history of colonialism in The Gambia and photos of the various British colonial masters. We of course visited the famous woman in Serrakunda that operates a tie and dye factory, where you can see the women demonstrating the process, tying the cloth with string, dipping it into various dye, then untying it and displaying the beautiful colorful fabric to the delight of the watching group. In the next fourteen years I would see this process unfold many times, and would marvel at the bartering skills and saleswoman ship of Kebba Dramah, the proprietor of this establishment. She is known all over The Gambia and really all over the world with the tourist from many countries who have visited The Gambia, as 'Mama Tie-Dye'. A wealthy woman with her Mercedes and mountains of tie dye that thousands of tourist annually buy. Employing her daughters, granddaughters, and nieces, extended family and others, a center of African commerce, vibrant, yet subtle. Kebba Dramah is a very successful business woman, shrewd, tough, and charming. This is the legacy of the African business woman, the backbone of the continental African economy, and perhaps even in the Diaspora. However in Africa it is more obvious, more pronounced, you see the mature African business woman traveling on the airlines often, to Europe, other African countries, and lately to the United States. Back and forth, trading, bringing African goods to various places and bringing back the European or American fashions and other Western produced items to a people that crave these products, and like the African American will find the money, some way, some how in order to have them. The women of The Gambia, understand that they have to make sure that there is food on the table for their children, so they hustle hard. Because they realize that they live in a society where there is little wealth, only for a few. They realize what being poor means, it means that their land was exploited, raped,divided so that the people would be fragmented and separate, bickering about whose European language was better, and who was better than who.

"Mama Tie dye
& others

Tie dye print

The Gambia is very small, because the Europeans treated it as a slice of pie, enjoying its fruit, getting fat off its richness, then leaving it alone and ineffective. In the marketplace it all becomes a skillful art between seller and buyer. The ladies of The Gambian marketplace in Banjul are good, they invite you to come inside their shops "come see my shop" "come, just take a look". These little "shops" that they have are little step-ins where many colorful cloth, dresses, wood carvings and other artifacts can be found. These were very nice little shops that were built that allowed each merchant the ability to close their shops with a metal gate. This came several years later though, a far cry from the market place in 1984. The sisters love to trade also, if you had some used bras, children clothing, they could cut you a good deal on the things that they had, that you wanted.

The Gambia has somewhat of a nightlife, they have a few clubs and restaurants, one of these clubs that I always enjoyed, which at this time I believe is no longer opened, is The Oasis. It was a comfortable club with a good dance floor, and some fantastic dance competition shows. There was a midget there that always tried to steal the show with his incredible and funny dance antics. The music was good and even though there was air conditioning in there, with the number of people and the energy of SeneGambian dancing you always came out of the Oasis with your clothes soaked, but feeling good about the night. The Atlantic hotel has its own entertainment with its dinner time dance and music shows, sometimes featuring the fantastic dance and acrobatic performances of the Puhl people from the Casamance. Their club and lounge always features a band and disco music for the dancing pleasure of the guests. It is a very nice and comfortable hotel, not fancy, not glitzy, it has three floors, on the beach, laid back like The Gambia and relaxing.

Fula acrobats

The Gambia would become for me, and many others that would travel with me in the future, an escape from the much faster pace of Senegal, or more accurately the hustle and bustle of the big African city that everyone talked about called Dakar. When you reached The Gambia, especially after the long tiring ride from Dakar, you kind of exhaled, wiped your brow and felt the relaxation of the pace. Not that The Gambia was without sin though, not that you were safe from criminals, and the like, you see because what slavery and colonialism has left Africa with is a hard tough life for the masses of its people, the broad masses. So even in a seemingly peaceful and calm environment, you will still find criminals, and you can still become victimized. I was a victim of what I am saying, I was conned out of $10,000 in a gold purchasing scheme by a guy who I later found out was a sort of Gambian Mafia. I usually do not use European models as an example. But I think that in this case it is okay, because the Mafia is a good example to show how members of a community can get fat off extorting each other like having notches on your gun for all the members of your community that you have murdered. The Mafia is a good example of one who can get rich off ripping off people, in and outside the community.

This was and maybe even today is what is or certainly was happening in The Gambia.

I was to have purchased some 22 karat gold from The Gambian Don Sehou Youba Cissou, from Seracunda. I gave him a deposit in August 1992, and he instructed me that when I returned to wire transfer more money, and also to locate a gold dealer who could purchase the gold for a good price and he would come to the U.S. to close the deal. I went to 47th street in Manhattan that had many gold and diamond dealers. After checking a few I had a serious conversation with Ira, he said that he was looking for a reliable contact for African gold because he had gotten burned a few times before and that he had many faxes and no results. He said that he would be able to take about 30 kilos at a time from me, cash and carry and no questions asked, I told him that we had a deal and that I was expecting some very soon.

My wife Safiya had gotten the guest room ready expecting this visit from The Gambian Don Sehou Youba, who never came, He kept giving reasons why he could not come, but told me that he was sending someone to bring the package. I waited at the airport with my sign for the courier who never came. Feeling that I had been had I called and threatened Sehou Youba, and he apologized and told me that the guy who was supposed to bring the gold could not get a visa. He said that he was going to re-route him through Europe and that it would take another two weeks. He also suggested that perhaps that he should send more gold since they had to wait to process the papers, so I should send some additional funds to bring the bigger package, which I foolishly did. You see greed is the real culprit here, this is what happens with gold, people are driven to obtain it and in the process do stupid unimaginable things, things that sensible intelligent people would not do. Some spiritual readers from Senegal felt that he had some Juju on me that was controlling my actions in this matter, they said that he had a reputation as a JumJum man.

After several failed arrivals I went to Senegal myself, I was planning to go as a guest of my business associate M. Moustapha Diop to be a part of the by annual Bienal Art festival. I figured this would be a good time to finalize this deal and I had with me the last thousand dollars that I was told was needed so that I could pick up the package.

The deal was finalized after several cancellations and changes. Two Gambian men came to my hotel room and we made the final exchange of money for 'gold'. I did not test the gold because I was trying to play the whole thing very low profile, because I worried that if the word got out that I had a bag of gold, I could get killed. So I had put it in a safe deposit box and told no one. When I left Senegal, I concealed it in one of my bags and did not declare it through customs when reaching the United States. I had a bag with five Kilos of 22 carat gold dusk. I hurriedly headed for my house and concealed it in a closet, my wife and I were excited about the prospect of having a few more dollars, and felt real good about this development.

The next day I went to Ira on 47th street with my bag of gold dust, his son was with him and they became excited when I told them what I was there for and refreshed their memory of my prior visit, particularly Ira, he was ecstatic. He went on to tell me that the future looked bright for us and that the next time I should take it through customs, that I could afford to pay customs on a commodity like this. As Ira and I were talking he had instructed his son to do a test and see if it really was 22 carat. His son hollered out from the back room, "Hey dad it's not 22" he said as Ira's attention began to shift. A few minutes later he hollered out again "Hey dad it's not 18" by this time Ira had his full attention on what his son was saying. Then finally the bomb hit, his son screamed out "Hey dad this is junk, this ain't shit" Ira went mad, he bellowed "They did it a fucking gen" he kicked the chair so hard I thought that he had broken his foot.

I was still, stocked, stunned, Ira was crying about what he could have made, I am like I got hit with a bomb because I'm the one who lost the money. He asked me how much did they get me for, I told him $10,000 Ira said "the sonsofabitches"

I tried every legal means to get my money back. I met with several people of some prominence and influence, a relative of the young man I had sponsored to go to school in the states who was a businessman, the Inspector General of the police. I sat down and ate Benechin with the Inspector, he promised to nail this guy Sehou Youba, telling me that they have been waiting for someone to come forward against this criminal. I spoke with a lawyer that my friends' uncle took me to. He said that he could help me to recover my money and that I should get certain documentation, such as the results of the test on the gold and wire transfer receipts, etc. I went back to the states and I took care of all of that, I sent everything to the lawyer, I heard nothing, he never returned my calls, I then realized he had been bought. I contacted my friends in The Gambia again and they connected me with a new lawyer, one they say could not be bought. He told me he could handle it but it would cost me a thousand dollars, I felt what the heck if it could get me my $10,000 back it would be worth it. I agreed but I was trying to make arrangements to wire the money then all of a sudden I could not reach him. Finally friends of mine in Senegal and some Gambians had the Gambian Don arrested, but he was out the next day, he was paying everyone off. This type of corruption that was allowed to happen in this small, peaceful and poor nation is because there was corruption in the government. I often tell people that are traveling with me on tours to Africa to keep their eyes open and their guards up like they were in the States, like in New York. That they should not relax too much and think that Africa has not been affected and influenced by the rest of the world, with drugs and crime. And here I am the leader, the organizer, falling for the con, it's the greed for gold, just like the gold rush days in California, the conniving, the larceny, the con games, the murder.

The Gambia's social environment is good, the capital Banjul is not a hustling metropolis, that brings with it fast and unsavory characters. The people are very friendly and hospitable. This hospitality I would experience time after time whenever I visit the compound, the home of Garbas' family from my first visit in 1984 through the nineties. Every Summer I bring a group of people from the states to the compound where Garba's mother and father and sisters prepare a large spread of delicious Gambian food that we devour. The family usually invites half of the neighborhood to join in the festivities, where we all dance to SeneGambian music and the Gambian women show the African American women how to do the local dances. We have a great time enjoying each other and sharing, them with their food, music and hospitality and us with our gifts, our laughter and our cameras. When we board our bus to return to Banjul there is a joy to hear the goodbye songs sung by the family and community of Baakow and a regret that our visit was ending.

Family celebration (Garba's House)

That Saturday evening we would enjoy our last night at the Atlantic hotel and a wonderful show and dancing at the hotel's club. The next morning would find the group preparing for an early departure from the hotel in order to catch the first ferry at 8:00am. Crossing the ferry we would again meet the same women that we met on the ferry coming to Banjul, trying to get in their last possibilities of sales. You have to admire these women for their steadfastness, and self-determination, after all they have to feed the babies.

Once we reached the mainland, we continued on into the bush in our drive to reach the village of Juffere, the ancestral home of Alex Haley, the writer of the Autobiography of Malcolm X and the smashing book and TV miniseries "Roots". The deeper into the interior we traveled we began to see more monkeys in the trees and bushes, people planting and weeding, boys herding cattle, when suddenly the vehicle we were driving in got bogged down in the mud. It had rained the night before or earlier in the morning and the roads had turned to mud, we had to get out and push the vehicle out of the mud. It was a lesson to be learned for the future that if it has recently rained then it is better not to try to make the trip to Juffere. This has disappointed many people on the trips, but the consequences of having a bus to push out of the mud, rationalizes this disappointment and letdown.

When we finally reached the village of Juffere, seeing the tiny insignificant sign, the mud and tin topped houses, the dirt and mud roads that snaked through the village. We were somewhat disappointed at the lack of grandeur, and the sameness as other villages we had seen in Senegal or The Gambia. I said to myself "is this the famous village that was one of the focuses of the 'Roots' story? It looked like any other obscure village in any part of Africa that one might visit, nothing indicating that this was an internationally known village, in fact I have seen more attractive villages than this one. The children were all around us begging and pulling, not quiet and gradually attaching as is the children in most villages in Africa. They were immediately aggressive, this I learned was due to the thousands of people that have visited The Gambia as a result of the 'Roots' story over the past 20 years.

This was once a hard working village of farmers, now it is a village of beggars, waiting for the next tour bus to arrive. One wondered what might have happened to the all of the money that Alex Haley made from the book, and film series, and why wasn't this developed into a real tourist spot, where a museum, gift shop, a restaurant or guest house was built.

It was said by the villagers, that Haley had promised to build a mosque, they took me by the foundation that had been laid and that is how it has stayed for 20 years. This place that is a bridge from past to present, a specific link to that past that African Americans seek, searching for their beginnings, as a child who does not know who its father is, at some point in its life begins to search for him.

This place that people of other races come to see, this link with a piece of history, satisfying their curiosity, is now just a tourist spot making money for tour companies and tour guides, while giving tokens and pennies to the chief, the village guide and a few others. Of course on the other hand I have heard that Alex Haley sent money but it did not go to the causes that it was earmarked for. Which one could readily believe, given the state of corruption in Africa. I must emphasize, that this unfortunate state of corruption in Africa is due to its underdeveloped condition, caused by slavery, colonialism and neo-colonialism.

Because there is nothing genetically wrong with Africa or continental Africans, just as African Americans we know that in spite of our culturally and economically dominated position in America, we are not as too many white people think genetically inferior. Somehow though I feel that Alex Haley could have done more to assure that certain projects would be completed, in spite of the problem of this possible corruption.

In spite of all these situations we had a very interesting, educational and meeting nice people tour of the village, which is how I look at Africa, I love Africa, and I am critical of her because I love her. I want us, all of us African people to get back to where we were in our historical glory days, powerful, organized and respected. We signed the big visitor's book, frayed by thousands upon thousands of people, flipping through its pages, it seemed to have most of the important people in the world's signature, political people, entertainers, sports figures, etc. This is where we met the chief and dashed him something in recognition of his position. Then we all gathered in a meeting place with thatched roof and open walls, sitting around in a circle and was introduced to Binta Kinte, a cousin of Alex Haley, the line on the other side that kept the name Kinte going for centuries, as in Kunta Kinte. Again the realization of history being re-visited, that link with the past, coming full circle, the understanding of the Kinte family being reunited after centuries of separation, this is the stuff that Hollywood is made of.

Binta Kinteh
house in Juffere

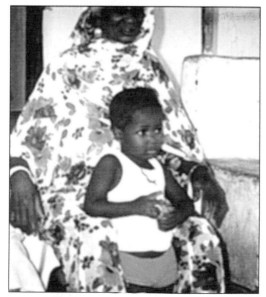

Binteh Kinteh & great
granddaughter

Some people actually believe that it was all Hollywood, that the whole thing is a farce, a fabrication, a plan by Haley and White folks to make money. During that period of the late seventies, there were many critics of the Roots mini series that gained a record of the most or one of the most watched programs in the history of television series. Some pointed out the Hollywood cosmetology, the curtains, and table cloths in the houses of the slaves in the scenes, not the harsh and stark reality of the slave quarters and life on the plantation. Some dismissed the book and the TV series as a complete lie, a hoax, a con game, however part of the story is true. I met a gentleman in 1987 in The Gambia, a griot (historian), a trade unionist, former scout leader, and elder statesman. His name is Al-Haji Cham Joof, I call him professor Joof. I organized a lecture by him, where he spoke on the history, customs, and family structure of SeneGambia while a Kora player played interludes of Gambian rhythms. The Gambia is famous for its world renowned Kora players. Then we had a naming ceremony where we all received names from the Senegambian Muslim influenced culture. The name I was given is Bakari Sanna, this now was added to a growing list of names from Senegal, Ghana, and now The Gambia. Prof. Joof was very instrumental in helping Alex Haley to find the village of Juffere, due to his designation of Scout Master he knew The Gambia and its geography, people, languages and customs. He told us that given the information that Haley had provided him with they took off by road and by boat to try to find this area according to Haley's account of the names and the river that the elders in his family had mentioned to him. Eventually after several excursions and speaking to countless people, as the surname of Kinte is very common in The Gambia and to find the right family was the challenge. Eventually they found the village, the accounts of Kunta Kinte were matched, several connections were made to confirm that this was the village that Kunta Kinte came from. Prof. Joof said that this was a time of great excitement for The Gambia and for Alex Haley and his family, both in the United States and in the village of Juffere. TV cameras came, newspapers and magazines from around the world, tourists came in droves, bringing their dollars, trinkets and candies. Alex Haley and Binta Kinte, his cousin and the matriarch of the Kinte family became celebrities, their pictures appeared together with the children of Binta, plastered all over TV screens, newspapers and magazines, all over the world.

Al-Haji Cham Joof first met Alex Haley at the Atlantic hotel in 1967, they would eventually start their search that would locate the village, which would result in Haley writing the book, and subsequently the mini series "Roots" would emerge in 1977. The book "Roots" was embroiled in controversy, not only by African centered scholars for its historical inaccuracies, but also by two authors charging Haley with plagiarism. It seems that award winning poet and novelist Margaret Walker had charged Alex Haley with taking from the story of her maternal grandmother in her book "Jubilee", she had sued Haley in court. There was a White author who also sued Haley, for taking information from his book titled "The Africans". Both of the cases wound up in court, the White author was given a settlement, Margaret Walker however lost her case. I asked Prof. Joof about this situation in the United States courts, and he said that he had told Alex to do it another way, stick to the truth and focus more than he did on Africa. Before the name "Roots" was decided on, there were several names and focuses for the book, one of which was "Before Disaster". It seemed that Alex Haley did not have enough information to create a substantial story on the United States side, and therefore he resorted to plagiarism to complete his project. Prof. Joof said perhaps he should have stuck to the original script and devoted most of his story to the African side of the family, where the information would be accurate and use his imagination and creativity to fill in the portion that would be the American side.

In any event the book and the mini series were very successful and Haley and others made some money. Juffere, and The Gambia however did not benefit very well, other than the flow of tourism from around the world. Back in the village of Juffere we posed for pictures with Binta Kinte, lis-

tened to the history of the village, and took pictures of and with the people of the village. We prepared to depart saying our good byes to the Kinte family, the chief, elders and people of the village. We made our way through the village with many children asking for dollars, as we boarded our bus and looked back at the tiny weather worn sign identifying the village, I wondered if this was a repeat situation of the exploitation of Africa in black face.

Al Haji Cham Joof

Part 4

Togo, West Africa

The country of Togo borders the North Atlantic Ocean, between the countries of Benin and Ghana. The total area is 56,790 sq km, slightly smaller than West Virginia.

Population is 4,570,530 (July 1996 est.). Ethnic divisions, African (37 tribes; the largest and most influential are the Ewe, Mina, and Kabre) 99%, European and Syrian-Lebanese are less than 1%.

Religions: indigenous beliefs 70%, Christian 20% and Muslim 10%

Languages: French is the official language, and the language of commerce, Ewe and Mina (the two major African languages in the south), Dagoma and Kabye (the two major languages in the north).

Togo gained its independence April 27, 1960 from France and became the Republic of Togo. It has a multi-party constitution, and a French based court system.

Togo grows coffee, cocoa, yams, cassava, corn, beans, rice millet, sorghum, meat and has a huge fishing industry. It exports phosphates, cotton, cocoa and coffee.

Its currency is the CFA, the French West African franc.

The Portuguese slave traders were the first Europeans to venture into Togo, in the 1884 division of Africa Togo was colonized by Germany until World War 1, following an Allied victory, the British and French took it away. The country was split between the two winners of the European war, and along with this the split and division of ethnic communities, as was the case in so many ethnic communities in Africa at that time creating adversaries and enemies of people who were related for centuries.

Togo like many African countries since their independence, has endured several coups that are most often influenced, instigated and planned by Western powers.

Togo has been in a state of economic and political instability for some time and does not have a competitive infrastructure for tourism. Its hotels are in a state of disrepair, and its roads barely passable. Togo however has much interest to those people looking for the traditional African way of life, with its Voodoo villages, marketplaces and shrines. It is a hub of commerce, with its exciting marketplaces, African cloth and artifacts from the indigenous people and surrounding countries.

(Internet and travelogue sources)

In most African countries the reality and effects of almost a century of colonialism has left its mark that 30 to 40 years of independence has not erased. Most countries have adopted the religion of those that have either invaded or colonized Africa, a few countries however, including Togo has for the most part maintained their traditional way of belief, that some might call religion. Voodoo is the prominent spiritual practice in Togo, vastly overshadowing Christianity and Islam. You can go to an open marketplace to purchase your good luck charm, or you can select any number of Voodoo priests to give you a reading on love and fortune. You do not have to sneak to see these priests under the cover of darkness, or receive your charm under the table, it is the accepted and dominate practice among the people.

I visited Togo in 1992 for a few days with a group of African American travelers. It was our first stop of a two country trip that also included Ghana, where we planned to spend 8 days. After arriving in the capitol of Lome on Air Afrique from JFK, we were met by Victor Kugzebeazor, a long time guide and friend from Ghana. He had crossed the border between Ghana and Togo with a bus to meet us and start our tour in Togo. After visiting Togo for a few days we would travel by road to Accra, Ghana. Leaving the airport in Lome we went directly to the Hotel De' Lapix, we were to experience the effects of an infrastructure that has seen its better days. The hotel's air conditioning system was not working and the worn and soiled splendor of Hotel De' Lapix became an unbearable hot box, and overrun with ladies of the night. The rooms however were okay, you could tell that the hotel at one time was a quality hotel, it had a very nice lobby, carpeted, though worn, interesting ceiling architecture, comfortable stuffed furniture, and the view of the Atlantic Ocean was quite good.

The next morning we started on a city tour of Lome', a small interesting city alive with the hustle and bustle of commerce. Lome' while not having a developed infrastructure to attract a sufficient number of tourists, is known as a haven for traders, Its marketplaces are stocked with crafts and items that African traders purchase and trade for other commodities from various West African countries and some European countries.

It is known that the African women traders that one so often encounter on the airplanes flying throughout West Africa, make Togo a major stop in the supply circuit.

My group had a great time bartering with the merchants in the marketplaces. One marketplace that was totally fascinating was the voodoo marketplace where people come to purchase their good luck charms, the stalls are overflowing with various animal parts, heads, tails, claws and body parts.

Most westerners would be appalled, some probably horrified at this overwhelming display of pieces of dried animals. However the indigenous people and others who consistently have been exposed to this, treat it as any other item for sale that one looks over and passes on to the next stall. Some of us decided to visit one of the Voodoo huts for a forecast, it was quite interesting. The voodoo priest read us one at a time while the rest waited their turn, there was an altar where alcoholic drinks were poured over shrines that consisted of small statues, sometimes a sort of rock that had a small mound, sometimes chickens were sacrificed, as one could see from the dried blood on the rock of the shrine.

For a small fee the priest would perform the ritual and give you a forecast for the future, telling you to beware, or prepare for a bright future in love and wealth. This was not a clandestine situation as you might find in some countries in Africa that have strong Christian or Islamic influences, it was open and visible.

As I mentioned earlier Togo was going through a lot of political turmoil at the time of our visit, there was an assassination attempt on the opposition presidential candidate and unrest was apparent with the presence of the military seemingly everywhere.

We had a very scary and I might add exciting experience when we were going to visit a village and some other interesting areas in the up country, north of the capitol of Lome. The political situation was that the government had its base and loyalty in the capitol, and other areas other than where we were going. We had entered the area of the opposition, while we did not know we were soon to find out. Traveling along the road, enjoying the sights of the countryside our bus suddenly came to a stop, we looked out and discovered that there was a huge tree limb lying across the road blocking our path. Then out of the bushes came a group of young men, some holding old rifles in their hands, some with machetes, our group which consisted of approximately 12 persons, mostly women, were all very frightened at this group of rag tag young rebels as they advanced on our bus. They demanded that the driver open the door and they came on board, looked us over with guns pointed and ordered everyone off the bus. They lined us up and began to search us. Patting the women down, everyone was stiff, silent and frightened. Our guide Victor gave the leader of the rebels some money and apparently it was sufficient because they told us to get back on the bus.

This we did with great relief, for this of course was not a welcomed experience. We continued along the road, talking excitedly about our narrow escape, when the bus once again came to a sudden stop. I thought to myself what now? Looking out the window lo and behold it was a repeat situation, there was another large tree limb blocking the road, rebel soldiers with antiquated weapons approaching the bus with guns pointed in our direction, we could not believe that we were once again experiencing this harrowing situation. This time they did not order us off of the bus but instead came on, guns pointed at our heads, looking at us, under seats and proceeding all the way to the back, looking under our baggage and feeling the outside of some. We suppose they might be looking for weapons, perhaps they thought that we might be gun smugglers or maybe we had concluded at this time that they wanted to shake us down for more money. Victor our tour guide again gave them some money and they left the bus and left us in a state of disbelief, wonder and concern. We all came to the conclusion that this was a shakedown and that these rebels were taking advantage of the political situation in the country and using the unrest to extort money from foreigners and visitors. So later when we were stopped incredibly for the third time by still another group of rebels we were not afraid this time. Victor just waved them off and told them that we were not going to give them anything and that they should get some money from their comrades who have already fattened their pockets. With that we just continued to move ahead and was not interfered with as we continued our journey to the villages and cultural areas north of the capitol of Lome.

Our visit to the northern area was an interesting and learning experience. We visited and shared the day with the indigenous people and culture of Togo, not too French, not too commercialized, the experiences that you usually have when leaving the commercial capitals of Africa and traveling into the rural or bush areas.

When we were finally ready to leave Togo headed for Ghana by road, we experienced another phenomenon that was the border crossing, it was a most busy, exciting and complicated time.Leaving the country of Togo, going through what seemed like several custom stops with the Togolese custom people, amidst the hawkers and vendors and hustlers that made the border their daily bread basket.

What seemed like purposeful complications and many dashes was, I suppose, part of the picture. After spending what seemed like hours at the Togo side of the border we moved a few yards to enter the Ghana side of the border, again a repeat performance, dash and confusion and hustling and the hot sun all meshing with the sounds of the day. I'm sure I must have previously mentioned that patience as a virtue was not just a wise saying but in fact a necessity for sanity on the African continent, and an African road border crossing was an extreme test of this virtue.

We finally went through all of the procedures and emerged triumphantly on the soil of the Republic of Ghana.

We picked up speed along the road to Accra, heading for the land of the chiefs.

Part 5
Ghana, Land of Kings and Queens

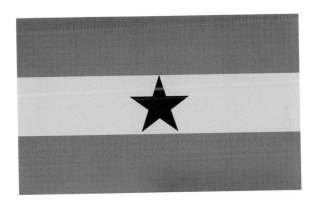

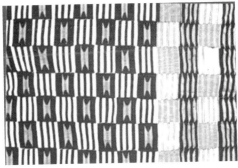

The Republic of Ghana who's name comes from the ancient kingdom of Ghana, which was actually located approximately 500 miles to the north of the present capitol of Accra. The actual name of ancient Ghana was Wagadugu. Some people of present day Ghana had ancestors linked with ancient Ghana. They can trace the family line to Mali, and the people of Northern Ghana, such as the Dagoma, Gonja and the Mamprussi people. The kingdom of Ghana controlled the trade in gold between the south and the Sahara routes. Copper, salt and other important minerals for export was the focus of Ghana. Ghana later became 'The Gold Coast' so much gold was found that the Portuguese then the British adopted the name Gold Coast. It remained with that name during the entire colonization period, until independence came on March 6, 1957 with Dr. Kwame Nkrumah as Prime Minister. On July 1st 1960 Ghana became a republic with Kwame Nkrumah as its first president. Dr. Nkrumah renamed the new republic after a great empire in the history of African people, hoping to reconstruct a new Ghana empire. An empire that would unite all of Africa in this thrust for independence and to restore Africa to its rightful place in history, to restore its humanity, its philosophy and its culture as a model for civilization.

Ghana has gone through tumultuous political turmoil since the overthrow of Dr. Nkrumah, who brought to Ghana an African socialist philosophy that the West was uncomfortable with. In spite of this reality and the adversarial relationship that it brought, Ghana has still remained a citadel of Pan Africanism, a bastion of intellectual debate, and a conglomeration of contradictions.

However Ghana in the midst of these contradictions has maintained the most visible, vibrant and cohesive African cultural structure on the continent of Africa that affect millions of people, and that is the chieftaincy. The

system of Kings and Queen Mothers, Chiefs and Priests that all of the people respect, the old, and young, the rich and those struggling to feed themselves each day.

This is the Ghana that I saw and felt, and this is the Ghana that I want to share with you.

Asantehene, Ashanti king

Vital Statistics

Ghana has an area size of 238,537 Kilometers, its 1996 estimated population is 17,748,400.

Major ethnic groups are: Akan 44% Mole - Dagoma 16% Ewe 13% Ga 8% European and other 0.2%.

The religions of Ghana are Christian 42.8%; Muslim 12%; Other religions 38.2%.

Ghana has 12,130 primary schools, 5,450 junior secondary schools, 503 senior secondary schools, 21 training colleges, 18 technical institutions, two diploma-awarding institutions and five universities serving a population of 17 million. So you can see that Ghanaians have relatively easy access to good education.

The official language of Ghana is English, the most widely spoken indigenous language is Twi of the Akan people.

Currency: Cedi - 2,640cd = $1us

(Internet sources)

Sounds Of Ghana

With the wakening of the dawn
with the rooster's call to life
and the birds chirps stirring the day
to the house sounds of Reggae and High Life
and fetched water being poured and splashed
and squeals of children in early morning cold baths
with voices slowly meshing with the sounds of the day
Ga sounds, and Twi sounds
& English accented sounds
& sounds along the highway
 calling out the various fruits and vegetables
an abundance of food
home grown and healthy is everywhere!
then market place sounds
the calling of wares
the friendly barters
the sounds of African commerce
the sounds of rifle clicks
and boots of soldiers & police cries
where are you going?
who are they?
open your trunk!
okay pass on
and sounds of Methodist & Presbyterian hyms
and drum & shakere sounds
and Baptist wails and drums
and shakereing the spirits
and fetish ancestral sounds
and the sounds of funeral mourns
spirituals sung
drums pounding out the sorrow of families
drums pound out the promise of tomorrow
and the mourners dance to the new day
the new dawn of passage
village celebration sounds
the excited voices of the children

the voices of village people gathering
the tuning of the drums
the sound of pageantry
as the chief & court enter among drums and staffs
and gold glittering against the sun
the sound of priests chanting libations to the
ancestors
for the visitors & friends, for mankind
the sounds of welcome
the sounds of tradition
then sounds of cars & horns blowing
& traffic jam sounds
& sounds of hustle & bustle
then sounds of bending tops of tall elegant palm trees
and splashes of ocean waves
against sandy beaches & Black rocks
and echoes of our ancestors painful wails
in rooms of torture and torment
in the infamous Elmina & Cape Coast castles
the link between the African & the Negro
the breaking ground & slave manufacturing plants
sounds of their cries and their resistance
and their struggle!
Sounds of Ghana

Reflections

Often I am asked if Ghana is my favorite country in Africa, and often I hesitate to give a firm answer as I love all of Africa and particularly those places that I visit often, such as Senegal, which has an excitement and passion that is like no other place. There is though a deep seated root in my soul and spirituality that is connected to Ghana. It reminds me so much of Blacks in the South, quiet and paced, Christian, yet African. Perhaps it is because of these things, or because it attempts to speak English in its own way, or maybe because of the long time relationship with Africa America.

Ghana has a nice feel and I knew immediately upon my arrival in 1985 that this place had a special meaning for me and for my soul. I was fortunate to meet a very special person in New York in 1983, a friend, a mentor, and a big sister. I must take this time to publicly thank brother Lionel, a good and spiritual brother who was attending Queens College at the time and told me of a lady who was completing an advanced degree. Being that I was the director of a cultural center that was a nucleus of activity, that I would find her interesting in that she was a Queen Mother from Ghana. My interest was immediately aroused. When he brought her to The Afrikan Poetry Theatre in 1983 it would be the start of an education for me that would open up the cultural doors of Ghana. It would connect me to a family and a culture that surely had to be where my ancestors originated, via Barbados and Charleston, South Carolina. This lady was Nana Boakyewa Yiadom II, Queen Mother of Adamorobe, and Amanonhene of Aburi, Akuapem, Ghana.

We met and shared the history of our people.

(Nana Boakyewa Yiadom II as Queen Mother)

I was to learn much about the Akuapem and the Asachari clan of Ghana, and Nana would become familiar with the history of the African Americans and the struggle for liberation in America, we would talk and share. She would come to the Center to teach the children how to make Tie & Dye print and tell them stories from Ghana. She would also lecture to the women about the role of Queen Mothers and share with them the plight of the rural women of Africa. Nana not only is an author of children's books and a teacher, but she is also a champion for the development of women in Africa, and serves in that capacity at the United Nations, working for a church based NGO (Non Government organization). Her late husband was in the Foreign Service for the government of Ghana, and served in that capacity in Ethiopia, Uganda (during the period of Idi Amin Dada) and several other countries in Africa.

This allowed Nana to really get to know Africa and its women. After serving the village of Adamorobe as Queen Mother for many years, and after the tragic death of the chief of the village Nana Kwa Kwa Sampong in a car crash in 1995, the council of Elders elected her to be the chief of the village. This is a very important and historical occasion, as she is the first woman ever in the history of Ghana to become a chief. There were female leaders in Ghana's history, but they were either Queen Mothers or stool Leaders never chiefs, such as warrior Queen Yaa Asantewa who led the Ashanti in war against the British. Nana Osei Boakyewe Yiadom II (a slight variation in her name that now has a male spelling and an additional male name) is also the chief stool representative of the Akuapem people who reside in the United States.

(Nana Osei Boakyewe Yiadom as a chief)

84

It becomes evident when you are in her presence that you are in the presence of a Queen, a person of royalty, a quiet, humble, but assured royalty. It was because of this lady that my first visit to Ghana in 1985 was a very special one.

She armed me with several letters as is the custom when someone is returning home, but also letters of introduction to some very important people in the cultural, political and business life of Ghana. In addition I was to meet some of the nicest people on all levels, the town dwellers of Aburi, the wood carvers, the farmers of Adamorobe, textile manufactures, bankers, ministers, chiefs, etc. I was traveling with a good friend and African traveling partner William Dyer, when we reached Kotoka airport in Accra, after spending many frustrating hours in Abijan, Ivory Coast, we were somewhat bewildered not finding anyone there to meet us. (We found out later that there was a mix up concerning the day of our arrival) The flight came in very late, it was after midnight, we eventually got a taxi and asked the driver to take us to Aburi.

We soon got a real quick lesson in the hazards of not pronouncing words properly with the accents in the right places, because after some 20 minutes or so the driver pulled up in front of a large darkened building in Accra, whose large sign read ABC Brewery. After a few more minutes of bewilderment I realized what had happened, it sounded to him that we had said we wanted to go to a brewery, and he took us to this beer brewery. After an exasperated chuckle we finally got through to him that we wanted to go to the town of Aburi in the Akuapem Mountains. Finally we arrived in Aburi, but not having an address, just the name of Nana's sister Mrs. Hammond, whom I had also met in New York in 1983, the driver did not know where to take us so he just let us out some where in the dark. And dark it was, no lights anywhere, pitch black, we could not even make out the houses across the street. After knocking on the doors of a few compounds, we were finally directed to the right house. The morning however brought a wonder to our eyes, the town of Aburi is a natural paradise, way up in the mountains where the air is fresh and clean, where the birds are chirping and everything is green. We discovered that we had moved from the center of town to the outskirts in finding the right house during the night, and was staying on the Aburi estate of Nana Boakyewa Yiadom.

It was a very comfortable setting overlooking the hills and valleys of the eastern region of Ghana.

The house was not new but nice, a 2 family house with the downstairs housing a small leather factory, and 3 bedrooms upstairs, with kitchen, liv-

85

ing room, bath and a small terrace with winding stairs leading to the ground. It is an artist or poet's joy to stand on this terrace, in the early morning or in the early evening, watching the sun rise or set.

Aburi

(View from the veranda/Nana's house)

Over looking lush green lands
rolling hills of trees, plants
fruit from the womb of mother earth
spring forth in abundance
cool breezes gently blow through
Tie-Dye and Kente caressing the natural essence
of my African being
crickets sing, crows, chickens, and ducks
randomly squawk & quack, birds chirp
creating an orchestra of natures
natural self
could this be paradise ?
tucked away in the hills of Ghana
the dawn is like a wonder unto itself
beginning with a mist of fog that slowly and
mystically drifts and reveals a site that is
breathtaking
that sparkles with greenness
as if being watered with the moisture of life
the sunset is like a gradual lowering of the heavens
It seems that you are equal to the sun
and the clouds are lower than your reach
in between the clouds and the green hills
is a burnt orange glow
then quickly, very swifly
the dusk is upon the land
and gradually the mist reappears
like out of some mystically genie's jar
could this be paradise!
tucked away in the hills of Ghana
Aburi.............village of the chiefs

Aburi, Akuapem

Aburi Botanical Gardens

The only inconvenience we found was that there was no running water, the water did not flow. Every day the children had to fetch water from the well across the road at the Aburi Girls School.

In the morning they would bring us a bucket of hot water that they would heat and a bucket of cold water. After several days I began to feel guilty that these children were getting up so early in the morning to fetch the water which was very heavy that they carried on their heads. My guilt was felt especially since I became conscious of the amount of water that I was using to wash and flush the toilet. I realized that I came from a culture that allowed one to leave the tap open and running when shaving or washing, and this was not possible here. I was using much of the water that the children were fetching and storing in a large barrel for the daily use of the compound. So feeling this guilt, I suggested that Bill and myself go with

Sisi "The Old Lady"

the children in the morning to help fetch the water, strong men as we were. In fact instead of fetching enough for only one day's use that we should fetch enough water for two or three barrels, for two or three days. The elders however refused the suggestions, and explained that this conservation idea would change the daily routine of the children. Which instills in them a discipline that requires them to rise at dawn and assume the responsibility of daily supplying water for the compound or village, for washing, cooking, and bathing. This was something that they took pride in and looked forward to. In fact we were told, they could not wait until they were old enough to learn how to balance the bucket on their heads.

I reluctantly accepted their reason for rejecting my suggestion, especially when I thought back to the children in the States and the difficulty we have at times to get them to rise early in the morning and to do their chores. It was a question of values and not convenience. I accepted the explanation as I searched my mind to find the balance for the 21st century, values and modernity.

I really felt at home in Aburi, and Nana Osei Boakywe Yiadom's mother who's name is Sisi, whom many call the "old lady" which is a term of respect in Ghana, because the elders are truly respected. When someone says the old lady said this or that, it is taken seriously and with respect. Call someone an old lady in the United States and you will have a fight on your hands. The old lady really made me feel a part of the family and community of Aburi. When I first met her she looked at me and told everyone that I was descended from one of the eighty Africans who were taken from Aburi and sold into slavery many years ago. Sisi is now a woman of approximately 97 years of age, and still as strong as ever.

Aburi is a paradise, with fruit trees all around and an abundance of food. Aburi is also known for its beautiful botanical gardens, the first in West Africa, its serenity and tranquility is unmatched. Reaching Aburi and the Akuapem area is an exhilarating experience, many people in the capital of Accra refer to the area as 'The Mountains' because when traveling to Akuapem your vehicle has to climb some extremely steep winding roads to reach the upper regions or the top plateau. The roads are very narrow and at certain curves in the road it will only allow one car either way to navigate the curve generously, so usually you would have to blow your horn to alert an oncoming vehicle that you were approaching the curve, which is a blind spot. If you looked to the right while climbing you will be able to see miles and miles of green valleys that seem so far below you, it seems that you are driving into the clouds.

Aburi, I suppose is the center of Akuapem (sometimes called Akwapim, this spelling was started by the British, are a part of the larger group called the Akan, who make up the majority of the population of Ghana. The Akan include: Asante, whom the British called Ashanti; the Akuapem, Fanti, Akyem, Swahu, Brongahafo, and Nzima.) or the Eastern region primarily because of the botanical gardens which attract many international visitors.

(The Aburi Botanical Gardens, opened in 1890, houses many rare plants and trees.) The capital of the Akuapem region however is Akropong, which is further up the mountain. In Akropong sits the palace and the seat of the traditional ruler, the Omanhene or Okuapehene, the paramount chief or traditional ruler of all Akuapems. The King of the Akuapems' is Oseadeeyo Addo Dankwa III, the traditional ruler who has been on the throne for twenty five years. There are many towns and villages in the Akuapem area, each has its own chief, regional chiefs and various traditional rulers. The traditional ruler of a particular ethnic group of people is represented in the National House of Chiefs, which represent the many ethnic groups and traditional areas in Ghana, are the Omanhene's (The Paramount Chiefs). The British called them kings, although there is no such word in the Akan languages, because of their royal nature and the respect they received.

The Ashanti paramount chief sits at the head of the House of Chiefs and is called the Asantehene. The Ashantis' because of their legendary military prowess in conquest, consolidation and federation of local groups, their resistance to European invasion, their vast gold fields and cocoa plantations gives them an historical place and status in the traditional culture of Ghana, and the world looks to the Asantehene as the king of kings. So Akropong is the cultural capital of the Akuapem people, as Kumasi is to the Ashanti.

There are many other important towns in Akuapem, one of which is Larteh. Larteh has its special place in Akuapem, and in fact all of Ghana, because it is one of the few places that has maintained its traditional spiritual religious beliefs. (We will discuss this in more detail later in the chapter, the dichotomy of Christianity and traditional African beliefs in a par-

Oseadeeyo Addo Dankwa III

ticular section and throughout this chapter on Ghana, because Christianity is woven into the fabric of Ghana) Larteh however is the place that many Ghanaians and Europeans are suspected of coining the term to describe the traditional and spiritual practices as 'fetishism', or the place of fetish adherents.

The term has a certain negative ring to it and conjures up visions of so called primitive practices, and is meant to suggest a level of so called uncivilized behavior. It is viewed as such by Ghanaian Christians and Islamic converts, and by Europeans, although quiet as it is kept, many Ghanaian Christian converts secretly visit Larteh for spiritual readings, counsel and direction. The priestess who passed in early 1996 (or as the saying goes 'has gone on to the village') Nana Okomfohemaa Akua Oparebea, was known as the powerful "Fetish woman" throughout Ghana and the United States.

The African American from Georgia, the late Nana Yao Opare Dinizulu was her first African American convert over 40 years ago, and who was responsible for bringing the traditional Akan religion of the Asante people to America, and teaching it to thousands of African Americans. In fact in the continuing controversy of describing and defining African religion and culture, we can surely say that Nana Yao Opare Dinizulu gave to America the cultural practices of the Akans through spirituality, language, dance, dress, customs and traditions, the very essence of the Akan people.

After visiting Ghana many times over the past 14 years, I am able to see many aspects of what Nana Yao Opare Dinizulu, has exported from Ghana that most would overlook, or not truly understand. As I am sure native Ghanaians recognize and are surprised to see its emer-

Nana Yao Opare Dinizulu

90

gence among African Americans in the United States.

It is Larteh and the Akonedi shrine in the Akuapem area that is one of the few places that has and maintains its traditional practices. These places are not only rare in Ghana, but in the whole of Africa, where it is difficult to find areas and cultures that have not been affected by Islam, Christianity, and/or Arabic and Western culture. When you do find them they are just pockets, remnants of grand and glorious cultures. These are generally the 1-5% of the population given after the high percentages given for western religions (Islam and Christianity), except for a few countries.

They are generally described as 'Fetish' or 'Anamist', terms that usually turn up the noses of "Western" religious converts.

There are many other interesting towns and villages in Akuapem, another one that I often take a group to is the town of Mampong. Mampong is known for its school for the deaf, its hospital and for its herbal institution, 'The Institute For Research Into Plant Medicine', a most fascinating place. This is a place that grow its herbs and plants on land that surrounds the institute, processes and evaluates its properties, and has an out patient clinic for the treatment of chronic diseases and illnesses, such as diabetes, high blood pressure, asthma, bronchitis, treats topical skin disorders, etc. It also tests and approves medicines, tonics and remedies of various chemists and companies that want to introuce these products to the Ghanaian public. It has a dispensary where one can purchase various herbal remedies that have been deemed safe after seeing the doctor and herbalist. The director of the center is a physician trained in western medicine, who is assisted by an herbalist. A regular tour of the herbal institute consist of, a visit to various rooms where charts are visible showing the different types of plant life and their usage. Other rooms contain specially controlled temperatures where live plant specimen and herbal products that are undergoing research are kept. Still other rooms contain the processing of plants, roots and herbs, large vats where herbs are boiled, machines that crush and sift, processes that take the herbs, roots and plants from its raw state to finish products such as liquids, powders, paste, creams and lotions, pomades, salves and teas.

Other rooms contain laboratories with many test tubes, ovens, purifiers and equipment for animal experimentation and testing. This is an institute that is sensibly supported and promoted by the government of Ghana, in the best interest of its people. Unfortunately for the people of America, the American Medical Association with its capitalist driven engines has profit as its main objective and not quality health care for Americans. This is another value system observation in assessing the true quality of life in various world societies.

Mampong herbal center

The Akuapem area is also a place where several wealthy Ghanaians build their vacation homes. The weather is cool compared to the low land areas of Accra and the Cape Coast, not many mosquitoes, the air is fresh and clear, and is covered with greenness. Ghanaians are known for building large houses, solid concrete structures, mansions with many rooms and servant quarters the size of 1 family homes in the suburbs of America. One such structure comes to mind in the town of Tutu in Akuapem.

It is the estate of Tutuville that was built by the late Ani, founder of Anitex, a textile manufacturing plant in Accra. I met Mr. & Mrs. Ani in 1985 when I first visited Ghana, Mrs. Ani is an old friend of Nana Boakyewe Yiadom, they were schoolmates in secondary school. Mrs. Ani is also a Pharmacist. I had dinner with them in their mansion in Accra that was an example of the upper echelon of Ghanaian society. But I was to be further awed by the estate in Tutu in the Akuapem Mountains. As mentioned earlier, many of the well to do Ghanaians have homes also in Akuapem, and for the Ani's, their estate was used for vacations, retreats and to entertain sizable groups and conventions for several days. The mansion is luxurious and opulent, from the main road that runs through Akuapem you can see the mansion looming large and impressive as the sun illuminates its white facade. Coming up the long winding driveway, you reach the front of the mansion and become enveloped in its massiveness.

The place is incredible, in addition to the family's private bedrooms, it has 15 guest rooms, each with a bathroom and sitting room. It has 3 formal dining rooms, and several parlors or living rooms. There are verandas on both sides of the bedrooms, you can step out on the balcony facing the sun or the inside balcony looking down on a courtyard in the center of the house, that has a huge tree coming up the center to the third floor. The number of bathrooms in the house (I counted approximately 26) had a special meaning for me, because in Aburi the water did not flow due to the condition of the pipes and the very high altitude and steep incline of the mountains. So it was somewhat of an inconvenience and a discomfort that I could not erase no matter how hard I tried. So upon seeing all of these toilets that flushed! I was so excited I had to suppress an urge to go from one toilet to the other and flush and flush and flush! I was truly fascinated with these toilets and inquired of Mr. Ani how was this possible given the water flow problem in Akuapem. He explained to me that the house is built on a reservoir, and that water is pumped into the reservoir by water trucks, much like a swimming pool, and that there are internal pumps that bring the water to the bathrooms and kitchens in the mansion. So in actuality the house is built on a swimming pool, what money can do. On further explanation of Tutuville we found that the estate was very much self contained, in that there was a small farm behind the mansion where all types of vegetables and fruits were grown, in addition to huge chicken pens and where livestock of pigs and cattle were bred. To complete the package we saw approximately half a dozen small houses where the numerous servants and their families lived. I had never been in such classy and opulent digs in the United States, Tutuville with its marble and glass, imported tiles and carpet, and rich carved and polished wood.

I always find the diversity of Africa very interesting, the difference between the upper class and the impoverished, the Tutuville's and the mud and straw or tin topped houses. The people in the middle, the so call middle class is extremely small in Africa. Either you have money or you do not, either you are rich or you are poor, either you own 2 or 3 Mercedes or Peugeots or you ride the lorry to work or market every day, cramped together like sardines in dangerous barely mobile converted buses, or you walk. So is the area of Akuapem, its rich and its poor, it is however a natural paradise to behold.

Another important and historical aspect of Akuapem is the fact that there is a higher percentage of Ghanaians who are western educated that come from this area, more than any other region in Ghana. This is because the first missionaries that came to Ghana came to the Akuapem area. These were the Basel Missionaries, in the nineteenth century, who set up the first formal school systems, so hence many of the Western trained intellectuals of Ghana hail from Akuapem. Of course we must understand that with western education comes a loss of African culture, simply because this education is couched and clothed in western views, values and philosophy. Just as it is in the lower grade schools, colleges and universities in America. It is all geared towards raising up paradigms of what is viewed as civilization and diminishing the national cultures of people of color. What it does is perpetuate the myth of White supremacy, and a myth is all that it is, if one truly knows the history of the world.

In Akuapem the Basel missionaries came with their education, with their schools, and their religion, with their images of God, white skin, blue eye, blond hair, and images of the savior of Africans. The rewards were attractive however, for those who converted to this European version of Christianity, this cultural imperialism. They were rewarded with material things that were different, some were rewarded with some technological items that the Europeans brought, but mainly it was the difference that fascinated them in the nineteenth century. In later times with the advent of modern technology such as cars and other trappings, and allowing some to go to England to be educated, which meant acquiring nice houses and such, the Ghanaians were hooked. Attending the churches and schools of the missionaries meant the possibility of acquiring these things in this life and a paradise in the heaven thereafter.

Of course there was a price to pay to be a part of this "civilized" society of missionaries, which meant challenging the practice of so called "Ancestral worship", worship of idols, the practice of animal sacrifice, the wearing of the cloth, the wearing of bangles and amulets. One had to give up all evidence of their tradition and customs, all manifestations of the culture in which they were born and bred, and they had to accept European Christian first names. Nana Osei Boakyewe Yiadom II, in our many discussions of Ghana, told me about growing up as a young girl in colonial Ghana and attending the missionary schools. She remembered that the girls were required to wear prim British dresses that had collars that came up to the chin, and frills around the cuffs of the sleeves. If anyone wore any African print, bangles or bracelets to school they would immediately be sent home. The missionaries were afraid of these things because they knew that they had meaning to them and they did not understand them, they wanted total control over the minds and souls of these Africans.

Nana has often explained to me the power of the cloth, in its patterns and its colors, certain symbols represent a language, such as symbols that you find on the Adinkra cloth, certain patterns on the Kente cloth, particular colors. Nana once explained that if a woman was having a problem with her husband and she was angry with him, all she had to do was put on a certain cloth and everyone would understand, they would know, no words spoken.

The Europeans understood this and banned all such dress. They called it backwards, uncivilized, and told the students that such things were shameful. And if they wanted a good Christian education that would civilize and educate them, where they could live good, then they would have to cease with these practices and that they better not bring certain items to school. This brain washing of course created a sense of shame in the students for things that were African, a sense of shame in their parents and the elders of their community. This sense of shame would further prolong the movement towards independence that was underway in the country. It would be several years before the energy of African pride and independence would emerge and propel Ghana towards independence under the leadership of Dr. Kwame Nkrumah.

The missionaries were able to suppress the national culture of Ghanaians who were in the leadership of Ghana, because it was those who attended the missionary schools that were rewarded with the jobs and positions of status, it was those who attended the missionary schools that subsequently were educated abroad. Even Dr. Nkrumah was an educated Christian that carried the Christian name Francis, and was a theology student. Dr. Nkrumah however was exposed to Africans who were some of the most progressive and radical on the planet. These Africans who for 400 years lived and struggled for liberation in the belly of the beast, the United States of America, the bastion of the western slave trade, and a government that has become the most clever of all the western imperialist. He also met, discussed, and collaborated with the intellectual firebrands from the Caribbean.

Ten years in America armed him with not only the impetus for African Independence, but provided him the ammunition to dismantle western cultural imperialism in Ghana. Nkrumah eventually suggested to all Ghanaians to be proud of their culture, to drop their Christian first names and to use their "Kra" name, the name that is given all Ghanaians for the day that they were born on. Nkrumah was born on Saturday, so his name is Kwame, the Francis was dropped.

Nana Osei Boakyewe Yiadom told me an interesting story about Nkrumah's drive to restore culture to the elite and her reason for the story was to also build confidence in myself that I would not feel so terrible about the fact that I could not wrap my cloth about me properly and keep it from slipping. She recalled the time of the big Independence Ball, cele-

brating the independence of Ghana in 1957. It was a grand affair, people came to Ghana from all over the world for this historical event, marking the independence of the first African country south of the Sahara.

Dr. Nkrumah in his drive for a Cultural Revolution, suggested to all Ghanaians who were planning to attend the ball that they should display this pride that was in their hearts and in their souls by wearing Ghanaian national dress. The women came with colorful dresses and the men draped in the traditional cloth, brilliant, colorful Kente and Adinkra, but what a scene it was. The men had such a time trying to keep the cloth on their shoulders. It was truly a difficult and embarrassing time for many. You see these people were the elite, the leadership of Ghana, these were the products of the missionary schools, the western educated intellectuals who were out of touch with the cultural practices of the indigenous people. Most of them had not wrapped a cloth about them ever!, they had quite a trying time that evening. This is all a result of the damaging effects that this missionary education, this western brainwashing had on the Ghanaian, and his

Kwame Nkrumah

appreciation of his culture. Nkrumah went on to say that this brainwashing was so complete that even when the British physically left the government to the Ghanaians, it was if they were still there because the Ghanaian was so trained it was as if they were still colonized. He related this condition of the African leadership mentality to many countries and governments in Africa that had gotten its independence from Europe. It was because of this observation, this condition, that he coined the phrase "Neo-Colonialism" (like colonialism) and that it was the last stage of Imperialism that the African must struggle against if they wanted to truly be free.

This looking at the White man as some symbol of what it is to be civilized must cease, we must as Dr. Maulana Karenga says in Kawaida theory, "View the world in our own image and interest" We must set the criteria for what is beautiful and good. We must be the model for own development, as Kawaida teaches. The representatives of the African nations made a mistake in the 60's. Remember when they came to their Washington, D.C. embassies and to the consulates and missions at the

United Nations in New York? They came in their colorful native dress, their flowing garments, this was new to the United States. The colorful ambassadors and consular were everywhere, very visible, so much so that some African American con artists were dressing up like these African diplomats in colorful garments and signing huge hotel tabs and restaurant checks. Eventually, except for a few, these colorful representatives settled down to the traditional western suit and tie. This accepted version of what was a civilized and dignified person. Who decided this? Why is the European always the one to set the standards for civilization? Psychologically, when the African adopted the costume of the European, he put himself at a disadvantage in the debating halls of the U. N., he was truly in the court of the European, wearing his uniform, acting and thinking like him. If the cloth or the Grand Bubba, or the Oshogba has the power to sway your shoulders back, straighten your back, step, and glide and emanate your Africaness, what makes you think the suit will not cause you to pronounce European rhythms.

It is why Nkrumah wanted the brothers to wrap themselves in the Ghanaian cloth, it is why he wrapped and took photographs for the world to see him in his wrap. And so the missionary education and brainwashing still persists to this day, in Africa, the United States, the Caribbean, South America, and around the world. In Ghana it started in Akuapem.

Unfortunately this mentality has caused me to insert an addendum to this section, at this point. In the September/October 1998 issue of "African Personality" magazine published in Elmhurst, New York, with the cover adorned with a picture of President Jerry John Rawlings in a resplendent Kente wrap, there was a story listed as "First African White Chief". I read this controversial story and responded with a letter to the Editor, in its entirety:

Re: First African White Chief

I had previously read about the "enstoolment" in Ghana of a European-American in one of the New York daily newspapers. I was surprised however to see an article covering this event and the story of Scott Morrow's trip to Ghana, in this magazine titled "African Personality". I expected to see such a story in the main stream White press. I was terribly disappointed to see this very colorful and informative African publication reporting on this cultural travesty without any evidence of criticism. In my opinion if a magazine is going to identify itself with an ethnic perspective, then it should report with a particular editorial slant. If it was a main stream publication then I could see it attempting to be objective, however it has taken on a particular identify and focus in the very nature of its name.

The magazine does live up to its name in the reporting of important news items that cover the continent and the Diaspora in the true spirit of Pan-Africanism. Then why break from the format to report on Scott Morrow? Is this another praise 'massa' story, where Black people all over the earth just love to please and make happy the slave/colonial master. Is this another piece of evidence that Dr. Franz Fanon was talking about in "Black Skin, White Masks" as he analyzed the slave/master relationship in his phenomenal book. The continental African and those in the Diaspora have always had this fascination with White people, looking up to them as if they were God. In fact because the artist Michangelo painted his cousin's portrait and passed it off as Jesus, Black people have had this admiration of White men as some one to look up to, praise, and worship, what ever makes 'massa' happy.

I have studied and have been involved in Africa history and culture for 35 years, have given my children, who are now adults, African names. I have been involved with African centered organizations for many years and founded a cultural center 23 years ago that has become a major African cultural influence in New York. I have become very intimate with several West African countries within the past 15 years, having traveled to Africa approximately 50 times during this period. I am a Pan- Africanist and cultural nationalist that believe as Dr. W.E.B. Dubois stated many years ago that the color line is the greatest challenge to the 20th century. And as one of my teachers and influences, Dr. Maulana Karenga states that the greatest challenge to Black people all over the world is the cultural crisis, ie. the crisis of views and values. The bottom line here is that I love Africa, she is my mother, in fact as we all know that she is the mother of all mankind. But let us be real honest, the European has not treated Africa and her children very well, they have ravished the continent, enslaved millions upon millions of her people, raped her of her natural resources and dominated her views and values with European cultural Imperialism. It is either chic to be French or British, not very much pride in being African, or Black. A very derogative and damaging saying that came out of African American folklore is "If you White you alright, if you Brown stick around, if you yellow you mellow, but if you Black stay back, way back" It is not popular to be Black on this earth at this time, history teaches us though that at one time being Black, being African was associated with greatness, with intelligence and accomplishment. There was a time when Europeans came to Africa to study at our feet, in our universities and temples, in our grand lodges, to learn our science, philosophy and art. They went back to their respective lands much richer with our knowledge and wisdom and spoke very highly of the people of burnt skin. What has happened to this world image of our race? Now we are looked down upon as incompetents, as unethical, and immoral, as niggers. And not only African Americans, Africans from all over, the Caribbean, from the continent of Africa, wherever we may be. Of course all White people do not think this way. There are many who are kind and considerate, many who have struggled with us on many fronts for our human and civil rights, many who have brought aid to the struggling masses in the United States and relief to impoverished villages and communities in Africa. We can never paint with such a broad stroke that we are not considerate of those who have helped us, some have even given their lives for our causes, we can never condemn them. In fact we should give thanks and praises to those Whites who have expressed their humanity in various ways. But we must not lose our faculties and make fools of ourselves by cheapening our culture, our customs and traditions that have been passed down from generation to generation for centuries and centuries.

It is a sacrilege to bestow upon a European such an important cultural title and legacy, calling him Nana, this our spiritual tradition, do you think the Queen of England would accept an African in the royal family?!!!.

There is a way to reward those of other races that have made a contribution to the African cause, I think that we should always do this, however we should be careful that our will to reward does not overshadow our respect for our culture and ourselves.

Finally I would ask what has Scott Morrow done to deserve this important honor, because he dances so well? Please spare me, there are countless Americans of African heritage that have preserved the cultural dance tradition of Africa for too many years to mention. We cannot be so eager about bestowing such important honors for such frivolous deeds.

The "African Personality" must consistently pay attention to the fundamental roots of this personality, and the history and humanity of its being. Funk & Wagnalls Standard dictionary defines an African as 'of or pertaining to Africa, or its inhabitants, a native inhabitant of Africa, a member of one of the African peoples; a Negro or Negrito.

All Europeans/White people who were born and live in Africa are not Africans, they are nationals of those countries, they are citizens and rightfully can call themselves Senegalese, Ghanaians, Nigerians, South Africans or what ever the name of their country of citizenship is called. But they are not African, this is our mighty race that gave civilization to the world.

My belief is that the African, not the European should be the model for civilization, that we should hold our head up high and let the resounding voice of the Honorable Marcus Mosiah Garvey's words ring in our ears "Up you mighty race you can accomplish what you will"

"Race First"

My response to the article that reported on the story of the "First African White Chief" was published in the January/February 1999 issue of the African Personality magazine.

To add insult to injury to this perversion of our legacy. I received a telephone call from a Ghanaian in mid January 1999 that Oseadeeyo Addo Dankwa III the Omanhene (Paramount Chief/King) of Akuapem was preparing to visit New York, and that he wanted me to call him in Ghana. I tried to reach him on two occasions but was not successful, as one time he was traveling in another part of Ghana, and the second time I tried he had already arrived in the States. I finally tracked him down on Thursday evening after contacting a cousin of Nana, he was staying at a mid town hotel. He told me that he was in the country to enstool someone at the United Nations. He said he arrived on Tuesday evening and would be leaving on Saturday. He invited me to attend the installation ceremony on Friday at 1:00pm at the U.N. Later I spoke with his cousin to find out who this person was and he told me it had to do with Ike "Bazooka" Quartey, Ghana's World Boxing Champion in the Welterweight division. He said he heard that Ike was being enstooled and so was his promoter/manager.

I asked was the promoter white? He said that he did not know, but I figured that it had to be a white promoter, while I do not know the boxing game, in fact I do not know anything about sports at all except what comes across on the news. I had only heard of Don King as a Black promoter of any note that might be honored at the United Nations. I was concerned and expressed this to my colleagues at the center and to my wife.

When I arrived at the United Nations the next day, I was met in the lobby by a Ghanaian in traditional wrap. He directed me to the elevator, and fourth floor where the program would be held. After hanging up my coat I entered an area where people were having cocktails, mingling and talking. I noticed that the majority of people were white, some corporate types, intellectual looking folks, press, and others. There were also several Ghanaians, some of the men in the traditional wrap, some in suits and ties, and the women for the most part in some African print and patterns. I recognized a brother from the African American cultural community, also the editor of African Personality magazine and some of the women of the Ghanaian association that I belong to.

I asked the African American brother what this program was all about and he told me that they were going to Enstool (install) a white man! I said that I had suspected that all along, he replied if he had known that, he would not have taken a half day off to be there. I told the editor that here is another case of our praising the white man, he replied that it was his job to cover these events, and that he welcomed differing opinions such as mine and that I should keep on writing. I told him that the only reason that I was there was because of Nana Dankwa, that I was one of his Ankobea's (advisor). I went to the front of the room to see if Nana was seated among several chiefs and others, which he was not. I was told that he had not made his appearance yet. I went to sit with the African American brother who mentioned to me that the affair was dead, no drums, no music, that it was not your typical gala African royalty affair. After a few minutes he left but I was for the sake of Nana going to see this thing out. The M.C. a Ghanaian skinin' and grinin' was trying to entertain the audience with his comments and trying to talk proper white talk with an accent. He began to talk about the promoter who was to be honored as a prominent millionaire lawyer, businessman, and boxing promoter. There were several boxing promotion people there, the president of Main Events, president of HBO Sports and several vice presidents of HBO Sports, and Bob Arum of Top Rank Promotions. Also present was Welterweight champion Ike Quartey who would be recognized and told that he would be so honored as his boxing mentor was to be in the near future. He was installed as a Chief in waiting, in that he would serve the needs of his white chief.

There was also a Black United States Congressman who read a citation from the Congressional Black Caucus congratulating Fredric G. Levin on his enstoolment as Barima Ofori Agyeman or Nana Ofori Agyeman I of Akuapem. These were sad words to my ears, bestowing such honors and titles on this person from a race of people who raped and colonized a whole continent.

Also present was His Excellency Jack Wilmont, Ghana's permanent Representative to the United Nations, and His Excellency Koby Koomson, Ambassador of the Republic of Ghana to the United States. Ambassador

Koomson spoke of the honor that was to be bestowed on Fredric Levin, saying how important a recognition this was and that no amount of money could buy such an honor, that this was for the good that Mr. Levin has done. The question arose in my mind for who? for Ghana? The shame full-ness of this whole sordid affair was that when the M.C. announced the entry of Oseadeeyo Addo Dankwa III, Okuapemhene of Akuapem Traditional area of Ghana. It was not with the Fromtomfrom rhythms of the drums, it was not with the fanfare and excitement of the entry of the leader of two and a half million people. When he entered no one even stood, it was so uneventful that I did not even realize he had entered until he was right next to me, as I was seated in the back of the room. As he passed me I stood up and some Ghanaian women seated next to me also stood, every-one else remained seated. Perhaps some of the Ghanaians did not realize he was walking down the aisle, perhaps some playing it by the rhythm of the white folks were afraid to be visible. The white folks themselves were either ignorant of what to do getting no leads from the Ghanaians, or just did not think that it was important to stand for this man. However a few minutes later, Fredric Levin entered with his entourage and everyone stood and applauded, except myself, I remained seated, the same Ghanaian ladies seated next to me unfortunately stood for Mr. Levin.

The ceremony went on with Nana sitting this person on the stool three times, each time giving away another part of Ghana, of Africa.

I left the United Nations, not with the usual high after leaving a grand Durbah among the chiefs, but with a depressed feeling of being once again robbed of our culture, feeling that nothing is sacred.

As we travel down the long winding road leaving Akuapem, we must visit a most special place, a place I lovingly call "my village". It is in the lower area of Akuapem, a suburb village of the town of Aburi. The village of Adamorobe, which is a Twi word for pineapple because it is the main crop in the area, sweet, succulent pineapples, in my prejudice I must say sweeter than Hawaiian pineapples, and they are in abundance.

I first visited Adamorobe in 1985, at the time Nana Osei Boakyewe Yiadom I was the Queen Mother of Adamorobe and had just celebrated her 10th year on the stool a year before. It was with great fanfare that my friend Bill Dyer and I were received in the village by the late chief Nana Kwa Kwa Sampong. The sheep was slaughtered, libation was poured, the peo-ple danced, the chief danced, the two of us danced and we were initiated into the village.

Adamorobe

Motor car on winding trails in Ghana hills
fresh wind whipping cool
gentle strokes across my face
descending concrete then dirt roads
to red clay flatlands
entering the mud hut, straw and
tin topped village abodes
past fences and goats
slowly blending with the children
and their games in the sand
and women pounding cassava
gathering clothes, fetching water
and washing naked babies in the sun
the elders and village leaders
gather and greet
the children slowly, curiously
began to draw near
and we stand underneath the tree
of history and magical properties
our eyes scan the village square
watching the daily activities
began to gradually cease
as attention is drawn to the visitors
the children come with smiles
and beautiful black faces
and some naked bottoms
and pretty red dresses
and the young men gather chairs & drums
the elders are seated and the visitors
and the people gather
as the drums began to beat
and the children dance
the welcome dance
and the old lady leads the women
in the dance of welcome

and the priest and elders pour libation
and chant words to the ancestors
to the gods
for the return of the family
and we bow to the wise men and elders
to the chief
and we clasp their hands
and dance to the hypnotic
rhythm of the drums
and the women dance around us
and twirl Kente in our faces
the drums of Adamorobe
of Ghana, of Africa
and the children cheer and sing
and the dusk falls
and the moon rises
and the village square becomes like
dots of light, as lanterns appear
like fireflies in the night
then we wander through village corridors
and black glistening bodies
shine in the dark
faceless but vibrant
bodies recognizable only by lantern light
the village is alive
dark but alive
and exciting and so natural
we wander through village corridors
and we enter the chief's palace
where aromas of hot fish soup
cassava, fufu, and Ghanaian beer await us
and we gather and feast
among chiefs and priests
and teachers and children
as lantern lights flicker
across blue black faces in semi-darkness
and we discuss the children's needs
among pledges of support
and realize that we are now family

citizens and members of this village
then we travel from compound to compound
hearing stories in the flickering night lights
and Mr. Crow, keeper of the history of Ghana
explains the history of Adamorobe
and the chief pledges upon our return
to perform the ceremony of entry of the elders
and visions of chief Kwa Kwa standing in the
carriage of Chiefs and Queen Mothers
on the shoulders of many
swaying to ceremonial rhythms of the drums
and finally we depart with well wishes and
goodbyes
from the children, the adults and the elders
as we drive slowly into the darkness of night
as lantern lights flicker, slowly dim and fade
as we disappear into the African night
the only sounds are the tires on dirt roads
and the faint sound of the distant drum remain.

The village of Adamorobe is a very special place, not because it is a place where you will find some of the nicest people in the world, a simple friendly and happy people in spite of the lack of electricity, running water and modern technology. And not because it has some of the most disciplined and beautiful children in the world, it is a very special place because it is where the Black stool of the Asakyiri clan is located. A clan that stretches straight to Kumasi, heart of the Asante/Ashanti people, many important Ghanaians are connected to this clan.

One year later in 1986, I returned to Ghana alone and after a few days of ritual I was enstooled as an Asafohene (military captain) to the chief of Adamorobe, Nana Kwa Kwa Sampong. In traditional times an Asafohene was a leader of the troops, in modern times an Asafohene works with and counsels the young men of the village, trains them to perform military presentations for celebrations, and is looked on as a leader and protector of the village. I was given the name of Osei, who was an Asafohene around the turn of the 20th century in Adamorobe. I was given a special hat, sort of a helmet made of deer skin that was used by Osei during that period and is what the Asafo's used during warring expeditions. The hat had many functions, and could be used for drinking water from the creek, for eating etc. I was also given the name for the day of the week that I was born, which wasTuesday, so my "Kra" name is Kwabena, my name then became Osei Kwabena II, after Osei I.

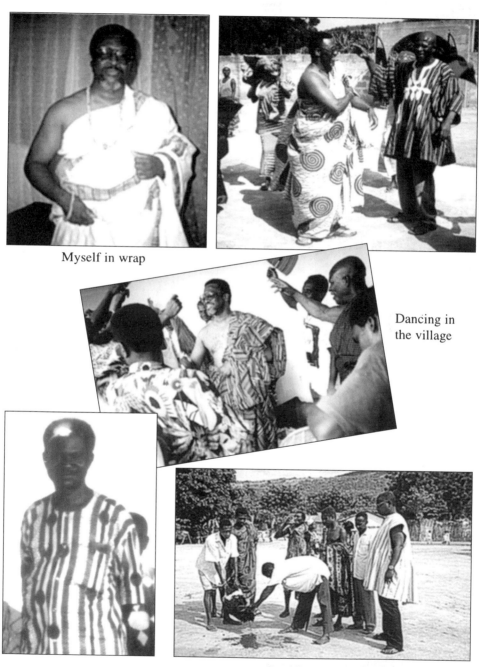

Myself in wrap

Dancing in the village

Sacrifice in the village

Village
compound

Residents of
the Village of
Adamorobe

Gathering of the council

It is interesting the organization that is chieftaincy, its structure and order, its systematic levels of leadership. Chieftaincy has somewhat of a government structure, if you look at its first level of recognized and respected leadership, the chief of the village we want to say governs the people of that geographical community, the village. There are sub regions of larger towns, which are called villages, these villages have chiefs, the next level would be the chief of the larger towns or communities, these chiefs would have an influential relationship with the sub villages.

The next level would be the regional chiefs, leaders of certain areas made up of towns and villages. Then you would have Paramount chiefs, and these are powerful chiefs who are leaders of larger ethnic areas and finally you would have the Omanhene, Paramount chief, the British called them Kings, they are the leaders of clans and ethnic groups. Going further up in the chieftaincy structure will bring you to the National House of Chiefs, where sits the Paramount chiefs of national regions and major ethnic groups. (Omanhene's). The chairman of this noble body of cultural leaders is the Asantahene, the number one Paramount chief of the Asante people, who sits at the head of this august body. The Ashanti as is commonly called gained fame for being great warriors, and resisting the British through the turn of the century. The Ashanti's are also noted for their gold mines and cocoa, but also because they consolidated a powerful state, and commanded a large land base and population. The Ashanti's are also the keepers of the culture and many of them wear the cloth every day. In Accra most men wear western clothes or politico suits, which some of us in the 1960's and 70's called nationalist suits. As you travel the road to Kumasi you will begin to see a lot of men wearing the cloth and particularly the black cloth. The Ashanti's maintained more of their culture and only succumbed to western culture, because of their defeat by the British.

Traveling to Kumasi by road is long and tiring but worth the trip. Stopping off at the various craft villages, such as the Kente weaving village of Bonwire, a place that can sometimes be pretty wild with the aggressiveness of the young sellers of the Kente cloth. It is however much worst in other places I can name, and besides you can get some pretty good bargains, depending on your bargaining and bartering skills. There is wealth in Kumasi, of course always along with the poverty that unfortunately seems to be a part of African society. Kumasi is a hub of commercial activity, with one of the largest marketplaces in West Africa. It appears to be more organized than Accra, and much better kept. There is much history in this city, right in the circle in the center of the city, on the hill overlooking the hustle and bustle of the marketplace, is a statue of Okumfo Onokywe commanding the golden stool from the heavens, as legend tells of the cherished golden stool that is the soul of the Asante people. Kumasi has a very important exhibit at the cultural center that is an example of what the King's court looks like, where you will see the rise and fall of the Ashanti empire.

Statue of Okumfo Onokywe

A recent addition to the history of the Ashanti State is a new museum on the grounds of the Palace. The Asantehene, the Ashanti king has many riches and a vast collection of gold. We are talking about solid gold rings and necklaces, and various other ornaments that adorn the king. During official high level public appearances the Asantahene has so much gold on his body that he has to walk slow, and when shaking the hand of someone he has to be helped to raise his gold laden arm by one of his attendants. I and the group that I brought with me in 1992, had a rare opportunity to see a magnificent gathering of royalty. The event took place on the grounds of the palace, the occasion was a scheduled visit by the Pope, whom however could not be there for some reason that I can not remember.

The event however went on as planned attended by a high ranking cardinal from the Vatican representing the Pope, it was a grand gathering. There were kings, religious and cultural leaders from all segments of the Ghanaian population. When we entered the green carpeted parade grounds, we saw the various kingdoms and areas represented by richly dressed royal leaders with huge entourages in splendid cloth, gold and elaborate embroidery. It seemed that every group that was gathered, was more splendid than the next.

Every gathering that we passed as we walked around the circle of splendor, I thought was the Asantahene and his entourage, only to see another that surely had to be the one. I was told to my amazement that the King of Kings had not yet arrived. The drums were playing, and around the parameters people were dancing to the rhythms. As we reached the 180 degree angle of the circle of royalty we saw the large Papal entourage, priests and bishops and attendants were gathered on a platform directly facing the opposite side of this huge circle that was approximately 100 yards away.

The gathering from the Vatican were dressed in gleaming white, trimmed in red, and wearing rich red skull caps, it was indeed an impressive group, in fact I have never seen such a colorful array of richness in the school of Catholicism before.

We found a place and continued to be entertained by the dancers and drummers, then we heard an orchestra of ram's horns blowing, announcing the coming of the African King. It was incredible, there were dozens of horn blowers, the sound was powerful and intense. Following were stool carriers, sword wavers, dozens of muskets being fired, huge and colorful umbrellas, there were literally hundreds of people in this incredible presentation of the representative of Ghanaian culture and tradition. Finally as the energy and variety of sound got louder and more intense, the Asantahene, Opuku Ware II the King of Asante came into view of all of the royal gathering. Everyone rose and the entire place reached such a crescendo, such a fever pitch of energy and emotion.

The king was walking very slowly, for this auspicious occasion he had on his best, his most expensive gold jewelry, solid gold, gold on his crown, gold on his chest, on his arms and wrists, on his ankles.

The Chief of chiefs was truly representing, as he walked the circle waving to, and touching the people, when he reached the place where the Papal group was gathered, the senior Cardinal representing the Pope, kneeled and kissed the heavy gold rings on the hand of the king. Then the Asantahene took his place at the opposite end of the circle, on his throne with dozens of his subjects all in beautiful golden Kente wrap, sitting at his feet. With courtesies exchanged, messages relayed, the cultural offerings began, and

what a presentation it was.

A gathering of this nature is very rare, some people in the country never get a chance to see the Asantahene, much less at a celebration such as this. We took photos, filmed with our camcorders and stored these experiences in our minds forever.

Asantehene in Royal Durbah

The Asanthene Otumfuo Opuku Ware II, King of the Asantes joined the ancestors in the eternal village in February 1999.

One of the disappointments was to see the state of the Ashanti library. I visited the library on one of my earlier trips to Ghana, the shelves were half empty, the books were in very poor condition, worn, frayed, in a state of ill repair. With a history so rich, this place should have been a reserve of information so that the children and people could read and know about the proud history of their people, the people who fought the European invaders to the bitter end.

This library should also contain books that tell the history of the continent of Africa, history of the ancient empires, the kingdoms and contributions of African people to world civilization. This library should also tell the story of the Africans who were sold and stolen, and sent to the West to be enslaved for hundreds of years, yet more than helped to build the United

States of America and the continents of North, central and South America.

Much work has to be done to educate the masses of African people worldwide to resurrect our history and preserve it so that we can teach future generations of African children to have faith in their own possibilities. However it is being done in Accra, where you have two very important libraries, one is the W.E.B. DuBois Pan African Memorial Center. Here you will find a collection of the books of

Bust of DuBois at center   W.E.B. DuBois Center

112

Tomb of Dubois and ashes of his wife

W.E.B. DuBois and of his wife Shirley Graham DuBois.

You will also find books written by men and women of the African race from various regions in the world.

This center for Pan African studies is indeed that, it fosters a concept of one people, people with a common experience, and a common history.

These writings are on the period of the ancients, when African people were looked up to with great respect, because they were the contributors to civilization, that they were the founders of human development. And the writings of the not so ancient empires and kingdoms, and the painful writings, the accounts, and stories of the slave trade and all of its unbelievable horrors. And the writings of the promise of tomorrow, the new day dawning for the rise of the phoenix, for the resurrection of life, for the rebirth. All of this you will find in the former house of the great African American scholar, who died at the age of 95, in 1963 in Ghana. This house is now a museum and a center that will offer you the opportunity to learn of the history, the building and struggles of Black people worldwide.

In addition to the collection of the literary works of Dr. DuBois, you will also find his robes, diplomas, photos, and other items that tell the story of this great activist scholar. The former bedrooms now house these items, with a special room that houses the books of Shirley Graham Dubois. There are photos that circle the main entrance room wall, that depict the images of some of the best thinkers, defenders, and doer's in the African race. Outside, close to the main house that houses the books and the former possessions of the DuBois', is the mausoleum, where the remains of W.E.B.DuBois lay in a tomb in the ground.

The stone gray cover, spelling out his name, looking up to you, and right beside the tomb of Dr. DuBois, are the ashes of Shirley Graham DuBois' in a glass and metal container. It is a serene place, an artistically circular room that many important and well known people from around the world have visited. The grounds are carefully manicured, adorned with an impressive bust and plaques that add to the story of this great Pan Africanist. W.E.B.DuBois.

The other important library in Accra is the George Padmore Library, another great Pan Africanist from Trinidad who worked with DuBois, Nkrumah, and the other great African leaders of the first wave for independence in Africa. This is a library that is fully stocked with books on all subjects, and it is a very active library, with several rooms and 2 buildings.

It was very encouraging to see the number of young people seriously engaged in study, quiet intense study. We went around to see what the students were involved with, we found that they were working on serious school assignments, researching information for papers that they had to deliver. There were no conversations between them, no whispering, no giggling, this was an exercise in discipline.

The Padmore library also had on its grounds a tomb where the Pan Africanist George Padmore is buried. A very impressive tomb, with the Black Star largely and prominently displayed, etched in the stone granite of the tomb. Yes Ghana is certainly the center of Pan Africanism, the heartland of Independence and Kujichagulia (self determination) although it has its contradictions, as most African countries.

A major dichotomy that has always puzzled me is the level of Christianity in the Chieftaincy. One would think that the chiefs being the keepers of the culture, those who officiate at the ceremonies and celebrations, would be involved in the traditional religion also, however that is not the case. The Paramount chiefs are predominately Christian. Earlier on I talked about the effects that the missionaries had on the people to push them further from their cultural base. Those who came through the educational system were converted to Christianity, and subsequently did not think much of this cultural involvement, and tried to avoid all public connection to it. However they did benefit socially and materially and dominated the ranks of the chieftaincy. As a result of this reward system, you will find that they are devout Christians, while at the same time they sit on the stool representing the traditional culture. (This dichotomy is the topic of the book "Christianity and Traditional

Women pounding FuFu

African Beliefs" by Oseadeeyo Addo Dankwa III) that examines and supports this historical reality. There are some chiefs who are not Christians, but not very many, the Paramount chief of the Ga people is not a Christian. In the very northern part of Ghana, the people are predominately Muslim and so are their traditional rulers.

In the book "Christianity and Traditional African Beliefs" which is actually a series of lectures that Nana Dankwa delivered at the University of Ghana at Legon, to audiences of students who were studying to be ministers. This book was published in 1991 by 'The Power of The Word Press', a division of The Afrikan Poetry Theatre. I wrote the introduction to this work. The lectures were intended to instill within the young student ministers that they should not be ashamed of their culture, and that Christianity came out of Africa, and that they should embrace their culture instead of abandoning it. On the other hand Nana critiqued the traditional customs of the Akan culture, and suggested that certain aspects of the culture should be done away with, stating that it no longer had any useful purpose and was just being continued because custom said that it should. Just to mention a couple of them here, there is a custom that says, FuFu (the national dish of Ghana, yam and cassava, or plantain pounded into a paste in which a sauce is poured over, and perhaps some meat or fish is added) should not be pounded after dark. This was a custom that had a purpose at one time. The reason originated in traditional times, in the villages of previous centuries, after the sun went down it was not advisable to pound FuFu because the sound of the pounding carried for a great distance in the still of the night. This was not advisable because enemies of the people of the village or encampment would know your exact location. Another reason was that you could not see if there were any insects that might crawl into your FuFu that might be mashed up in your dinner.

These were fine customs at the time, they had a purpose, they made sense, but there is no need for them now, villages are not at war, we now have electricity, (at least in most urban areas) and the fear of insects crawling into your food is not a concern. Certain rituals that involved the spilling of blood, Nana had some concerns with for health related reasons. This position, which appeared to a reformist one, angered some of the elders on the traditional councils, and did not contribute to Nana's popularity, in fact it caused him serious criticism. However his objective was to help to balance the young ministers who would have an influence on the people who they would minister to. He certainly was not suggesting that they abandon Christianity, for in fact he was a devout Christian, even though he had accepted his place on the throne. He was telling them to be Ghanaian, be African, respect your culture, and at the same time be a good Christian. Some would argue that this was not possible, that it is a contradiction, because the African thought being a Christian was the same as being White. The European missionaries and colonialists had made Christianity synonymous with European culture. Nana's position was it came out of Africa, that it also belonged to the African, and that African culture belonged to Christianity. There was a problem however in applying this theory when it came down to identifying the race of Jesus Christ. Most Ghanaians would say that the color did not matter, Christ was universal. The question of the race of Christ, was brought up in question and answer periods, several times when Nana was giving lectures on the topic of 'Christianity and Traditional African Beliefs'. For groups that I brought to

Nana Dankwa during book promotion with Nana Boakyewa Gary Byrd of WLIB and myself

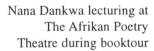

Nana Dankwa lecturing at The Afrikan Poetry Theatre during booktour

Ghana, or during his visit to the United States that I organized to promote the book in 1991. Nana's answer was the same as other Ghanaians who were Christians, in spite of his broad learning experiences, in spite of the fact that I had sent him a few books by Dr. Yosef ben-Jochanan, and other African centered scholars from the United States. He certainly displayed the information he had received from reading these books in the way that he weaves this information through his lectures on history and religion, but he also consistently says that the color does not matter. The usual reply from African Americans who take radical racial stances, "If color does not matter, then why not make Christ Black?", the African American would argue, because of being as it is said "in the belly of the beast", meaning the United States of America where race is a critical issue. Where W.E.B. DuBois said at the turn of the century, that the main problem of the twentieth century would be a problem of the color line, and usually there was not a significant response to this question. One year I brought five dozen posters of the Black Christ to Ghana, a Christ with wooly hair, dark skin, and quotes from the bible at the bottom of the poster supporting this image. I gave a few of these posters to Nana Dankwa, asking him to give them to people he knew, and distribute them to family and friends in Ghana. I was happy to see them displayed at a few places.

The color of Christ becomes a central issue for African Americans when visiting Ghana, because you see so many pictures of Christ everywhere, being sold at marketplaces, at roadside stands, on billboards, on vehicles, and always the blue eyes, blond hair, with very red bleeding hearts and halos that glow in the dark. These white pictures of Christ appear to be like the ones that were visible in the United States in the earlier part of the twentieth century. However the Black community in the U.S. had begun to replace these White images of Christ with Black images in the Cultural Revolution of the 1960's. A story that brings a smile to my face was told by one of the students in our Afriquest program that sends high school and college students to Ghana for 4 weeks in the Summer. She said that she was having difficulty getting to sleep in one of the Christian villages where the group was staying. She kept tossing and turning, and looked up to see this picture of a White Christ hanging over her bed and glowing in the dark. She said it was so bright that it kept her from sleeping, we concluded that It must have been painted with glow in the dark paint. Again the pictures were everywhere, I thought to myself that the people who lived in the city were truly indoctrinated with Christianity and with this White Christ. I thought surely the village people, the rural people practiced more of the traditional customs and that I would find refuge from these Michelangelo cousin's images.

On my first visit to the traditional village of Adamorobe, I was thinking. "Here it is, a perfect place where the traditional belief is practiced, where we sacrifice the sheep, pour libation and beat the drum," It was a great disappointment to find when entering the chief's house, sitting down and looking up to see once again on the wall, the white image of Jesus Christ I screamed to myself, not again! It seemed that I could not escape it, not in the city, not even in the bush!

Ghanaians have learned to assimilate Christianity into their culture and customs very well in some cases, an example of this is Sisi, the mother of Nana Osei Boakywe Yiadom II, the first female chief of Adamorobe. Sisi invited me to attend church with her, this was a Methodist church where Sisi, or the 'Old Lady' was a matron. It was a most fascinating experience, a true example of this so-called dichotomy working well together, African and European culture woven together in a strange pattern. There were European Methodist choir songs in English, then Twi, there was organ

Myself in wrap, Okyeme and others pouring libation

Sacrifice in the village

118

playing and drums beating, matrons in starched white, and African prints and colorful Kente and Adinkra wraps. A most interesting and creative experience was the 'collection'. We all assembled at the rear of the church in the center aisle, the drums began to beat and we danced down the aisle to the collection basket and dropped our contribution in the basket, all with the rhythm of the drums, and back to our seats. Quite an experience, but I must add, all the while looking down on us from the front of the altar, was the ever present image, a huge picture of Christ, white, and blond and glowing.

Sisi was also an example of this blending of Akan culture and European Christianity, she was an involved matron of the church, busy with her responsibilities, in the center of the Methodist rituals, and later she would reveal another side of herself, another side of Ghana. When we visited the village where I was initiated, she then took the role of the elder priestess, covering me with powder, and preparing me for the ritual. It was like being in two worlds, but the transition seemed quite normal to her, this switching of roles, this moving from one culture to the other was taken all in stride.

Ghana is certainly the foremost country in Africa that has maintained its culture and Chieftaincy structure, but it also has incorporated Western Christian values into its lifestyle.

Accra, the capital of the country, is a city where you will find representatives of all the ethnic groups in the country. It is however where you will also find the majority of the Ga people. It is said that the Ga people at some time in history migrated from Yorubaland. In terms of religion you will find Ga's who are Muslim, some who are Christian, and some who are so called 'Fetish' The Ga's Omanhene, Paramount chief interestingly enough does not adorn himself in gold as does the Akan Kings. He wears beads most often, and appears to project more of an association with the so-called 'fetish' and the role and practices of the Okumfo priest.

The infrastructure of Accra has improved greatly since the mid 1980's, new hotels have been built, new roads, a national theatre designed by the Chinese, and the Kwame Nkrumah Memorial Park, which contain the remains of Dr. Nkrumah in a beautiful mausoleum and tomb in a pyramid shaped dome, an impressive and imposing statue of Nkrumah that looks out over a lagoon with several smaller statues of chiefs in their wraps on both sides of the statue with water blowing out of horns that announces the coming of the king. This imposing arrangement is surrounded by green, expansive manicured lawns, and cool lagoons.

In the rear of the mausoleum, that is surrounded by water canals is the museum that has displays of artifacts, books, and photos depicting the

Kwame Nkrumah Memorial Park

years of the leadership of Ghana, by Dr. Nkrumah, and the drive towards independence.

The Kwame Nkrumah Memorial Park is a national splendor, a Rockefeller Plaza Center of Ghana, so to speak. It is a place that many African Americans are also proud of, as Dr. Kwame Nkrumah is a hero of the Pan-African world. To that end The Afrikan Poetry Theatre and its friends and supporters have contributed money to the maintenance and

Statue of Kwame Nkrumah

upkeep of the park. In February of 1997 we presented the sum of $2,000 that was raised by Paul Knox and associates, which was received by the office of the Minister of Culture for the government of Ghana and the director of the Kwame Nkrumah Memorial Park. This sum while it may appear to be a small amount, translates into 4,200,000cd (Four million, two hundred thousand cidis) in the Ghanaian local currency, a significant and appreciable amount to the Ghanaian public.

In the village of Adamorobe in the Akuapem area approximately 10,000,000 Cidis was raised for the electrification project. This is really just an extremely small example of the financial help that the African American can bring to Africa, because of the value of the dollar. What we should be examining is the investment and manufacturing possibilities on the

Tomb of Kwame Nkrumah

continent of Africa as a whole. When we look at the impact of what a few thousand dollars can make in a third world economy, then we should began to see what we should be doing with our dollars.

Often I hear of the wealth of Africa, well in most cases and places I do not see any wealth, I see a few with some extremely lavish digs, some more just making it and most impoverished.

Of course if we know anything at all about Africa, we know that much of the world's most precious minerals still lay in its earth, after centuries of exploitation. We must begin to look more at Africa as the place to launch a development and economic attack on the western world, namely the United States, Europe, and Japan in the East. We need to look at Africa for production, to take advantage of the value of the U.S. dollar compared to the local African currency. To manufacture and produce items and products to flood the International markets, and to raise the quality of life for Africans, through higher wages and more available cash flow. Imagine building finely carved African furniture, with fine fabric, like the Senegalese company Afriland. Provincial furniture, French Provincial, Italian Provincial, why not African Provincial.

Africa has the best wood carvers in the world, imagine having quality African furniture in the many comfortable and affluent homes in the United States. This is just one example of the items that can be produced in Africa. The large manufacturing companies, giant retail firms are relocating outside of the United States because the labor is cheaper, they however exploit the people in the countries where they build their factories. Paying them pennies an hour for merchandise that is put in high priced stores in the major cities of America. America is the market place, so is Europe, and Japan should also be in the mix because they have a lot of capital in which to spend. They are making a lot of money selling products in the States. African people must do the same, we need to understand that America is

121

the biggest marketplace of all, we have to produce and sell products here also. The African American is producing very little, of course there are some success stories, some encouraging signs along the way, but we are still the biggest consumers of all. There are hundreds of billions of dollars being spent in the African American community each year, this money is coming from hard work and labor, and we be giving it right back. We are really not producing in the U.S. and Africa is also not producing anything, where is the African automobile?, a whole continent can not produce a car?!

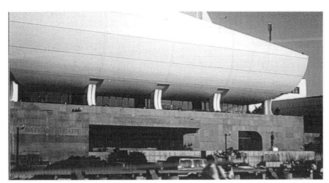

National Theatre, Accra

Black Star in Independence Square, Accra

Billboard in Accra

We have to come together and make some commerce, Africa has always been the rich continent that has made the European very rich, what can it do for us, what can it do for itself?. We can cause a flow of cash that can oil up the continent and get it back in the mix, its been too many centuries, too long ago. So in Accra it is that spirit of Pan Africanism that is alive and vibrant, where you can perhaps see a play, watch a cinema that deals with some issue that affect the lives of the people. And its night life, the High Life is still there but I think that it is losing ground to the sounds from the West, at least among the younger generation. I remember hearing more Hi Life, finding more places to dance to Hi Life into the night.

The Volta Region

There is another very important area in Ghana, that we will visit, and this is the Volta Region. The Volta Region is a fertile farming region, where I made a brief visit to in 1985. We went straight up the Volta until we reached Ho, the capital of the Volta Region.

Ho is a large and prosperous agricultural center for cocoa, tobacco, and teakwood. One of the main ethnic groups in the Volta Region is the Ewe. It is said that the Ewe migrated to Ghana, that they are not indigenous to Ghana, as some of the other groups, such as the Akans, with their various geographical areas, speaking slightly different versions of Twi. The Ewe people however speak Ewe, a different language than the Twi that the Akan speaks.

Even though the Akans from the various geographical areas speak different versions of Twi, they all can basically understand each other, but Ewe is completely different. The people in the Volta Region are mostly farmers, not traditionally a wealthy group very generally speaking. Many made their way to Accra as domestics, eventually became a part of the rat race to survive on a continent that has been exploited.

We saw the massive Akosombo Dam, 105 km from Accra, a 400km long hydro electric situated on the Volta Lake built by Dr. Kwame Nkrumah. This dam is the major source of hydroelectric energy for the nation, and it also supplies hydroelectric energy to neighboring countries. Lake Volta, 210 km northeast of Accra, is one of the largest man made lakes in the world, with fresh water fishing, and numerous farming villages.

The president of Ghana, Jerry John Rawlings was born in the Volta Region.

Cape Coast

Located in the Central Region, the Cape Coast houses the horrible history of the Slave Trade, with its forts, castles and dungeons. A beautiful area of Ghana, near the water, with its tall elegant palm trees swaying in the breeze from the Atlantic Ocean, its sandy beaches and bustling fishing industry. The main ethnic group in the Cape Coast area is the Fante people.

In the Cape Cost region there are 42 forts and castles/dungeons, most of them are in ruins or just shells. The two that are open to the public are Elmina Castle, which needs a lot of work to preserve it. And Cape Coast Castle, which has had some renovations, and in fact has a very interesting museum which was built in the early 1990's. When you visit this museum they show you a video of the slave trade that is gripping and captivating.

I first visited the Cape Coast in 1985 when there was no museum and other areas of renovation. I remember when Bill Dyer, Kwabena, and Kwame (my adopted family) and myself, were travelling to the Cape Coast, this was a time in 1985 of great political strife in Ghana. A few weeks prior to our arrival there was an espionage plot uncovered with the arrest of an African American woman, Sharon Scranage. On July 11, 1985, Ms Scranage a CIA operative who was initially sent to gather intelligence data on the government of Head of State Flt. Lieutenant Jerry John Rawlings. This woman however fell in Love with a Ghanaian, Michael Soussoudis, a businessman and first cousin of Head of State Flight Lieutenant Jerry John Rawlings. She was arrested when she was transferred to Washington for passing on CIA secrets. Including the names of American agents operating in Ghana, the names of their Ghanaian inform ers and details of the Agency's communications system there to George Agbotui Soussoudis, brother of Michael, and also a cousin of Head of State Flight Lieutenant Jerry John Rawlings.

She became a double agent, as is usual in such cases. The CIA "turned her around", working with the FBI, the CIA got her to arrange a meeting with Soussoudis, who had arrived in Washington. Even though Scranage a trained CIA operative and a woman who had an intimate relationship with a man can warn someone that something is amiss, even though the FBI was listening to her conversation, she did no such thing and set Soussoudis up for arrest. He arrived in Washington, DC from Ghana and was to meet her at the Holiday Inn motel in Springfield, Virginia. In a classic FBI movie type operation, he was picked up when he turned up for the assignation. Sharon Scranage was nowhere to be seen as the FBI pounced on him. At a hearing Michael Soussoudis stated that he was not associated with the intelligence service of Ghana, that he was just related to the Head of State.

Sharon Scranage is just one example of the habit that the CIA has of using Black people in African countries. Especially those with a history of Pan-Africanism and whose people are therefore more Black conscious than usual to penetrate African society in ways that would not be possible for White agents.

(1) Source of information: Africa Now magazine August 1985 issue.

This became a problem for us as Americans we were to discover on our journey to Cape Coast. The four of us driving along the road to the Coast, we were stopped at one of the regular police barricades that you find along the roads in Ghana, even to this day the police can stop you to ask of your destination, etc. We stopped at the barrier and a sharply dressed officer with a swagger stick inquired of Kwame who was driving, of our destination, and who was in the car. Kwame explained that the passengers in the back were Americans and that we were on our way to see the slave castles.

As soon as he said that we were Americans we knew that we were in trouble by the immediate reaction of the officer, he said with intense fervor "Americans! Step out!" He demanded," open your trunk!" Kwabena went around to open the trunk of the used white Mercedes. The officer saw all of the video equipment that we had and bellowed "what is this?" We explained to him as tourists and officers of a cultural center that we were here to document our visit, so that we could show African Americans the beauty of Ghana and the history of slavery from Africa, the other side. He retorted "Do you know that your government tried to overthrow the government of Ghana?"

I replied, "yes we know but the United States is not our government it happens to be the government of the country that we live in.

We do not support that government, we in fact struggle against the policies of that government for our civil and human rights, and support the governments that oppose these U.S. policies."

I continued explaining to him that some African Americans oppose national and international US policies and speak out against them whenever we can. I then took out a book of poetry that I had published about a dozen years earlier that contained militant poetry that spoke out against racism and the US government. I showed him a page that had a poem denouncing the US government and a graphic drawing of the caricature of Uncle Sam with top hat and striped suit, being hung after being sentenced to death.

The officer exclaimed "You wrote this in your country?" He was obviously surprised that I was able to get away with this. I offered him a copy of the book and some T-shirts, which he took, but that was not enough to let us go. Perhaps we should have offered him money, we thought of that later, however I am not sure if that would have helped in this situation because this guy was fired up on revolutionary rhetoric. Kwabena

125

explained to him that we were friends of Nana Boakyewa Yiadom and her sister who was at that time the Deputy Minister for Fuel and Energy, and a top officer of the Bank of Ghana. In addition that we were also friends of Oseadeeyo Addo Dankwa, the Okupahene (king) of the Akuapem region. He said that he would have to check on this information and that we were officially detained. They sat us on a bench with several guards and a blue armored vehicle with treaded wheels and a long gun barrel pointing in our direction. After some 2 to 3 hours he returned and offered his apologizes for our detention and explained that they must be very careful at this time in the country.

This experience with the military forces was the first time, but not the only time that I would be suspect to the police and military government of Ghana. In 1991 it was a very political, very volatile time in Ghana. The presidential elections were scheduled for the coming year, the ban on political parties was expected to be lifted very soon, and this represented a return to elections after more than 10 years.

Many people were beginning to secretly organize their political organizations, and were quietly trying to raise money. One of my traveling buddies and business partners Lewis Matthews and myself had met with an attorney and business associate of Oseadeeyo Addo Dankwa III, Omanhene of the Akuapem people and also a friend and associate of ours. Nana was sharing an office with Harry who was one of the central figures in a new political party that was trying to organize in this period before the lifting of the ban on political parties. The reason that the activities were secret was because the ban was not officially lifted yet and meeting and planning political activities was still unlawful. At that time the Chairman of the military government, Flt. Lt. Jerry J. Rawlins was unannounced but planning to run for the presidency in what would be a newly created party.

The opposition parties thought that the government would not give them much time between the lifting of the ban and the date of the elections, so they decided to get an early start to raise the necessary money and support.

A few of us who traveled to Ghana often during that period decided to respond to the request of Nana and Harry to make a financial contribution to their political efforts. We donated $1,500 to the cause, towards campaign literature, vehicles, etc. Lew and I along with Harry, met with other people who were trying to formulate political entities. We went to the house of one of the old line Nkrumahist, Kojo Botsio, a former speaker of the house in the government of first president Kwame Nkrumah. One who you can see in the photos that was at Nkrumah's side in the speeches at dawn and post independence. There were people from the Ashanti and other powerful people in Ghana. The discussion was around the lifting of the ban on politics and the coming elections.

We pledged in addition to the money that we brought with us at the request of Nana and Harry, who was with Nana when he visited the United States in the Spring of 1991, as the guest of The Afrikan Poetry Theatre. That we would help to raise additional money, and other material support. We found ourselves backing this opposition to Jerry Rawlins because Nana is our cultural leader, and it seemed that all of our friends in our Akuapem cultural circle of important people were against the continuation of Rawlins running the government. Our position was not clear, we were influenced by the reports from Pan African international sources, progressive media and such that painted a picture of a progressive, socialist, revolutionary Rawlins, however we had received and heard from the people stories of military atrocities, imprisonment's, and extortion's. We also witnessed the heavy handed manner in which the soldiers treated the people. However on the other hand we applauded the method in which Flt. Lt Rawlins dealt with corruption and along with his wife worked to improve the conditions of women and the people in the urban areas, the poor and uneducated, the little 'people. So we were on the border line but we went along with our people, who were not of the corrupt major forces in Ghana, but in fact were a fringe political group associated with the old guard who no longer wielded the power of the old days. After we left the house of Kojo Botsio we went to a Chinese restaurant to have dinner, yes a Chinese restaurant in Africa. There were four of us, Nana, Harry, Lew, and myself. We had begun discussing the political situation when a man who appeared to be a drunk came into the restaurant and stumbled near our table, the personnel of the restaurant asked him to leave as he was disturbing the customers. We thought that it was a very strange incident indeed, we started to think spy, agent, under cover operator. After dinner Harry dropped me off at the hotel that I was staying at, and went on to drop Lew at the house of a friend that he was staying. The hotel where I was lodging was the King David hotel, a small but clean hotel with a good kitchen. I retired a little later after packing my bags as I was catching a plane early in the morning, going to London for a few days and then on to the U.S. my friend Lew was staying for another week or two.

I was suddenly awakened during the night by banging on my door, I jumped up and went to the door "who is it? " I asked "police!" came the response. I opened the door to find 4 to 6 men a few in uniform and a cou-

127

ple in civilian clothes. "What is the problem I asked?" "Can I see your passport?" the leader of the group asked. "Sure" I replied, and went to the drawer that had my waist pouch that contained my passport. As I made this move the leader of the group put his hand on his gun that was on his waist. I thought to my self what is going on with these guys. "What is the problem here? What is going on?" I asked "We suspect you of having drugs" the leader answered. "That's ridiculous" I responded "We would like to search your room?" the leader asked. "I resent this" I responded, "I am a citizen of another country, I have friends of importance in this country, and dropped a few names". "Well if you do not let us search your room we will have to take you down to headquarters." He said. I thought what the hell let them search, I didn't have anything and I did not want to be delayed where I might miss my flight in the morning. I told them that they could search, which they did and found nothing, I demanded an apology from them and told them that I would report them to my friends and associates. I figured that this was a climax to the night of intrigue and surveillance. I gave a letter to Nana's chauffeur who came to pick me up to take me to the airport. In the letter I explained the incident and what I believed was the connection to the political meetings of the previous night. Later I was to find out that there was a formal complaint lodged against the police and the inspector who searched my room and intimidated me. The complaint was brought by Harry the lawyer, and as I understand an apology was given. The excuse was that the King David Hotel was a place where drug dealers met and I was a suspect because I was a foreigner and had aroused some suspicion.

We were visiting the Cape Coast during a very festive time of year, this was the first week in September, the period of the largest festival in the Cape Coast region, the Fetu Afahye, the Fante celebration of the harvest, the New Year celebration. The Fetu Afahye is equivalent to the Homowo that the Ga people of Ghana celebrate, and the Odwira celebration of the Akuapem and Ashanti people. This is a time that the town is jumping with activity, just as is all the other harvest and New Year celebrations. The Fetu Afahye is 7 days long, with various activities taking place during the week. The last day there is a huge colorful Durbah, the gathering of the chiefs, Queen Mothers, government officials, and people that come from all over the country. The hotels were full, the streets were packed with people, the air was festive with the excitement of the impending Durbah that was scheduled to take place the next day, which was the last day of the festival.

We continued on through the winding streets until we reached the Cape

Coast Castle. The Castle is a big white washed fort that changed hands over the centuries from the Portuguese, Dutch, and finally the British. The worst part about Cape Coast Castle is the dungeon, walking down the sloped surface into the darkness, it seems as if you are being swallowed up by a giant whale, as we disappeared into its belly the darkness consumed us, making us blind with its intensity. Gradually our eyes became accustomed to the darkness and we were able to see the cobbled floor and trenches where the African urine flowed. Our guide explained the various rooms in the near pitch blackness of the dungeon and we then gathered around the shrine that was built to the ancestors.

We watched and participated as the old man, the priest poured the libation to those who went through the "door of no return".

Cape Coast Castle

Cape Coast

Cape Coast Dungeon

We continued on to Elmina Castle, the dreary one, the big dark and dank one. Elmina still has the smell of the African in her walls, still has the sound of the wails and screams in her sordid chambers.

Unlike Cape Coast Castle with its whitewash facade trying to conceal centuries of torment and torture Elmina stands looking out on the Atlantic, dark and foreboding carrying the nightmarish sins of eternity. We visited the rooms and holes where they kept the rebels, the rooms where the slave traders stayed, where they brought the young female slaves for sex, the auction room and the infamous door of no return. Leaving the slave castle/dungeon, walking across the now dry and dusty moat that helped to keep other Europeans from overcoming the castle, I looked back at this huge edifice of cruelty and inhumanity and realized that this slave trade of Africans lasted for centuries in places such as this.

Elmina Castle

Slave dungeon

Female passageway

"Door of No Return"   Elmina Castle   Dungeon (Elmina)

Later, we went on to Oyster Bay motel, on the Atlantic with huge waves crashing against the rocks and creating wet sprays several hundred yards almost to the doors of the bungalows.

The bungalows were nicely designed, though in need of some renovation were still quite quaint with their circular design.

Oyster Bay in fact was in need of much renovation at that time in 1985. It is much more developed today, but still is no more than a 2 star establishment. The pool now has water in it, still not properly renovated, but at least it is now functional years after it stood empty and barren. The food at Oyster Bay however is excellent, and the out door setting is quite nice. It was sort of quiet and laid back this particular night, some highlife music was playing over the speakers, some folks sitting in the booths with their thatched hut roofs, sipping beer and enjoying the music and light conversation. The round half -walled outdoor dance floor was empty this night, but tomorrow would be a different story.

The next day, Saturday, would be the final day of the Fetu Afahye, the parade and Durbah (gathering of the chiefs and the people). We went to sleep with great anticipation of this famous festival and the excitement that it promised, with the cool breeze from the nearby Atlantic Ocean blowing through the louver windows lulling us to sleep.

Oyster Bay bungalow

The next morning the four of us sat down to breakfast and discussed our plans for the day. We left the motel and went to the house of Kwabena's fiancé' Marian, there we collected her, her mother and a friend and then headed out to the streets for the big parade that would precede the Durbah. The streets were already crowded with people, early in the morning, people came from all over the country for this festival, not only Fante's but people from many other ethnic groups. The varied smells of food caressed our nostrils as vendors started to prepare their food for the day's consumption.

We found a spot along the parade route where Marian's mother said we would be comfortable and would be able to see everything. It was in front of a bank of stores with a low ledge where we could sit, yet not be blocked by the huge crowds that would soon gather. The parade finally started about 2 hours after the scheduled starting time, which is typical of the time schedules in Africa.

In the States Black people have similar patterns of being late or starting events late, we call it CP time (Colored People's time), in Africa I call it AP time (African People's time). It was well worth waiting for though, there were no floats as we know them, the Paramount chiefs and Queen Mothers however were carried in Paraquets (hand carved sitting carriages with lavish cloth) that are carried by the subjects on their shoulders. Each Paraquet is preceded by a contingent of people carrying stools of the Clan or family/village grouping, sword carriers, horn blowers and drummers. The chiefs, Kings and Queen Mothers were decked out in their finest cloth, gold colored Kente, beautifully designed Adinkra cloth, gold and more

133

gold glittering against the sun, waving their ceremonial swords and joyfully acknowledging the crowds. Each contingent seemed to out dazzle, out drum, and out dance the other. Not all of the groups carried their leader on their shoulders, some chiefs, family heads, and leaders walked and waved with small to large to huge contingents surrounding them, blowing rams horns, shooting off old muskets, and vigorously playing the drums.

Fetu Afahyse (Annual festival)

The Asafo groups, (these are the young men who in traditional times were the soldiers and warriors), entertained the crowds with their acrobatic displays of playful warfare. Twirling the Asafo banners and flags in a playful aggressive manner, the opponent had to get out of the way by jumping over or ducking under with very rapid and agile moves. It delighted the crowd and lent to the air of merriment and celebration. This was truly a parade of royalty and proud kinship.

The highlight of the procession was the appearance of the king of the Fante people with the largest and most colorful entourage of all. After the parade was ended the people all gathered at the Queen Victoria Park, the display of entourages of chiefs was awesome. There were thousands upon thousands of people gathered there.

There were many dance troupes that performed, libation poured and several presentations made to the King. The park was a great festival everywhere we went, even on the fringes other activities were going on. Drumming and singing, food was everywhere, and of course all of the best tasting beer in Ghana.

One of the highlights of the celebration was the appearance of the chairman of the Armed Forces Council, the head of State of Ghana, Flt Lieutenant Jerry John Rawlings. We heard all this commotion and excitement, then the crowd parted and coming through in a caravan of 4 wheel drives was the very popular, yet hated head of the government of Ghana (at that time). His head was protruding through the roof of his vehicle and he was waving to the people. What struck me was the absence of the big black shiny limousines, Rawlings in his people oriented image, was as usual in his army fatigues and the jeeps and 4 wheel drives, conveying the message that the government does not spend the people's money unnecessarily. He of course addressed the crowd, wished them well in the celebration of their New Year, and urged them to work together to build a strong and united Ghana.

When the sun went down the people began to disperse and went on to continue to celebrate the end of this weeklong celebration with numerous parties that would take place that night.

That night at Oyster Bay was one of those parties that took place and what a party it was. Folks danced High Life and drank beer and danced High Life and drank beer and danced until the sun rose. The band was the famous A.B. Crensil, the master High Life bandleader, who had won the number one spot as king of High Life several times during those years.

High Life is the national popular dance music of Ghana. During that period of time, the early and mid eighties there were many places and establishments where one could dance to a live band. I loved the outdoor dance floor of the old and now defunct Ambassador hotel, The Metropole was another dance and watering hole, it still exists today, but it is only a shadow of its former self. The disco clubs are the popular spots with the younger people, and with it comes the Western baggage. The women are not in their African dress, like they were at the High Life dance spots, the record mix however is Western and Ghanaian, it is an example of how Ghana integrates her culture and religion. The disco clubs also bring the Lebanese and European men looking for the young women in their seductive Western clothes and straight hair.

The next morning after breakfast saw us preparing to leave, headed back to Accra. Things were sort of quiet that morning, Cape Coast had partied itself out. Those that were able or willing found themselves in church that Sunday morning, after all the libation pouring, all the drumming and dancing and sacrificing of the sheep, they will once again give praise to the blond hair, blue eyed, Jesus, not the Jesus of Nazareth, but the Jesus in the mind of the European artist Michelangelo, and the image of his cousin. On the way back to Accra we stopped for lunch at Krokrobite a very nice resort off the Atlantic Ocean. While we waited for what seemed like hours for our food to be served we looked around the grounds. There were some half way decent chalets where one could get a room for a very reasonable price. Krokrobite is owned by a Danish woman and her Ghanaian husband, Moustapha Tettey Addy. Moustapha is a world renowned master drummer, who travels quite often, fortunately he was there at that time and we were treated to a masterful performance of his drummers and dancers. Krokrobite also houses the Academy of African Arts and Science, which is a training institute founded by Moustapha Addy to train Ghanaian youth in drumming, dancing and folklore. We found out that every Sunday, there was a 2-3 hour performance and that it attracted a lot of people from Accra, various Europeans, Ghanaians, and African American expatriates.

We met several African Americans there that have been living in Ghana for many years. Earlier at the W.E.B. DuBois Pan African Center we met some of the first African American expatriates, such as the Lee's, who were both dentist and some of the first that heeded Dr. Kwame Nkrumah's call to his old friends, and some former class mates at Lincoln University in Pennsylvania, to help him build the new Republic of Ghana in 1957. Mrs. Lee was my gracious host who showed me some very important film footage, during my second visit to Ghana in 1986, and told me a lot about the time when Malcolm X visited Ghana in 1963. Mrs. Lee is no longer alive at this time, she died from complications and a broken heart. Her son who was born in Ghana was executed by the government for a shooting death that he was tried and convicted for. We continued from Krokrobite on to Accra, and eventually up to Aburi where we would spend a few more days before heading back to the states.

The airports in Africa are usually a very trying experience, though the situation at Kotoko airport in Ghana has improved tremendously since the mid eighties, patience is still a very necessary virtue. However in 1985 it took more than patience, it also took whatever Cidi's you had left and what ever extra US dollars you might have in your possession. Corruption, is a routine practice in Africa, and particularly at the airports. After a grueling time of weighing our bags, dashing some handlers and custom agents

137

(Dashing is equivalent to 'greasing the palm'), we sat down for a traditional wait for the Ghana Airways plane to Abijan, Ivory Coast that was always coming but never there. Ghana Airways in 1999 however has improved greatly, but always keep a watchful eye.

As we boarded the plane our friends and new found family were still seen waving to us as we settled down in our seats, relaxing and enjoying the memories of our visit to the land of history, Kente, Kings and Queens, and a bastion of Pan Africanism and cultural pride.

As the Ghana Airways jet left the runway of Kotoko airport climbing into the African sky heading for Abijan, another expression of the massive African continent, visions of Fufu, Queen Mothers, and Fromtomfrom rhythms dance in our heads, and memories of a warm, friendly and evenly paced people.

Traditional stool

Part 6

Cote D' Ivoire

Cote d' Ivoire, also known as the Ivory Coast is located in West Africa, bordering the North Atlantic Ocean, between Ghana and Liberia, it is slightly larger than New Mexico.

Population is approximately 14, 800,000 (1996), and ethnic divisions include: Baoule 23%, Bete 18%, Senoufou 15%, Malinke 11%, Agni, foreign Africans (from Burkina Fasso and Mali, approximately 3 million) Non-Africans 330,000 (30,000 French and 300,000 Lebanese).

The religions of Cote d'Ivoire are: Muslim 60%, indigenous 25%, and Christian 12%.

The official language of the Ivory Coast is French, there are 60 native dialects with Dioula the most widely spoken.

Cote d' Ivoire gained its independence from France in 1960. Cote d' Ivoire is a republic with a multiparty system headed by a president. The first president was Felix Houphouet-Boigny from independence until he died in office in 1996.

Since 1983 Yamoussoukro has been the capital, although the former capital Abijan still remains the administrative capital, the business center, and where foreign governments maintain their official presence.

Cote d' Ivoire is among the world's largest producers and exporters of coffee, cocoa beans and palm-kernel oil, other primary exports include pineapples and rubber, trade and banking. The Ivory Coast's economy has maintained some measure of stability due to these exports and to offshore oil and gas discoveries, financing and debt arrangement by multilateral lenders and France.

Some of its natural resources are: petroleum, diamonds, manganese, iron ore, cobalt, bauxite, and copper. Cote d' Ivoire is mostly flat with northerly mountain areas, the country had at one time the largest forest in West Africa, but has been cleared by the timber industry.

The climate is tropical along the coast, semiarid in the far north; three seasons -warm and dry (November to March) hot and dry (March to May) hot and wet (June to October) 'the rainy season'.

Cote d' Ivoire is a member of the French commonwealth and its currency is the Communaute Financiere Africaine franc CFAF (CFA) which is regulated by the French Zone currencies

Abijan, Ivory Coast

The Ivory Coast for myself had a reputation that preceded itself among African American travelers, long before I actually visited there or before I had the opportunity to at least experience its airport and its capital of Abijan in transit to Ghana in the mid 1980's. This reputation was one of complaints that Abijan, the people of the city and the airport were too French, very aloof, cold and uncaring concerning the questions and concerns of African American, and English speaking West African travelers. If you did not speak French, you were virtually on your own and at the mercy of uncaring French speaking African airport personnel. Since Abijan is a connection hub for West African travelers on Air Afrique, Ghana Airways, Ethiopian Airways and several other West African and European airlines, you did not have a choice but to come in contact with the airport at some point or another.

My first encounter was in 1985 while traveling to Ghana. At that time the only connection from the United States other than traveling through Europe, which I did on a couple of occasions after that on KLM and British Airways, was to fly on Air Afrique to Abijan, and then take Ghana Airways

Air Afrique at that time did not fly to Accra, so we had to, (my traveling partner Bill Dyer and myself) disembark and layover in Abijan for approximately 13 hours until the next flight to Accra on Ghana Airways. Trying to find out how to get into town, find a restaurant and such was a most trying experience. However a little dash kind of opened some dialogue for us and we found ourselves in the beautiful city of Abijan, with its wide boulevards, impressive architecture, skyscrapers and chic restaurants and clubs.

We visited a few areas, ate lunch and wound up spending the rest of the time at the fabulous hotel Ivoire'. This is like a hotel city, with its lagoons surrounding the complex, its promenades and shops, restaurants and lounges, its casino and clubs.

We easily willed away the time listening to the live bands, sipping drinks and talking to various people. Later we headed back to the airport in time for our flight to Accra, picked up our bags, which we had left in storage and without incident boarded our flight to Accra.

It was however on our return from Accra, passing through on a 3 hour layover for the next flight on Air Afrique to JFK airport in New York that I had a problem. Usually when the Ghana Airways flight comes in to Abijan transit passengers have to present their boarding passes to receive a new boarding pass for the flight on Air Afrique to JFK. They told us that our boarding passes were not ready and that we would have to wait some time. We casually did and then they started giving out the boarding passes 30 minutes before departure time, my partner Bill received his along with all of the others that were scheduled to board. I inquired about my boarding pass, and they told me to wait it was coming. Well the time kept ticking away and I told Bill to board and that I would catch up to him, meanwhile I questioned several people regarding the whereabouts of my pass and no one seemed to understand what I was saying. I of course got angry and frustrated and confronted an official, he just continued walking past me and I gently touched his shoulder to get his attention. He abruptly pulled away saying "Messier unhand me!" My reply was "Messier my ass, I want my boarding pass!" He continued to ignore me, at that time a man who identified himself as a Liberian, said to me "man you better just get on that plane these French Africans are crazy". At that point I began to run to the plane, through the door onto the tarmac, to the steps of the plane. The flight attendant at the bottom of the steps asked for my boarding pass, I told him that I did not have it that they lost it and showed him my ticket stub and baggage tickets. He said "Messier you must have a boarding pass". I immediately raced up the steps to the plane. I was stopped by a flight attendant who again asked for my pass, and I again explained to him the situation. At that time the captain came to hear what all the ruckus was about. I told him that I was not getting off the plane, my baggage was on board and that I had a ticket stub, and that it was not my fault they had misplaced my boarding pass. I was told to take a seat and continued my voyage back to the States fuming with anger and vowing to never again set foot in that country. Of course that was a promise I did not and really could not keep due to the fact that Abijan was indeed the crossroads of West Africa. It was unavoidable as was Dakar being the first stop when traveling anywhere in Africa on Air Air Afrique (Air Africa), coming from the United States. I did pass through Abijan again of course due to my yearly trips to Ghana at that time, and I did have problems with the airport, its personnel and trying to get back to the States again.

On another such occasion as my first negative encounter with the airport, when I was again traveling with my friend and traveling partner Bill Dyer from Ghana back to the States. I again had a problem trying to get a seat on the plane back to JFK, not Bill just me again! When we deplaned at Abijan, had gone to the transit area where we were to be issued boarding passes, I was told that I would have to wait on standby because the plane was full and there was no seat for me at the time. Of course I was livid!, this was practically the same situation as before, the first time they could not find my boarding pass, this time there was no seat for me! I asked how could I not have a seat? I was a transit passenger, I was not getting on in Abijan, I had a seat from Ghana, how could it be that now I do not have one? They told me that my name was not in the computer for the flight to JFK. How could this be I said?, my ticket indicates the flight and if I had a confirmation for the flight from Accra on Ghana Airways, how could I not be confirmed on Air Afrique? the ticket was the same. They told me that I would have to wait, it seemed that this was a case of dejavu, Bill had his ticket and was boarding when the call to board came and here I was still waiting for a boarding pass. This was incredible! I was again frantic, going from one official to another, until I reached one of the top airport officials in his office where I tried to explain my problem. At that time due to the difficulty in communicating effectively with these Black folks who spoke French with such pride and arrogance that they refused to speak English even if they could to some degree, I thought that just maybe I needed to learn French. But of course as a long time Cultural Nationalist, I was opposed to learning another European language, with all of its nuances, particularly French with its subtle cultural Imperialist influences. However I found myself at the mercy of these French speaking African airport officials. Finally I was told by an official who had taken me to see the person in charge, that if I had $150.00 he would see to it that I got a seat. This was the real deal, here was the cause of all these problems, corruption, a pay off, the selling of seats, which is one of the reasons for planes being full when they finally arrive in Dakar for the flight back to the States, AKA bumping. I told the official that all I had was $75.00 as I was ending a trip and was out of money, of course he accepted this and in a few minutes he produced a boarding pass. I knew that I had been ripped off, stuck up, extorted, but I wanted to get back to the states and chalked it all up to the corruption of inter state travel in Africa.

In 1989 while Bill and I were traveling to Ghana with our wives and a group of people, we decided to spend our layover period of 13 hours in Abijan in a hotel and with a guided tour. The Grand hotel is a very modest hotel to say the least, but with an interesting garden and fairly good food. Our tour of Abijan was quite rewarding, we visited the incredible open air public laundry, a place of extreme hustle and bustle, where hundreds of people from Mali and other places wash the clothes of the wealthy Ivorians with their hands. These people were practically naked, some of the children actually were, as they washed tons of clothing in the river and laid them out for what seemed like miles on the hills surrounding the river. We actually began to see the clothes as we drove on the highway getting close to the area. It was such a spectacle! the sound! the excitement! the splashing

Public
Laundry

Public Laundry

the area. It was such a spectacle! the sound! the excitement! the splashing of water and quick sounds of African dialects clashing with each other. The colorful clothes dotting the countryside is an incredible spectacle not to be missed by the visitor to Abijan.

We had a great time in the marketplaces of Plateau, the public laundry and Trechville where you will find a Casbah like atmosphere of small stalls in winding close knit corridors where merchants from several West African countries have set up shop to sell wares from those countries, Senegal, Ghana, Nigeria, Togo, and other African states. We enjoyed delicious Ivorian food in a very nice African restaurant. This trip was without much incident, except for the customary dash that it took to get our baggage on the flight to Accra.

My ongoing relationship with the Ivory Coast was one of a transient, passing through the crossroads of Abijan to either Accra, Ghana or Lome, Togo for the next 5 years (1989-1994).

In 1993 Air Afrique began to fly into Accra and hence eliminated the 13 hour layover for the Ghana Airways flight to Accra. The layover now became approximately 1 hour and 45 minutes for the continuing flight to Accra on Air Afrique.

1994 saw a change in the itinerary for the Ivory Coast and a new more intimate relationship with the city of Abijan and a more expanded view of the country. Firstly the important thing to do to really get to know the country and its inhabitants is to move beyond the city limits of Abijan. The city of Abijan is influenced by the Francophones, those Ivorians that are trying desperately to be French, in their appearance and customs, speaking only French, etc.

The outlying areas however is where the real Ivorians are, and I had a chance to visit some of these areas during a 3 day tour in August of 1995 with a group of approximately 14 people.

We had just arrived from Accra and had cleared the customs in the arrival section, where we were met by Kofi, a guide that was employed by IVT (Ivorian Tours). Kofi turned out to be a very good guide, personable, informed and organized.

We had a more extensive tour of Abijan, visiting several marketplaces, the timber industry, cathedrals, and other places of interest. He gave us information on the commerce and development projects of the government and Ivorian businessmen.

Our impressions were that the French had a lot to do with the developed infrastructure of the city, Kofi however told us that many of the skyscrapers and impressive architecture were built by Ivorians (Africans) and not the French. This of course we had doubts about, as we understood that the government and businessmen of Cote d' Ivoire are under the influence of the French, to put it mildly.

Our trip to Tiegba was a trip that allowed us to see the countryside and to become involved with the traditional culture. Tiagba is an area that is perhaps 2 hours outside of Abijan, on our way there we made 2 stops, one to a rubber plantation, a most fascinating experience. We saw the rubber trees, and how the white stiff rubber grew out of these trees, oozing out like some substance from a horror film. This white stiff growth is the stuff that winds up on our cars and bicycles, and in the industrial industries in the Western world. Some of us took a piece with us as souvenirs, for how often do you see rubber in its natural state. From the rubber plantation we moved on, traveling on a winding roller coaster that took our vehicle up and down twisting, wet, red clay roads until we reached a Cocoa plantation. There we had an interesting visit to see the Cocoa pods in their early stages of development and to also see the fully developed Cocoa beans.

This was a rich and dense plantation, a sort of Cocoa forest if you will, a cool, and green atmosphere. After the plantation we continued on the roller coaster road, up and down the hills, we almost got stuck in a couple of places where the red mud became soft and the tires became bogged

Finally we reached an area where the road ends and we can not go any further, at this place we took a small canoe across the river to the village of Tiagba. Before we did we had lunch at a nice restaurant that is extended over the river. After we cross the river in groups of three, the boat being small we load 5 persons each into the boat with two boys, one rowing the boat, and the other dipping the water out.

The ride is only about 15 minutes, but it was for some a very long time, seeing that the boat was so small and the water was rising over the bow. When we reached the other side we were delighted to find that we had picked a good time to visit the village because there was a festival of some sorts in progress. The village was alive with people and music, and the festive sounds that permeated the air.

We walked past several compounds where the inhabitants were drumming and dancing, and preparing all kinds of delicious food.

The people were friendly, they waved back to us, smiled and posed for pictures. One thing that struck me about them was the way they were dressed, many of the men were wearing the 'wrap' as they do in Ghana, the women's hair was short cropped also like the women in Ghana. They were dressed much different than the people in Abijan, I was to learn that these were the Akans, we were in the area of the ethnic group that is also in Ghana. Of course this was yet another example of the geographical division of the continent of Africa by European countries at the start of the colonial period. Having just left Ghana we were pleasantly surprised to find several of the cultural practices the same. We approached a real get down party that was going on in a sort of indoor-outdoor dance hall, a circular concrete floor with a three foot wall, topped with a straw roof, and speakers blasting out African and Reggae dance music. We jumped in with the people and danced our butts off. After, we paid a special visit to the chief of the village in his quarters, which was a most unique type of dwelling. Some of the dwellings were constructed over the water, in that you entered from solid ground, but as you continued in the house you found yourself in rooms that were built with bamboo and wood slats over the water. It was quite interesting, not very sturdy, as the floor swayed as you moved or walked, there was furniture, beds and various items that one finds in a typical house where people live.

We visited the chief in the first part of the house where the ground was solid. He welcomed us along with several of the elders and we sat as we delivered our message of our mission through our most able guide Kofi. We then went to the room with the bamboo floor where libation was poured, and we sipped the schnapps that was offered and was additionally surprised that they had the locally distilled fermented palm wine, that is called Apathusi in Ghana.

We shared in the libation, sipped the schnapps and Apathusi and made our contribution to the chief and members of his village.

We said our good byes and headed toward the shoreline and the small canoe to begin our short journey back to the other side and the road to Abijan.

On our trip back to Abijan we savored the time that we spent with the villagers, talked about our pledges to stay in touch with and send items back to some of the people.

It felt good to meet the real people the real Ivorians, not just those who lived in the capital, competing against each other in order to sustain themselves and to prove who is more French than the French.

Not all of those who live in Abijan are that way though, in fact it would not be fair to the genuine people of the city to paint them all with such a broad brush. We have to be more analytical about these observations, however there seems to be a sort of consensus that point in the direction of the Ivory Coast being one of the more Francophone countries in the French speaking West African community, French culture being the model for civilization for them.

In fact we spent time with people that were related to a good friend, and member of The Afrikan Poetry Theatre. Djaze Serpika is from Cote' D'Ivoire, and a proprietor of a book store and hair braiding salon called Afrikan Bookstreet in Jamaica Queens, next door to The Afrikan Poetry Theatre. Jazzy, as we pronounce his name around the Jamaica area is a perfect example of ambition and hard work. When Jazzy first came around the Center he sold me some framed drawings of Toussaint Le'Oveture and Desalline, two important heroes of the Haitian revolution. He could speak very little English and asked me if I knew someone who could teach him English. I arranged for a bilingual teacher that I knew to work with him, and that proved very fruitful. Jazzy later came to me and asked me would I take out a license so he could sell and distribute literature and promotional materials in the new Jamaica Center subway station.

He also rented a room at the theatre, which was common as we had a student from The Gambia, a brother from Nigeria and several African American young men live at the center at some point in time over the years. Jazzy eventually opened up his store, and in fact has two shops, the other being solely a hair braiding salon.

It was through Jazzy's family in Abijan that we would really experience

148

genuine Ivorian hospitality.

In the Summer of 1994 with a group of African American tourists arriving in Abijan from Accra, we met Jazzy's brother and cousin at the hotel, we arranged for an evening of dinner and entertainment. They picked us up the next evening and took us to a nice African restaurant as we requested, a place that was in a sort of nite life cultural hub. We passed through a little dirt road area that was enclosed with several wooden structures that housed local eating establishments, drinking bars and dance halls where lively sounds of Soukous, Hi-Life, and African popular music blared through scratchy speakers. It was a festival mood that permeated the air.

This is the stuff of Black life that is universal, be it in Harlem, Compton, Accra, Mississippi, or wherever African people gather to have a good time, we felt comfortable, people were friendly, and were having fun.

We entered a restaurant that had a thatched hut roof, was simple in décor but was clean and intimate. All of us agreed that we did not want continental food that we wanted to taste traditional Ivorian cuisine. We ordered starches such as yam, a small grain called Attieke, vegetables of various kinds, a few people in the group were vegetarians and did not require meat, the rest of us, some who ate fish and chicken, a couple who ate red meat inquired about the choices available. We were told that fish and chicken was available, but that if we wanted to experience authentic Ivorian food, we might try Agouti. "Agouti" we asked? "What is Agouti?", "it is a meat" we were told, we further inquired about the kind of animal that it was, Jazzy's brother and cousin, the waiters, could not describe it in relationship to the various animals that we compared them to. Was it like a rabbit we asked? a deer? Did it taste like chicken? Was it sweet meat? The only description that they could offer was that it was an animal that ran through the bush. I immediately thought of Ghana and what they call bush meat there, or another word for the animal that ran through the bush was 'Grass Cutter'. One of the waiters said that he would bring out the head of the animal for us to see, and when he returned with the head on a platter, it was clear to all that this animal was a member of the rodent family. We quickly and respectfully declined the offer for Agouti and settled for something that was more familiar to our taste.

Later we went dancing at one of the local clubs and after, returned to the Novotel.

In the Summer of 1995, the group that I brought to Abijan was again met by the family, and this time instead of going out to eat and party, we were invited to Jazzy's brothers' house where we had a big spread of all kinds of delicious food. No Agouti though, and all kinds of drinks were available. There was a large table set in the middle of the courtyard where we feasted with several family members and community. Later we danced to Ivorian Hi-Life music, sweated and enjoyed the warm hospitality of the Ivorian community.

In 1996 while briefly visiting Abijan alone while passing through to Ghana my host was Dr. Horodias Ahimon whose family showed me a grand time, taking me to places of interest, dining and a show.

These experiences helped to change my attitude about the Ivory Coast, and allowed me to view the country in a more analytical way. It is true that many of the people are cold to visitors who do not speak French. But I think for the most part these are people who are victims of French cultural Imperialism, who have no appreciation of their own contribution to civilization. True a lot of them live in the very cosmopolitan city of Abijan, but they also have counterparts that live in cities and suburbs of the United States, and other affluent places in the world where emulating white customs, ethics and values are cherished and are models to strive for.

The majority of the people however, especially those in the towns and villages, are friendly, as they are in all of the countries that I have visited. These are the real people, these are the people that unless you go there you may not find so readily in the cities of Africa or America. Cote d' Ivoire however is a country trying to keep up with the world's movement towards the 21st century, in spite of its denials.

Part 7

Nigeria

Official name: Federal republic of Nigeria

Location: West Africa, between Benin and Cameroon

Total area: 923.770 sq. Km, more than twice the size of California

Climate: equatorial in south, tropical in the center, arid in the north

Natural resources: oil, tin Columbite, iron ore, coal, limestone, lead, zinc, natural gas.

Population: 110,532,242 (July 1998 estimate)

Ethnic groups: Hausa, Fulani, Yoruba, Ibo, Kanuri. Ibibio, Tiv, Ijaw

Languages: English is the official language, Hausa, Yoruba, Ibo, Fulani

Religions: Muslim 50%, Christian 40%, Indigenous beliefs 10%

Nigeria gained its independence from U. k. in 1960. It has a legal system based on English Common law, Islamic law, and tribal law. The national capital is in Abuja, which was officially moved from Lagos in 1991. It has been ruled by several military governments since 1983, until the recent elections in February of 1999 when Onesegun Obasanjo, former military ruler now civilian was elected President.

Before 1914 there was not a country known as Nigeria. The people that lived in those areas that is now present day Nigeria, were part of four different empires that stretched even beyond the current boundaries into areas of present day Ghana and Cameroon.

The Calabar Kingdom was the oldest kingdom founded in the year 1000 Ad, had the oldest contact with Europeans and the oldest church built in Nigeria dating back to 1850.

The Northern Empire, composed of the Borno Empire, the Hausa states, and some other groups.

The Oduduwa Empire consisted of two main groups, the indigenous people whose religious and cultural life was Ile Ife, who now make up the Yoruba people and was called Yoruba land. The other group were the Berbels, who eventually formed the Hausa and Borno states. This empire has many interesting stories and legends, in which Oduduwa is considered the creator of the earth, and the ancestor of the Yoruba kings. It is said the Oduduwa founded the city of Ife and sent his sons out as priests-kings to establish other cities and to preside over the cultural rituals.

The Benin empire was also powerful and stretched into present day Ghana, well known for its African sculpturing. Independence came in 1960, in 1963 Nigeria became a republic. 1966 saw the first military coup, and what was to become a succession of coups.

1967 saw the Biafran civil war that was to devastate the country, which lasted until the section of Nigeria under the leadership of the Ibo's surrendered in 1970. The early 1970's saw an oil boom that brought a lot of revenue to Nigeria that some say benefited those in government and a few others.

(Internet sources)

152

My first and only visit at this writing to the country of Nigeria was in 1986. I spent only one week there, I left Ghana to travel to Lagos and returned to Ghana after the visit. Nigeria has a reputation that precedes itself, a lot of what you hear is negative, Nigerians are thieves, criminals, if you go there you will get ripped off. The things you hear today will definitely discourage you from entering the country, the atrocities of the military government, the hanging of Ken Sarowiah and others, the imprisonment of presidential candidate and self proclaimed winner of the presidential elections chief Abiola. In 1986 things were not as bad as they are today, but there were massive social problems and criminality was at a high rate then.

The Nira at that time was approximately 3 to 3 1/2 to 1 Us dollar, today the Nira is approximately 95 Nira to 1 US dollar. The economy has taken a tragic plunge, what was once a booming economy in the early to late 1970's is now in shambles, massive unemployment and an alarming increasing gap between the masses of people and the businessmen and political people who are swimming in wealth. However in 1986 the situation was somewhat better, but the signs were there.

Before leaving the states I had made plans to connect with the brother of a Ghanaian travel agent who was operating a travel agency in Lagos, at that time the capital of Nigeria. Today it is considered the commercial capital of Nigeria, the official capital and seat of government is in the city of Abuja. Even though Nigeria is going through serious political and economic trials and tribulations it is still a country with great wealth and natural resources.

When I arrived in Lagos, I found a very busy airport, I caught a taxi and went to the office of the travel agent. I had asked his brother to have him arrange for me a hotel to stay in and for a guide to show me around.

He introduced me to my guide who's name I have forgotten at this writing 13 years later, but I do know that he was a very nice person and traveled with me for approximately 6 days, taking me many places. He was very knowledgeable, courteous and professional. He was a good companion, and drove a very clean and comfortable Mercedes Benz, that would afford me a very respectable means of traveling around Nigeria. My guide checked me into a hotel that was not too expensive yet one that was clean and decent.

The hotel was located in Ikegia, an area outside of Lagos proper or downtown Lagos. If you are familiar with New York City, it might be compared to the areas in Manhattan like lower Manhattan and Harlem, or the areas surrounding the borough of Manhattan, such as Queens, Brooklyn or the Bronx.

Lagos is quite a place, in spite of some of the negative things that one might find, as you will find in any large city in Europe or the United States, the fascinating thing about Lagos is it is an African metropolis. Usually people in the West do not think of Africa in terms of large cities, with skyscrapers, highways, fast food restaurants, and massive traffic jams.

The uninformed images many people have of Africa are huts, animals, rivers and jungles, and people half dressed. Lagos, Nigeria defies that entire image, it is very much like New York, the hustle and bustle with a huge population trying to survive and feed itself.

LAGOS

Lagos Nigeria Africa
Lagos Nigeria Africa
Lagos Nigeria Africa
Lagos Nigeria Africa
Stone buildings/tall glass neon signs
Tower bridge honking Peugeots and Mercedes
Hustling Mr. Slick got what you want
Afro beat knee peeping big ass gerri curls
strolling cool and hip/feeling the force
the western winds blowing big apple chills
and power vibrations/smack dab in twentieth
century motion madness
riding the waves of Yoruba musical rhythms
and dancing dialects
Oyomi Yo Oyomi Yo Oyomi Yo Oyomi Ye
Oyomi Yo Oyomi Yo Oyomi Yo Oyomi Ye
Hamburger joints washed down with powerful
Guilder brew/and yam in hot soup and sticky
fingers and bubas and El -Haji cooling and
praying to the east/and African reflections
in corporate strongholds and hip struttin
cool dudes and multi colors and African Shriners
cool out in the wake of Fela's worldwind

as they dance to his essence
are melancholy of his absence
and long for his return
as Afro beat be jammin from superbox
and horns blow/ and traffic jam outside
and open sewers flow
and magnificent architect glow
and stick up grown kids
play cop and blow
and Africa cries
and Europe and America smiles
and lick their slimy chops
and Black America recoils
and Africa America dreams
and we all dance to the multi-rhythms
the freak dance/the drug jig
the ancestral rhythms
and rattle dice made of cowrie shells
for the next move.
Lagos Nigeria Africa
.Lagos Nigeria Africa
Lagos Nigeria Africa
Lagos Nigeria Africa

Lagos is cool with me though, I can relate to it because it has a rhythm and a beat like New York, with its diversity, all Black that it is, but varied, very varied.

The diversity was very interesting, the wealthy, with cars that were so expensive that not many Black folks in the U. S. could afford. Incredible homes, mansions, and other palatial abodes, in a country where the masses of unskilled workers make less than $100 a month. Lagos, a city that has so many people bursting at its seems, so many automobiles, so many big city ills. After seeing a lot of the city my driver brought me back to the hotel, later trying to get some sleep my phone rings and I hear a voice "You want to have some fun?" said this sultry, provocative voice. Of course I wasn't interested, but this is an example of the level of prostitution and street life that one might find in overcrowded, impoverished Black cities, in the US and in Africa.

I was able to visit a couple of homes due to my meeting with a brother called Yomi. Abeyomi was a dance teacher, a Yoruba language and cultural teacher, and was involved with a Nigerian cultural theatre group. He had discovered some information on the Afrikan Poetry Theatre and wrote to me of his interest in doing some cultural exchange work with the theatre, and would like to come to the states and teach the Yourba culture though language and dance. I wrote back to him to inform him of my plan to come to Nigeria. He had given me his phone number and I called him upon my arrival. He met me that next day at the hotel with a friend who was driving and we went to visit his home and the homes of friends. The traffic jams in Lagos are incredible, cars going every kind of way, and I don't mean just north, south, east and west, I mean all in between. Horns blowing, cussing and name calling, I looked for traffic lights and systems of order, but could only find a frustrated police officer waving his hands and blowing his whistle against the deafening sound of countless horns honking, trying to move traffic that was going nowhere.

Later that night the three of us Abeyomi, myself and his friend, went to visit Fela Anikulapo Kuti's night club. Fela is an internationally known musician, one who is credited with merging Jazz, popular African music, along with traditional Yoruba rhythms to form what has been popularly known as Afro Beat. Fela had recorded more than fifty albums of music that has a funky beat, a sensuous rhythm, in fact Fela (who's name was Fela Ransome Kuti in the beginning) was called the James Brown of Nigeria and Africa, his beat is so cool, so funky. Fela 's music is also very political and consistently criticized the government of Nigeria. He was a person who had formed his own political party, and ran for the presidency of Nigeria on more than one occasion. Fela's mother was a politician involved with one of the opposition parties, and was a powerful person in the political life of Nigeria. This was an asset to Fela in his trials and tribulations with the authorities in Nigeria.

Fela's mother was jailed on more than one occasion, her political and private properties invaded by soldiers and police, and she and her political allies became the victims of government aggression, through harassment, violence and murder. It is said that Fela's mother was killed by government forces. Fela himself was imprisoned several times on a number of charges.

He was a controversial person in Nigeria, not only was he disliked by many mainstream Nigerians for his criticism of those political people who were corrupt, stealing the money from the people, but also his charges of Nigerians wanting to emulate White people. He criticized Nigerian women for trying to get away from doing things and acting the way that birth and culture had given them.

He said that they wanted to be like the White woman and chronicled this charge on one of his most popular albums with a tune called "Lady" "She gon say me be lady O". Fela was also controversial because of some of his social cultural practices, he was a multi polygamist, he did not have just 3 or 4 wives, Fela had 27, 28, 30 wives at a time. Many parents and people of high social status in Nigeria were complaining that Fela was luring the young women into his movement and had created a cult. Many of the young and beautiful women of Nigeria became involved in Fela's Shrine, as dancers, singers, members of the Shrine, and/or one of his numerous wives. Fela was also known to light up a blount, a reefer, marijuana on stage before thousands of people. He also publicly bragged about his sexual prowess, how many times a day that he had sex. His music is infectious and he developed followers and listeners to his music in Africa, Europe and the U.S. He most often presented a large group of musicians that consisted of the traditional big Jazz band, a chorus of African drummers and dancers that grooved to the rhythms with accentuated sensuous body movements, and singers that echoed his refrain. Fela was multi-talented, he sang songs of protest, culture and power, blew a mean saxophone, and played the electric keyboards, in addition to dancing and leading the huge ensemble of 30 to 35 people. Fela's music would not hit you full in the face, like most of the Yoruba influenced music does not, it builds up slowly, consistently, getting tighter, stronger and rhythmic, hypnotic, as when you saw him in concert you would see and feel the effect of the music on the audience. When we reached the club we were disappointed to find out that Fela was not in the country, that he was performing in Europe with his band. I found however my visit to the club quite interesting, the music was happening, women were everywhere, so was the pungent smell of marijuana that was openly and indiscreetly smoked in the indoor/outdoor club.

Tropical life brings with it another kind of architectural consideration, many of the traditional High Life and Afro Pop dance halls have walls, and usually no roofs so that the air can be the natural air conditioning for dancing and drinking beer. For just like Ghana, drinking beer in Nigeria is a popular pastime, they have some of the beer sold in Ghana, also Guinness, and their own famous and powerful beer.

Fela's club is a most popular place for contemporary African socializing, it might be looked at by the police as part of the 'Red Light District'.

Fela Anikulapo Kuti passed away in 1997 at the age of 59, from complications associated with Aids.

Fela Anikulapo Kuti

Fela You bad man !
You come on like a whirlwind
Like cosmic energy
Like Shaka and Coltrane
Like Bird and Mongo
Like a Caribbean wind storm
Like cascades of African drums
Like James Brown and Little Richard
You blast your way from Africa
to New York's Felt Forum
you philosophize, stimulate the mind
and testify to the real deal
and waves of rhythmic African
polyrhythms began to build and ride
and build and ride
and horns call out in their individual voices
and answer in their collective refrain
and sweet African voices, and sharp voices

and rapid vocal cries encircle your voice
and feeds you its energy, its sensitivity
its power
and Egypt 80 cooks and burns and swells
and drives and pulsates
and mellows
and grooves
and floats
and African vibes be all encompassing
African rhythm be king
be the force
be spiritual
be strong
be determined and sure
be groovy
be bad !
and African women dancing to the groove
swaying and shimmying
rolling and vibrating
and energizing the very air
Fela your Yoruba musical voice rhythm
rises and falls and races and demands
and stops and starts the changing rhythms
as it calls for freedom liberty and self
determination as Egypt 80 responds
calling and responding
and riding the African waves
calling & responding
calling and responding
and the audience breaks loose
responding to your calls
clapping & crying & screaming your name
Fela ! Fela ! we love you Fela !
the roar of the crowd is thunderous !
seems to feed your energy
and it refuels that super musical machine
Egypt 80
when you ask we give it up
submitting our sensitivities

our emotions, our souls
to the rhythm of Africa
Fela you bad man
you leave in a flash
in the twinkling of an eye
leaving a trail of energy & sound
like the combined winds of the world
like the thunder of all the oceans
like a million African drums
and thousands of voices and horns
calling your name

Fela! Fela! Fela! Fela! Anikulapo Kuti

November 1986

Abeyomi would be in New York within the next month and a half, living at The Afrikan Poetry Theatre. After my visit to Nigeria I began to put in motion the process for a visa that would allow Yomi to come to the United States as a guest of the Theatre for two months, to teach African dance and Yoruba language and culture. It was a very productive time that Yomi spent at the Theatre, teaching and sharing his culture with the participants of the workshops. His dance class was very popular and he became a part of the APT family.

When his time was up to return to Nigeria, he asked me if it was alright for him to extend his visa for another few weeks, I told him that yes it was okay to extend it for another month. At the end of this period it was time for Yomi to leave, I asked my wife to prepare dinner for a few people for a mini going away party, we also had a small gathering at the center for him, recording the event on video tape.

One night approximately two weeks later I received a telephone call at home from Yomi, I said "Yomi you're calling me all the way from Lagos?" Yomi answered "no bro. John I am in Baltimore, MD" "Baltimore?" I hollered, "What are you doing in Baltimore? You are supposed to be in Nigeria, don't you know that you can get me in trouble for this? You tricked me, you had this planned all along, before you came to America, you had this all planned". "No, I just decided that I wanted to go to school and I know how you felt about me returning to Nigeria" he said, "you do not know how difficult it is in Nigeria bro. John" he said. I was furious, I had been tricked, been had by a slick ass Nigerian I thought, beginning to blame all of Nigeria for the trickery of this sorry ass. Bro. Garba, the young Gambian student who was also living at the theatre asked me to forgive him some time after this took place, said that he had spoken with him and that he wanted Garba to talk to me and ask for my forgiveness. I refused of course because I felt that he had planned the whole thing. I later found out that a sister that was associated with the theatre drove him to Baltimore.

I did spot him at the African street festival in Brooklyn, about a year after that time. I have not seen him since then but I believe he is still in the U.S. In spite of how I felt about how he had deceived me I still would not let that turn me against all Nigerians, but it gave me a warning in how to deal with people and this visa situation.

The next morning my driver picked me up at the hotel and we continued our exploration of the people and places of Nigeria. We visited the National Theatre, an architecturally impressive building, with its circular shape and well kept grounds, this building houses a performance space, exhibit rooms, artifacts, a library and film archives. There I also saw books and paintings by prominent African American artists, Nigerian artists and artists from other African countries and the Diaspora. I was shown film footage from FESPAC, the International African festival on culture and the arts held in 1977 in Lagos, Nigeria. Unfortunately I had not begun to travel to Africa just yet in 1977 and did not experience this important cultural 'extravaganza. This monumental event drew thousands of people from around the world to Nigeria to participate in a world festival of arts and culture. Musicians, scholars, artists and participants from the Africa world, would participate in concerts, symposiums and exhibits.

Nothing of this magnitude has been done on the continent of Africa since that time. PANAFEST (A Pan African festival) in Ghana has been held on four occasions in 1993, 1995 and 1997 - 1999; and FESTAM (An international festival of music and art) in Senegal held in 1994, 1995, 1998 and 1999. Neither of these festivals or other mini festivals held in Senegal and the Ivory Coast during the early and mid 1990's would match the level of international African involvement and money invested that FESPAC did.

National Theatre

The following day my driver and I found ourselves traveling across highways and byways heading towards the Western region. I was impressed with the roads and highways in Nigeria, this was no dusty bush country, we are talking about a huge country with lots of wealth, primarily from the rich oil reserves, and other important minerals. At the time of my visit Nigeria had 19 states, now it has more than thirty states, reorganized I suppose for better management or other political reasons.

I enjoyed traveling on the smooth highways in my hired Mercedes, chilling in the back with air conditioning, Afro Beat and JuJu music playing softly in my ears from the cars' radio. My driver and I would have occasional conversations whenever he pointed out various landscapes and points of interest to me.

We arrived in the city of Ibadan, a huge industrial complex, where the hustle and bustle of commerce and industry permeates the air. We continued on to the University of Ibadan where we visited various areas of the campus, met the brother of my driver who is a professor there, and had an interesting lunch of Nigerian food that is quite similar to food in Ghana, yam and cassava and other starches.

We visited the zoo at the university, which was my only opportunity to actually see any animals in Nigeria. It was quite an organized zoo compared to some of the others that I had seen in Ghana, and a few other West African countries. It was very thoughtful of the university to include this operation in the scope of their activities. Having this facility to display these animals, as it is unbeknownst to many people in the West, who do not realize that you will not see lions and elephants, and other large animals roaming loose in West Africa. Particularly in a country like Nigeria with

162

over 100 million people.

Our next stop in the Western region, where the Yoruba speaking people have a very strong presence, is Ife, land of the Yoruba. A place where as soon as you arrive can feel the musical rhythm of the people, in their voice, their walk and in their body language. Ile Ife is where the head of the Yoruba culture resides, the Omi, his palace is huge and seem to stretch for several blocks. I unfortunately was not able to meet him or see the palace, as he was not in his residence at this time. I enjoyed visiting the various places in Ife and mingling with the people, at the marketplace, and the areas where they live. My visit was all too short, I wish I could really spend more time in Ife because I loved the atmosphere and rhythm of this city of the Yorubas. In fact I need to visit Nigeria and spend more time to really see and experience the country. However in terms of leading people on tours to Nigeria, I must honestly say that I will wait until the political climate improves for the benefit of visitors from the West. Nigeria is a dynamic country, an important country not to be dismissed, it contains almost one fifth of all of the population of Africa. The bad rap that Nigeria gets then concerning drugs, corruption, rip off schemes, etc. may be due to its tremendous population and the number of people involved in such schemes, as opposed to the labeling of an entire people as corrupt and criminal. We must understand the facts that Nigeria has many honest professionals and business people, many doctors and accountants, and architects, and people with several human interest skills that contribute to the world and its development. In reality if we talk about corruption in government and in the society of any country, the United States of America has to be the number one culprit. A country with a legal system that allows and supports cheating people out of their meager resources, like the concept of being responsible for any kind of corrupt scheme that is supported by the court system because you have signed on the dotted line. No matter if it is an unethical scheme, no matter if the signers are old, or cannot read very well. They tell you to read the fine print and fine it is, instead of the legal system determining if the deal is a fair one, is an ethical one, if you sign you are responsible. This is the corrupt system that you find in the United States of America.

In conclusion those of us in the West must be very careful how we judge Africa for its corruption, while condoning the cancerous corruption that one finds in the so called bastion of democracy called the United States of America.

163

Ile Ife

Part 8
Mali

Located in West Africa, southwest of Algeria, Mali is in the West African savanna region, between the coastal rain forest and the desert. The northern third of the country is within the Sahara Desert and is sparsely populated. Mali is almost twice the size of Texas. It also borders Mauritania, Guinea, Senegal, Cote d'Ivoire and Burkina Faso.

Note: Mali is landlocked (The Niger River flows through it)

The climate is subtropical to arid, hot and dry February to June, rainy, humid, and mild June to November, cool and dry November to February. 65% of the land is desert or semi-desert, 10% of the population is nomadic. Inflation was 35% in 1994.

The terrain is mostly flat to rolling northern plains covered by sand, savanna in the south, and rugged hills in the northeast.

Natural resources are: gold, phosphates, Kaolin, salt, limestone, uranium, bauxite, iron ore, manganese, tin, and copper.

Agriculture accounts for 50% of GDP, livestock products accounts for over 70% of exports.

Population: 9,375,132 (July 1995)

Ethnic groups: Mande 45% (Bambara, Malinke, Sarakole) Peul 17%, Voltaic 12%, Songhai 6% Tuareg and Moor 10%, other 10% (Dogon - Approx. 705,000)

Religions: Muslim 90%, indigenous beliefs 9%, Christian 1%

Languages: French (official language), Bambara 80%, numerous African languages.

Capital: Bamako - 8 regions: Gao, Kayes, Kidal, Koulikoro, Mopti, Segou, Sikasso, Tombouctou. (Timbuktu)

Independence: September 22, 1960 - from France

Currency: CFA franc

Various Internet sources

When you utter the name Mali, you speak of history, empires, Timbuktu, mud cities and Dogon, conquering Khalifah's, Sultans, and tales of conquest. Tales of trading in gold, ivory and salt and wealthy merchants.

There were three great ancient West African empires whose histories are traced to the stone ages through carvings, rock paintings, and other archeological finds. Mali was the second of the three great empires, Ghana being the first, and the Songhai Empire being the last. Mali was a small state from 600AD until the twelfth century when Sundiata Keita, a prominent Muslim leader achieved many conquests that turned Mali into a great, rich and well organized empire. The religion of Islam was spread with veracity, zeal, and aggressiveness that was uncompromising and unparalleled in the history of the world.The expansion of Mali into an empire was synonymous with the spread of Islam. In 1324 A.D. the Sultan Mansa Musa organized one of the most regal pilgrimages to Mecca, bringing with him an entourage of 60,000 people, 12,000 servants, 500 slaves, and almost 100 camels carrying tons of gold to be distributed to the poor. On his return from Mecca he brought with him master architects and builders who constructed the libraries and other magnificent buildings in Timbuktu.

Timbuktu also spelled Tombouctou in French is historically important as a major trading post on the trans-Saharan caravan route. It is found on the southern edge of the Sahara desert, and a few miles from the Niger River. Timbuktou was a center, an intellectual and spiritual capital, it was home to a prestigious Koranic university, the university of Sankore. The three great mosques built at that time still remain today.

Timbuktu was founded about 1100 A. D. by the nomadic Tuareg people. It became a part of the Mali Empire around the 13th century by the Muslim leader Mansa Musa who built a tower for the great mosque and a palace, or royal residence, there is no trace of the latter today.

The Tuareg from time to time during the 14th century regained control of the city, but this did not stop the continued development of the trade in gold and salt, because they ruled from the desert, plundering periodically. In fact there was a significant settlement of Muslim scholars and North African merchants, during this period.

Mali began its decline after 1400 due to weak leadership, internal disunity, and civil war. In 1468 Timbuktu was conquered by Sonni' Ali, the Songhai ruler, who was not endeared to the Muslim scholars which led to conflict and disunity. His successor Askia Muhammad I of Songhai (1493-1528) however reversed this trend and utilized the scholarly elite as legal and moral counselors. During the Askia period, the dynasty period of the Askia Muhammad rulers (1493-1591) Timbuktu was at the height of commercial and intellectual development. The city's scholars many of whom had studied in Egypt and Mecca attracted students from a very broad area. Timbuktu declined after being captured by Morocco in 1591. The Moroccans were repeatedly attacked and conquered by the Bambara, Fulani, and the Tuareg until 1893, when the French captured the city. In 1960 it became part of the newly independent Republic of Mali. Timbuktu is now an administrative center of Mali, where small salt caravans still arrive, but there is no gold to offer, sub trans-Saharan commerce no longer exists, and Islamic learning survives among a handful of aging scholars.

(From Mali Home Page and various Internet Sources)

My first visit to Mali was in January 1994, I had left Dakar, Senegal and landed in the capital of Bamako after a one hour and twenty minute flight. I was again full of quiet excitement on entering yet another African country for the first time. It brought back to me the reality of the immense size and diversity of the African continent. Many people in the United States still do not understand the reality that "Africa is a continent, not a country", quoting the title of Dr. Arthur Lewin's book, a professor of Black studies at Baruch College in New York City. There is an initial excitement as one enters the continent itself, and that same excitement repeats itself as you enter country after country, experiencing yet another culture, different indigenous languages, food aromas and smells, different rhythms and sounds. Yet it all seems familiar, it all seems the same, the lines going through customs, the patience of the travelers, the European language, either French or English, the hustle and bustle of the capitals and large commercial cities, the commerce and bartering, the sound of the drum. It is what makes Africa so interesting, so exciting, its diversity and its familiarity and sameness.

Finally passing through customs I looked for my host and saw a sign with my name on it and walked over to the gentleman holding it and recognized Jibril Traore, owner and director of ATS (African Travel Services) one of the more prominent African owned tour companies in Mali. I had met brother Jabril a month or so earlier in Dakar during a Bienal Arts festival that brought prominent African American, continental African and European visual artists and lecturers for a week of exhibits, symposiums and concerts in Senegal. It was a week of grand events, cocktail parties, banquets, etc. that involved many of the intellectual, cultural elite, politicians and business people of Dakar, including the President and many of the top government ministers.

Jibril Traore, and I became acquainted at several of these festive events. I was happy to see him and to be in his country. We left the airport and got in his 4wheel drive and went directly to his office in downtown Bamako. There I met his staff and later we went to lunch at a very nice restaurant where I sampled Malian food. Some of the selections were similar to Senegal, but although they had some fish on the menu it was not as available as it was in Senegal, however lamb and beef was more than enough. After lunch I checked into the Grand hotel that was seeing its last days in the condition that it was in. A couple of years later the Grand would open up with a new face, a renovated look. However at the time that I stayed there, it was in quite a state of disrepair. I managed though and also managed to escape from the onslaught of many ladies of the night that frequented the lobby and halls of the hotel. Later that night Jibril picked me up for dinner and took me to one of the finest, most elegant and cultural restaurants in Bamako. This was Djenne, named after the famous historical mud cloth city further north. It was owned by one of the most renowned designers, decorators, artists and businesswomen in Mali. It was draped with magnificent African prints and mud cloth everywhere, on the walls, hanging from the ceiling, on the furniture, the pillows, it was gorgeous, the subtle lighting and table settings, the expensive stuffed couches and arm chairs, the plants. This was a most delightful way to dine in an elegant African atmosphere with delicious food and interesting company. Jabril's wife had joined us for dinner and we spent a most enjoyable time that evening. I mentioned that the restaurant Djenne was one of the finest restaurants in Bamako, because there was another one that topped even this one and that was San Toro, larger, more elegant, with a boutique that was like a comfortable museum, and an elegant showroom. San Toro is also a cultural center, it has a lovely outdoor garden and performance space, where drummers, dancers and musicians perform for the guests.

The food was exquisite and so was the professional service and concern of the staff. This cultural center/restaurant is also owned by the lady who owns Djenne. I was introduced to her by Jabril at Djenne and discovered that she was a frequent traveler to the U.S., in fact one of her daughters attended Stonybrook University in New York, and had as her Black literature professor, Amiri Baraka, the well known poet, author, playwright, and political activist. This gave us additional information in which to engage in meaningful discussion. In future visits to Bamako in 1995 and 1997 I would take my group to SanToro for their farewell dinner where they enjoyed the comfort, décor and fine food that San Toro offered. It is truly an elegant, African experience.

The next morning I was to get a good look at Bamako. Being on the edge of the desert it was a somewhat dusty town. Bamako however was a busy commercial city with exciting market places, motor scooters outnumbering the cars, and people moving to and fro, buying and selling, trading and bartering.

My guide was a Dogon brother who was working at the time for ATS with Jabril Tabore, his name was Guire. He was an excellent guide who shared a lot of information with me about the extraordinary history and scientific pursuits of the Dogon people. I am not a scholar, although I have always been interested in the history and scientific accomplishments of the

Dogon people, who inhabit the Malian cliffs.

Guire and our driver took me to one of the interesting outposts in Bamako, up a steep hill and winding road to the top where you could see the whole city of Bamako before your eyes, This place was called 'Point of View', a. magnificent view. After we descended, we paid a visit to the National museum, which is an historical treasure house, carvings and ancient towns unfold before your eyes, history encascd in glass, ancient artifacts, wood carvings and musical instruments suspended in time. These museums are extremely important in that they connect with and give reality to what many of us students of history have read in books about ancient African history. Here you are able to translate this information into a visual connection to this history. This museum is an important resource in the resurrection and reconstruction of the true history and contributions of the African race.

One of the most exciting and amazing marketplaces that I have visited in Mali, and in fact in all of my marketplace visits in Africa, is the metal market in Bamako This place, believe me is incredible, this is a place where all types of products of metal are made. Household items, garden and yard items, industrial tools, etc. While this may not seem like such a big deal, I think that this may be a case where words cannot describe what the eyes and ears will reveal. The metal market is a place where people literally work, hard work, physical work, creative work, and practical work.

Often you hear from detractors of the African race, those who attempt to put down Black people as lazy, not willing to put in a hard day's work. And even some Black people who may have been fortunate in their careers, and of course those who have worked hard to achieve their success, have also been quick to criticize other Black people who have not been as successful, describing them as lazy. The metal marketplace in Bamako defies this false impression, this place is an incredible exercise in hard and productive work. Please let me attempt to describe the operation of the metal marketplace. If you start at the entrance or is it the exit of the marketplace, you will find old metal car doors, empty oil drums, huge pieces of sheet metal, and large scraps of metal from various discarded machines piled in heaps. Much like you will see in the junk yards, and scrap metal places.

As you began to walk through the lanes or isles the noise of banging and burning metal attack your eardrums and nostrils in a most ferocious way. Men and boys are seen manually banging the curves and dents out of twisted metal. Round oil drums being straightened out by the sheer strength and the consistent banging of these men, literally hundreds of men and boys banging at the same time in the same area, the sweat, arms rising and falling with force and rhythm, changing these varied shapes into flat sheets. The noise is deafening, the motion and energy intense. We move on through the lanes and began to see the next stage of production that our nostrils had already experienced. The burning of the metal, hot torches burn, melt and shape the flattened metal into varied creative shapes, then the banging again to shape them into products described earlier as household, industrial and yard products.

This is the mid stage, products in the rough. The next and final stage of production is the finishing stage, the smoothing of rough metal edges, the grinding noise of file on metal, rounding off the edges. And finally the painting and designing of some of the products, turning them into artistic and practical products that are on display at the end isles of the market. Here in the purchase areas you will find the products all stacked in categorical displays, cooking utensils in polished silver, garden tools, pots and clothes chests, and various containers, with bright painted designs glittering in the hot Malian sun.

If you have been in industrialized, mechanized or automated factories and have experienced the energy and intensity of production. Or even in a more manually comparable massive sweat shop, then the intensity of the Mali metal market will leave you with a sense of guilt in what you have complained about what you do as hard work, with your coffee breaks and all. Commerce is always present in Africa, people are always selling something to someone. Women have little stands and benches where food is sold to the workers, girls walking around with containers of cool water so that the workers can quench their thirst. This market is an example of the high quality of hands on creative production, much as you see also in the wood carving industry, where men are literally taking tree trunks and turning them into beautiful hand crafted masks, statues and other wood items.

Imagine if this process was in some way mechanized, where production could be accelerated. Imagine if these wood carvers all over Africa that make and sell their wares were mechanized, and organized into a lucrative furniture manufacturing industry. Given the quality of craftsmanship of these African wood carvers, this could be a substantial quality industry in America and Europe that could rival the popularity of French, Italian Provincial, and Mediterranean quality furniture. There is a Senegalese owned furniture company in New York called Afriland that manufactures furniture made with wood from the Cameroon and Senegal that is exquisite in design, sturdy in structure and uses beautiful African designed fabric. Not only can this furniture stand up to the most qualitative European designed furniture, but with its unique designed fabric and hand crafted work can in fact surpass the marketability of the others.

The next morning Guire was at my hotel with the driver to began our journey into the interior of the country. On this first trip I would not visit Mopti, Dogoland, and Djenne but would visit Segou and other areas along the Niger River.

The Niger is one of the great rivers of Africa, stretching over 4,000 km (2,500 miles) a great arc that extends northward from Guinea to Mali before turning back towards the south and making its way through Niger and Nigeria to empty into the Gulf of Guinea. Mali sits at the northern apex of the curve, where the river splits into a vast inland delta before reforming itself to return southward. The Niger is of vital importance in Mali, providing irrigation for agriculture and serving as a major transportation artery. For visitors the Niger offers a magnificent and leisurely means of travel and touring. During the high water months (between August and November) large river boats ply the river, traversing more than half of the country over a period of six or seven days. Smaller and slower vessels also offer passage, including pirogues, Africa's small traditional canoes, and pinasses, slightly larger and motorized boats.

I had a most interesting time during my first visit along the Niger, in Segou where I spent the night at a Lebanese owned motel and restaurant. The involvement with the Lebanese in small and medium sized businesses in Africa as mentioned in an earlier chapter, is not just confined to the cities of Africa. You will also find them in the remote areas doing business of one type or another, general stores, restaurants, fabric stores, hotels, etc. In Segou one of the main gathering places for visitors to this area is at the Le'Auberge restaurant where one can find delicious African and French cuisine. It is, one can say a sort of Oasis in the desert, a very nice garden area where you can also have dinner, only you will have to fight off the mosquitoes while trying to eat. The sleeping quarters were quite comfortable, air conditioning, TV, and many of the amenities that you might find in hotels in the cities. I must admit though it annoys me to see foreigners in Africa controlling the businesses and economy of Africans.

You will find Lebanese and Europeans everywhere in Africa, in the cities, in the bush and remote areas. It is true that they are very adventurous, I certainly wish that African Americans were as adventurous, but the paternal attitude that Europeans and Lebanese have towards the people smacks of a master/servant relationship.

Along the Niger in Segou there are several areas of commerce, some of which are fishing and brick making. Watching the workmen make bricks was very interesting to a city boy like myself who is used to bricks as the stuff buildings are made of.

The visit to the Bozó people's villages along the Niger was most interesting, where they shared with me their culture, homes and hospitality. This particular visit to Mali was an exploratory one where I wanted to get an idea of how the country was, in terms of the possibilities for bringing African American tourists there. The other trips that were to follow for the next three years would prove to be more extensive and involved.

Woman & children in Bozo village

The Road To Mopti & Dogonland

In July of 1995 I brought a small group of people for a five day tour of Mali. We had just come from Senegal where we completed a five day tour, and were now ready for the adventure of Mali. I had made the necessary arrangements with Jibril Tabore of ATS tour company to handle our accommodations and tours. We were met at the airport in Bamako by Amadou Traore, I was hoping that I would get the Dogon Guire as my guide again but I found out that he was working for another company. Amadou however turned out to be a very fine guide, very personable and informed about the country. This trip was a more extensive one that took us by road from Bamako to Segou where we visited areas along the Niger, a mosque and Koranic school, and peoples homes. Many of the buildings in the Segou area have Sudanese styled architecture, some with a mixture of Sudanese design and others with French colonial design. Some of the buildings were large, wide with arch type windows, and intricately designed roof facades.

After lunch we continued on the road to Mopti, stopping on the way to speak and take pictures with the local people along the road as we occasionally made a 'bush stop', you know when nature calls. As we were traveling along we spotted two men riding on camels along a ravine, we pulled over and offered them some money to allow us to take a short ride on their camels. It was my first time attempting such a thing, and I am sure it was the first time for the group.

I was a little surprised and somewhat unsettled to hear the sounds coming from the camel, particularly when it put its front legs and head down, it started making these strange noises and I could not control its movements. Finally it straightened itself out and I rose on its back to its full height and I began a short but curious ride.

Camel ride

We continued on the long dusty road further north until we reached Mopti, the hub of commerce that has been influenced by the blending of the Niger and Bani rivers.

The Fulani people are the major ethnic group in Mopti, or the Peul people as they are also called. They are known for the intricacy that they put into weaving blankets, and other wool wraps to protect themselves against the elements. The Fulani are devout Muslims, as is the Bambara.

Mopti is a busy port city with lots of commerce along the river. Boats are constantly going up and down the Niger transporting merchandise and people. We stayed in a fairly decent hotel, The Kanga , it might be classified as a 2 1/ or 3 star, it had rooms off of a grassy walkway and air conditioning. It is probably one of the best choices that you can make in Mopti given the shortage of adequate accommodations for tourists. However our stay was pleasant and the food in the hotel's restaurant was quite good.

The next morning after breakfast found us eagerly boarding the bus and excited about our trip to Dogonland. We were riding more than an hour when we turned into a road that took us into a desolate area where the landscape began to change, the trees started to disappear and the land became barren, rocky. We were in an area that had strange rock formations, this was a place that you might envision in a science fiction movie, it looked like Mars or the surface of a planet. As far as the eye can see there were these barren rock formations, still and desolate. Some suggested that perhaps it might have been the bottom of the ocean thousands of years ago. We took photos standing or sitting on the precariously perched ledges of the rock formations.

We continued on further into the interior in search of the Dogons, we traveled over hills, down ravines, through what appeared like small rivers through uninhabited areas until we finally began to see some life, some activity. We started to see people

Myself and guide on rock)

175

working the land, engaged in some small farming, they waved to us as our vehicle drove by, the children excited about the welcomed intrusion into their daily routine. We stopped at one compound to take pictures and give gifts to the children. We noticed for the first time the pointed top granaries, like little thatched top houses that stored the grain for the coming dry season. Finally we reached the village of Sangha, which is on the crest of Bandiagara escarpment, steep treacherous cliffs and natural erosions. Sangha overlooks the village of Banani which is at the base of the cliffs, it is a village of 21,000 inhabitants. A large number of Dogon, approximately 200,000 live in the cliffs of Bandiagara, the total population of Dogon in Mali is approximately 705,000 people.*

(1986/87 census) * (Internet sources)

Some of the land in Sangha is owned by the residents, the rest is owned by the government. The village of Sangha is known for its circumcision ceremonies and its intricate rock carvings, it also has one of two rest houses, the other being in Bandiagara. We stopped at the rest house where we were able to get cool drinks, use the rest rooms and relax a bit. Sangha also has very interesting shops where we purchased items on our return from the cliffs. The region is a major center for Dogon culture and is noted for its rich ancient traditions and rituals, art and folklore. According to archaeological evidence, humans have occupied the cliffs for more than 1,000 years. However the Dogons were not the first people to occupy the cliffs, there were four ethnic groups that were there before the Dogon, these were the Dyon, Ono, Arou and Domno which migrated from the land of Mande'.

We continued on to Bandiagara, on the way we stopped to look at some of the fascinating yet somewhat spooky cave cemeteries, where you could see human skeletal parts. We reached the Bandiagara plateau, the Bandiagara cliffs and the Seno plains.

The plains consist of ancient eroded terrain of flat tablelands, messa and sandstone, the plateau comprises sandstone and rock slabs riddled with holes, caves that connect with springs along the cliffs. The cliffs are shaped with irregularities and indentations, ravines and rocky passages that connect the plateau with the plains. The cliffs are extremely steep and dangerous to the visitor, they however protect the architectural

Cave cemetery

Cave cemetery

structures which for centuries, have been the heart and soul of traditional, secular Dogon culture.

It is said that the cliffs are one of the most impressive natural landscape features in West Africa. Looking out from the plateau to the plains it looked as if you could see as far asTimbuktu, looking down the height made me dizzy. Our Dogon guide who had now taken over from Amadou our main guide who being a Bambara was not as familiar with the Dogon cliffs. He began telling us the history of why the Dogon had fled to this area and had inhabited the cliffs. They were fleeing their enemies, some say that they refused to submit to the religion of Islam, not wanting to give up their indigenous beliefs which they still practice today, they fled from the Muslims who converted those who they conquered to Islam. I could almost see the pursuing Muslim armies as they chased the Dogons across the desolate plains, where the Dogons finally found refuge in these treacherous cliffs. Treacherous they were, our Dogon guide pointed to a village down at the bottom of the cliffs, where due to the great distance I could hardly make it out, said that we were going to go down the cliffs, I said to him "are you crazy? how are we going to get down there? with a helicopter?, where are the ropes?" He said "we are going to walk, please follow me".

We began one of the most daring and dangerous treks I have ever undertaken. Our Dogon guide said "Step where I step", and we followed him as he placed his feet on certain rocks that were firmly rooted in the hills. We started on the main plateau, and as we started to descend there appeared to be smaller plateaus or ledges, I thought to myself that I must be a complete nut to try to walk down these dangerous cliffs, with no defined path, just stepping from rock to rock. At the beginning the hill was so steep that I slid on my butt from one rock level to another until the rock path became less steep as we continued to descend. We did have help from some of the young Dogon boys who were on each side of us, each taking one hand to help us balance as we tried to manipulate the rocks.

The vision of the women loom in my head as they gingerly stepped from rock to rock at the same time being propped up by the young Dogon men. I must admit though that I also needed the young men at times trying to get from one rock to the next at the same time continuing in a downward direction. The most incredible thing about descending the cliffs is that one slip and its bye bye! As we continued our descent the cliff life of the Dogon people began to open up, we passed cave cemeteries, women washing clothes in the rock pools that are found on the horizontal sections of the cliffs. Rice and a few other crops are also grown in these cultivated rock pools and gardens. Dogons rely on spring lines that run along the base of the cliffs for permanent water supply. We began to see life unfold among these cliffs, family plots (compounds) are arranged around a courtyard with domestic animals. Millet and wheat are stored in granaries, which are fortified towers that are set above the compound's courtyard, with their pointed capped thatch roofs.

Granaries

We saw several women with large pails of water on their heads, some with huge piles of fire wood, and babies on their backs, taking the cliffs in stride, passing us by as we cautiously navigated our way to the bottom and the plains that lay before us. Finally we reached the bottom with great relief and the heavens full of our prayers.

Photo by TEDDY WILSON

We rested for a bit, sipped our water, looked up at the top of the cliffs and marveled at the distance and the reality that we actually came from the top. Our guide explained to us that centuries ago, the Mande people used ropes to maneuver the cliffs.

We visited a nearby market place where we bartered for Dogon doors of various sizes, Juju rings, rattles, and elaborate spiritual masks and headdress.

We began our climb back up the cliffs, taking a different rock pathway up. Stopping at several compounds to visit people and an interesting gathering of men sitting on a rock in a 'house' with no walls

and a very low roof, so low that if they stood up they would bump their heads. We were told that this was the Hogon (village chief), and the council house where he was holding court with other men.

We continued our long arduous climb back to the plateau at the top, stopping to catch our breath and to sip water, also to take photos of the activities of the women and their children, washing clothes, making meals and engaging in the general chores of domestic life. This would not be so unusual as this is the description of life in the typical rural areas of Africa, this however is taking place on a mountain, imbedded in the sides of the cliffs! Here we were taking

Council house

great care as to how and where we were walking, and these folks were going on as if they were on level ground.

We gathered ourselves once again and continued to climb. Let me say that climbing the Dogon cliffs is not an exercise for a weak heart, or for one who is excessively overweight, it is however a good workout for the body as long as you take your time, rest at intervals, drink water and breath regularly. This was my first time climbing the Dogon cliffs, and it was a difficult yet exciting and exhilarating experience that adventurous folks would love. We finally reached the top with relief and a sense of great accomplishment. This experience however was minor compared to the next time that I would visit Dogonland and descend and climb the cliffs.

Climbing the cliffs

We then went back to Sangha where we had the opportunity to see and visit the 5th day market. *The Dogon are known for their astronomical beliefs, knowledge of satellites of the planet Jupiter and rings of Saturn, in addition to knowledge of Sirius B, a companion to the star Sirius. The Dogon have a traditional interest in the sky and astronomy including Sirius, the brightest star in the sky and the center of Dogon mythology. They knew that Sirius B orbits Sirius and that a complete orbit takes fifty years.

*(Internet sources)

181

Many scientists believe that without telescopes and scientific equipment this knowledge must have come from extraterrestrial beings, that perhaps the Dogon had made contact with an advanced technological civilization. They used another system to measure the days and the years, they function on a 5 day week instead of 7 days, on the 5th day the Dogon have their market, and what an exciting time it is, hundreds of merchants selling wares of all types. We saw how they made the local beer, powerful stuff that will rock your boots, we understood that a lot of the men drank this home brew and were still able to navigate the cliffs, even at night.

5th day market

Dogon religious art is found in masks, door carvings, and terracotta figures. There are four main tribes or ethnic groups in Dogon society, and they are believed to be descendants of the four original ancestors of humankind. The villages are ruled by the old men and are patrilineal, male and female circumcision is practiced, and so is polygamy for some.

Traditional Dogon Temple

182

Dogon temple

Dogon dwellings

Two years later with another group that I brought to the cliffs of Bandiagara, this would, as I told myself later be my last time to climb. I had at that time to say the least a most challenging experience. I did not know it at the time but I had what would turn out to be a very severe case of Malaria. We had just left the country of Benin after spending several days in the bush (remote areas), and at one poorly maintained 'hotel' I was bitten by Malaria carrying mosquitoes. I wasn't feeling very well the day before and did not go out with the group for dinner. That night I had a bout with nausea and fever, in the morning I was better and contributed it to a 24 hour virus.

This time in visiting the Dogon cliffs I was not feeling that great, when we stopped at the encampment at Sangha, I had to find a bathroom real quick as my system was loosening up real fast, I took a few charcoal pills to settle my stomach and joined the group so that we could start our trip to the plateau and our descent into the cliffs of the Dogon. We had gathered at the top of the plateau on an edge that had to be the steepest part possible where our guide decided to have a lecture. The children and people of Bandiagara gathered around us, our backs to the cliffs and the vastness of the plateau. Our guide explained to us how we would descend the cliffs and at that time the numbers of our group suddenly decreased as two members decided that this was not for them. The rest of the group started our descent behind our guide down the rocky cliffs, as we picked our way, slid on our butts in some cases down the first two levels, which were the steepest, I remember one of the women cursing me out for getting her in this mess. She was screaming how she was going to kill me when we got back to the States, but at the same time feeling the excitement of the moment. Words can not really describe the experience and utter insanity of going down those cliffs, it is like stepping into space.

Going down this time we came upon several women coming up the cliffs, I stopped to video tape them as they ascended in a sort of train, baskets of merchandise on their heads. One of them, an old woman grabbed my arm and demanded money, I refused and tried to pull away but she kept a good grip on me, I had to forcefully pull out of her grip as she angrily said some words that I am sure were not flattering and spat on the ground. She was fuming, I figured it was time for me to move on and continued our descent down the cliffs. Reaching the bottom I was out of breath and asked someone for water, as my water was in my bag that a Dogon brother was carrying. After buying some items at the marketplace we started our climb back to the top. I became very weak, sweating profusely, gasping for air, the young Dogon brother who had been serving as my personal support in coming down the cliffs gave me water to drink, I gathered myself and again started to climb.

It became extremely difficult to go more than a few yards without getting out of breath, and I could not get very far, I collapsed on a rock, panting and gasping while the young brother was fanning me and giving me water. Several people were coming up the cliffs looking at me curiously as I sweated and gasped, then a very old man, white hair and long beard came up the rocks stepping quickly, took a look at me and the situation and asked "Fatique?" (fatigued?) Of course I was more than embarrassed that this old man was stepping so well and it looked like I was dying trying to reach the top. I mustered up enough energy to continue until we reached a ledge where some of the others in my group were resting, I ran out of water and asked one of the sisters for some, I took a drink, felt nauseous and ran to the rock to throw up. I began to feel weak, started losing consciousness and began to crumble on the rocks.

The Dogon brothers immediately came to my aide, turned me upside down and started rubbing my ankles, soon I began to regain consciousness and was able to stand on my own. I was very thankful of the Dogon brothers and the methods used in reviving me, I thought to myself that perhaps they used some JuJu magic, and as I thought of JuJu, I also thought that maybe the old lady who cursed me and spat had put some bad JuJu on me. We finally reached the top and went to the encampment at Sangha for food and drinks, where I had another bout with nausea and realized that I was sick but I thought that it was due to dehydration, as I had not drank enough water while climbing the cliffs and it was extremely hot. Later I felt much better and was able to complete the rest of the trip with no major complications, however I was to discover approximately 2 weeks later after having returned home and then one week later leaving again for Senegal, that I had contracted the deadly Malaria.

I would however recommend that people who are physically able should the opportunity arise, to climb the exciting, historic, and spiritual Bandiagara cliffs of the Dogon people.

Dogon house
in the cliffs

After leaving Dogonland we returned that evening to Mopti, had dinner and slept well after a very tiring, but interesting day. The next morning we rose early, had breakfast and started on our journey south to the fantastic mud city of Djenne'.

Djenne' like Timbuktu is an ancient city that was mighty in its time, the grand trans-Saharan trade routes brought great wealth, as many merchants profited from the gold, ivory and salt that was transported to the Mediterranean until the sixteenth century. Djenne, as Timbuktu became the stuff of legends of exotic wealth in Africa for centuries. The more renowned Timbuktu has little that remains of its ancient structures, Djenne' however seems to be frozen in time, its structures still remain five centuries since its decline, a magnificent architectural city of mud. Constructed on a small island in the Niger Basin, Djenne' was also a communications center for Islam, and possessed a large naval fleet. Djenne' today is a small town in central Mali with a population of approximately 12 thousand people, most of whom are Fulani, Bobo, Markas or Sonrays. To reach Djenne' we had to take a ferry, our driver drove the vehicle on to the ferry and we waited to hear the sound of the motor cranking up which never came, in fact there was no motor, we were told that it was in Mopti for repairs. Meanwhile 4 to 5 men inserted long bamboo poles in the water to push this huge ferry forward. Needless to say it was a very long ride to the other side to reach the city of Djenne'. I was immediately impressed with the place, this was the famous city that is made of mud, the place where you will find some of the finest mud cloth artists and intricate architecture made of mud. The Great Mosque is the centerpiece in Djenne', it is a very large structure, at least one square block in radius, with spirals and minuets reaching into the sky. It is constructed with an architectural style that is typical of the Sudan, as is the city of Djenne' itself. A very large market sits in the shadows of the Great Mosque, it is the largest mud building in the world. It is also a testimony to the genius of the African mind and will, to create something not out of nothing, but in fact out of everything. Mali is known for its mud cloth, internationally famous, and Djenne' is known for producing the finest quality of cloth and artistic design. This is because it is a mud culture, the people have taken the mud, the reality of their geographical location and made a great civilization from it. Usually when a person is doing bad, has sunken to the bottom of human society, it is said that they are 'wallowing in the mud' they have hit rock bottom, on the skids.

But the people of Mali have taken the mud to a higher level of civilized and human development. They have taken the mud and built cities and temples, great monuments, created art, and indeed have incorporated mud into their culture, shaping and molding their environment. The architectural structures of the city of Djenne' are not ancient remnants of a past society, they are in fact a living and functional testimony to history and building for eternity.

We visited a few apartment complexes in Djenne' and was amazed at the architectural structure of these buildings, I compared them to the tenement buildings that you might find in the urban inner cities of the United States, with an African domestic setting.

They were basically two, three and four story buildings, where you entered a main door that had a staircase that led to the first level, where you would find three or four flats, or apartments, with a hallway/balcony. Where you could look down and see the courtyard that was the center of activity for the complex. Here you would see people washing clothes, mud cloth murals drying in the hot Malian sun, on clotheslines strung across the yard.

The courtyard was in the center of the building. Enclosed with three sides of the buildings, with the fourth side enclosed by the neighboring building. The staircase continued to the second level where you found the same structural setting, then on to the third or in some cases the fourth floor. This was a most interesting observation in that these building are centuries old. Usually when one thinks of Africa before the coming of the Europeans, if you are not a student of ancient African history, you might think of primitive huts or simple and primary dwellings. Such as mud and straw 'huts', not realizing that not only did the ancients build great and grand temples and monuments, but they also built multiple dwellings in which to house their people.

We visited a very famous mud cloth artist in one of the apartments where she had a sitting and viewing room for her murals and pieces. We sat down and bartered for some of her very exquisite designs, this lady was the subject of National Geographic Magazine some years ago, which she proudly showed her dog-eared copy to the visitors. We went on the roof of the building where we were able to see the roof tops of the immediate neighborhood, the backyards of some of the smaller dwellings, the activity in the streets and the huge Grand Mosque basking in the sun.

These were flat roofs that reminded me of the Harlem tenements, where in some cases you could jump from one roof to another. Standing on the roof overlooking this great and ancient city of Djenne' the feeling one gets is a realization that history lives.

It is one thing reading about ancient places and people, ancient history if you will, but to experience it is a most gratifying experience. It brings things to a reality, full cycle as it is said when visiting the slave dungeons of West Africa, or as some have said when visiting the temples and pyramids of Egypt. It verifies the fact that African people were a great people, a respected and powerful people. Often this notion is questioned by other races, sometimes it's questioned by Africans themselves. However the proof is in the vision and reality of this place and places like this on the Mother continent, the cradle of civilization, and center of human development.

Standing on the rooftop, the African sun beaming on me I take a moment to meditate, closing my eyes with the warmth of the sun calming my anxiety and racing active mind and receive the energy and spirit of the ancients.

Rooftops of 2 and 3 story buildings

Rooftops in Djenne'

Mosque of Mud

As we leave the great city of Djenne' we pass a large gathering of people, we stop to see what is going on and learn that there is a wedding ceremony and fest that is about to begin. There are many beautiful women there with intricate jewel stones around their neck, and in their ears and noses. Here we have seen multiple examples of the legendary beauty of Malian women, in their colorful dresses and garments of gold and elaborate embroidary, these were indeed the African Queens that are the stuff of legends. We continued on to the ferry and the road to Segou.

The wheels from the vehicle stirring up dust clouds gave the spirals of the Grand Mosque seen in the distance a mystique that is known to the culture and essence of Mali, land of ancient history and culture.

Part 9
Benin
(Land of Voudoom)

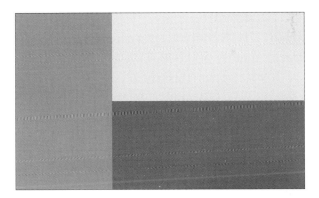

Benin is located in West Africa, is bounded to the east by Nigeria, to the north by Niger and Burkina Faso, and to the West by Togo. Benin stretches approximately 700km (435 miles). Benin can be divided into five natural regions, a coastal region, low and sandy; a plateau of clay and marshy dips; a wooded Savannah; a hilly region, and a plains area.

Climate: Tropical; hot, humid in the south, semiarid in the north. Benin has unusually dry conditions, the great part of the country is under the influence of transitional tropical conditions. Rainfall is not as abundant as found in areas with the same latitude.

Natural Resources: Small offshore oil deposits, limestone, marble, and timber.

Exports: Crude oil, cotton, palm products, cocoa.

Industries: Textiles, cigarettes, construction materials, beverages, food Production, petroleum

Population: 5,341,710 (1994 est.)

Ethnicity: African 99% (42 ethnic groups, major groups are Fon, Adja, Yoruba, Bariba) Europeans 5,500

Religions: Indigenous beliefs 70%, Islam 15%, Christianity 15%

Languages: French (official) Fon and Yoruba (most common spoken languages in the South) tribal languages (at least six major ones in the north)

Capital: Port Novo, population: 164,000

Cotonou: Main port city, Benin's largest city, the commercial capital. Total population is approximately 500,000. Densely populated, middle class settlement north of town, upper class near the airport, lower classes near the lagoon and the west of city center. Islam has more influence and presence in Cotonou, than in the rural areas. Cotonou is also the site of the International airport, and most government, commercial and tourist activity.

Currency : CFA franc (CFAF)

History: Benin was traditionally a sophisticated center of African culture, with kings going back hundreds of years. Benin was used as a trading post during the 18th and 19th centuries. The male population was severely depleted by the slave trade by the 19th century. France first occupied the area in 1872, and in 1904 the territory became incorporated into French West Africa as Dahomey. On December 4, 1958, it became the Republic of Dahomey, self governing within the French community, and gained full independence on August 1, 1960. From 1960 through 1972, saw a succession of military coups which brought about many changes of government, which finally brought to power Major Mathieu Kerekou, who headed a Marxist-Leninist government that remained in power until the beginning of the 1990's.

In late 1990, a student movement helped to force the government to the polls, and in 1991, the principle opposition led by Prime Minister Nicephore Soglo was victorious, and led to a transition from a 'dictatorship' to a pluralistic political system.

(Benin homepage and other Internet sources)

My first visit and introduction to the country of Benin was in July 1997, and I must add that it was a most memorable one.

Of course I was fascinated with the history, culture and geography of this place of ancient culture and spirituality, but it also marked an experience in my African travels that I could not easily forget.

Here is where I contracted the deadly Malaria. I had previously prided myself on not ever remembering getting a mosquito bite, many times I was in the same physical space, at the same time as others and they would be slapping themselves on the arms and legs as the mosquitoes feasted on any visible part of their flesh. I would be oblivious to this problem, they would not bite me, I don't know how many bites folks would be showing me that they had gotten from these African mosquitoes who were Draconian legends. I do not know why they did not bite me, I thought that perhaps it was my oil, for many, many years I had been known for wearing these rich body oils that come from Pakistan and Saudi Arabia. Or I often told many that it was my Juju, that the mosquitoes were afraid of my aura, that I was protected by the African gods. That myth however was shattered by the severe case of Malaria that resulted from this mosquito attack in Benin. This has not changed my overall feelings about the country though, for it has truly been an experience with an ancient and living history and culture that is evident in Mali and a spirituality that one finds most dominant in Togo. Reaching the country of Benin has truly lived up to the theme of this book and the essence of my tours to Africa, that is 'Journey' To The Motherland. In a nutshell it was a long and tiresome travel itinerary that took almost 24 hours of travel time, including approximately 4 1/2 hours layover in Senegal and The Ivory Coast. The flight on Air Afrique to Dakar was not bad as usual, including the layover of approximately 1 hour, it was however the 3 1/2 layover in Abijan, just sitting in the airport that was the killer. Eventually we boarded the next Air Afrique flight for the 3 hour flight to Cotonou, the main port city. This was still better than traveling on a European airline, that would take you to London, Amsterdam, Italy, or some other European city that took 6-8 hours and then another 7 or 8 hours to Africa, including most often a 6-10 hour layover in these European cities. So I suppose considering, it was not that bad, however it would have been difficult to try to convince my group otherwise, veterans that they were and all.

There were 8 persons in our group including myself, which was fine for a rugged trip such as was planned for this one which included Mali for 6 days, for a total 12 day tour of both countries. These were people who had traveled with me at least on two or three different occasions, they were prepared for this bush trip. Our problems started actually in New York at JFK, when we realized that one member of the group who was traveling with her mother, did not get her passport and visa back from the Mali consulate, where she had mailed it. Although she was instructed to mail it with a return over night prepaid self addressed envelope, she failed to do that and when she called to inquire why it was taking so long, she was told that they sent it back by regular mail. Of course it had not reached her in time for the trip so without her passport she could not travel.

We had to leave her at JFK, the new manager of Air Afrique, Mr. Komoclou was there to assist her and assured us that she would be on the next flight as soon as she received her passport. This was the first obstacle in this 'Journey'

I did not actually know how bush it would be, but I did know that Mali was a very adventurous experience, having been there on two other occasions. On this trip to Benin however I relied totally on the information that my travel agent had given me, which sounded very exciting, and looked so interesting. This is not to say that it did not turn out that way, however it was perhaps much more than I had anticipated. I was given a more updated itinerary at JFK airport in New York by a former director of Air Afrique airlines, who used to be in charge of North American Air Afrique traffic. I was told by my travel agent the he was an associate of our ground operator in Benin.

When we arrived in Cotonou after clearing customs which was not so difficult, we were met by a middle aged African gentleman who helped us to claim our baggage.

I asked him if he was our host and he replied that no he was not but that the owner of the company was outside and was waiting for us. He then went on to tell me that the owner was white, a Frenchman.

I was somewhat disappointed as I would have liked to give my business to an African, but realized that the former director of Air Afrique in New York, being a French man, that this was of course a friend and fellow European.

I told him I could live with that and we proceeded to clear customs and meet our host on the other side. Here the disappointments would began to become serious, first our host a French national who as he proudly stated later had been living in Africa for 15 to 20 years, was married to an African woman, and was not by any stretch of the imagination a cultured person. He had a car and an old small bus waiting to take us and our luggage, the door to the back of the vehicle was stuck and it took some time to free it so that the two African men could load our baggage. The next shock that we received was that not only was he our host, but also our guide because he was unable to get an African guide who could speak English. He had an African man there who he said was an excellent guide, a historian, a cultural specialist, dancer and drummer, who would be with us, but his English was limited.

He said unfortunately for us he would have to be our guide and that he realized that my people would probably not be happy with this arrangement, coming from the States to visit their ancestral homeland and have to be led by a big fat White man, his words exactly. When I explained this to the group they were just too through, totally upset, I explained to them the situation with the unavailability of an English speaking African guide, and they said that well we had no other choice so they would have to deal with it. The final blow to our excitement about being in a new African destination came when he told us that we were headed for the bush, "the bush?" I asked, "are you saying that we are not staying in a hotel in the city?" "No" he answered your itinerary says that you are staying in Grand Popo, but it is quite nice, better than the city, much cooler, it is right off of the ocean, a very lovely area" I was really upset, the group became quiet, I said "You know we are very tired, we have been traveling for 24 hours without any rest" He replied "you mean you came straight from the States?, usually the groups will spend a night in Abijan, then come in the morning when they are refreshed" I said "that was not our plan, I did not know that we would have to travel further once we reached Cotonou" He said "well it will not take long" I asked "how long are you talking about?" "Oh about 45 minutes" he replied, or rather lied, because it took almost 2 1/2 hours to reach Grand Popo, after traveling through several dark towns, across bridges, bumpy roads and what appeared to be washed out roads. We finally reached there about midnight after initially landing in Cotonou around 8:00pm.

We were exhausted, mad and really unfriendly, however we were met with a lavish spread, all kinds of delicious food, bottles of wine, cold beer and other delicacies, sitting on an outside terrace several yards away from huge waves splashing against the beach. Everyone began to relax after awhile, and even began to loosen up enough to laugh with our jovial host who had introduced his wife and several other Africans. This guy, whose name escapes me now was a real card, one who bragged all the time about his businesses, his years of living in the States, and his world travels and ventures. He was originally from France, but loved Africa he said. Of course he was one of those typical White men who knew everything and everybody in Benin, the government officials, businessmen and people of important affairs he claimed. But I must admit we did began to feel better after literally feasting and enjoying the cozy atmosphere of the ocean side setting. We commented on our missing person, and hoped that she would join us soon on the next available incoming flight.

After dinner he showed us to the sleeping quarters, which required us walking across an expanse of grass, of course we could not see very well at this late hour in the pitch black night of Benin, and reached a huge wooden structure that might have been a colonial mansion at one time. It had two sets of wooden steps that were situated on either side of the two story structure, with rooms on the first landing which was a wooden porch that surrounded the entire house on both levels with rooms off both sides on both levels.

The rooms were sort of nice, simple but quaint. They had a rustic look, wooden floors and walls, beds with big posts that held huge mosquito nets. Some of the rooms had a short staircase where there was a bed, below was another bed.

It had a bathroom with cobble stone floors and a shower situated outside of the washroom and toilet with only cold water. We all learned to wash and jump from the coldness of the water hitting our skin, in the chill of morning. It wasn't really that bad though, and it was great sleeping with the breeze from the ocean coming in through the wooden shutters, and the roar of the ocean caressing your dreams.

The next morning we awoke to a most beautiful sight of the surrounding foliage and the ocean waves rising and falling against the sandy beach. We walked across the grass to the main house, the restaurant and lounge area, passing a small pool, a sitting area under a thatched roof canopy and to the deck outside of the restaurant/lounge where breakfast was being served. We had an opportunity to take a good look at the property, and some of the other guests that stayed at the beachfront resort if you will.

It was a nice little set up that one could relax and enjoy the peacefulness, the sun and the roar of the mighty waves.

There were some French guests who also stayed there, and we found out that our guide and host was the owner of not only this establishment, but also two other such small hotels and a large restaurant in Cotonou, Benin's largest city.

Our itinerary for the day was a visit to the surrounding areas of Grand Popo and a picnic lunch on an island. Our host also suggested to us if we would like to participate in a voodoo ceremony that was going to be held later that day, and if we wanted to we could visit the village after lunch. The price however would be approximately $20 per person, after discussing this with the group we all agreed that we would participate.

We headed out for a drive around the area and also passed a little pool of water that had a boat and a man who would paddle you across to the other side, which was the country of Togo. The width of the water was so narrow that it seemed that you could almost jump across and be in another country. We got a pirogue, a large motorized canoe type of boat and visited a village off the coast where we met the chief and the people and visited a voodoo shrine and the shrine of Elegba. Elegba is a voodoom diety who protect the home and the village, you will find an Elegba outside of most homes, small ones, sometimes large ones, and a huge one that protects the entire village. Elegba is made to look like a half human with a face of sorts, much like an African mask, with a base for a body and an elongated penis that sticks out from the base of the body.

We were able to to see that this cultural practice was an ancient one that came from the ancient kingdom of Dahomey, and was in fact the base of knowledge that went across the Atlantic to Brazil, Haiti, and the Caribbean during the trans-Atlantic slave trade.

After visiting the shrines, talking to the people and giving gifts to the children, we got in our boat and continued on to an uninhabited island where we had a very delicious and interesting lunch. Our host and his wife prepared us a very nice lunch that was so complete, with silverware,

Elegba

cold beer and sodas, hot and cold food. It was truly a unique experience. We had the entire island for ourselves, it was not a big one, and not that much grass, matter of fact we had to search for the most grassy section. It was mainly sand and sea weeds that appeared to be more grassy than it really was until you got up close on it. We had a great time, lunch on an exotic island in West Africa.

After lunch we got in our boat and continued on to another part of the mainland, where we were about to participate in a most fascinating experience, a Voodoo celebration.

We entered the village among the tuning of the drums, people gathering, and children curiously looking to see what different kind of excitement was going to happen today.

We took seats along a wall on a row of benches awaiting the festivities to begin. In the center of the village square was a huge Elegba, encased in a sort of house with a roof and walls that came up half of the way. This was a very big one with a huge elongated penis rising from its lower part. The drummers began to play exciting intoxicating rhythms that started the children to dancing, it seemed after awhile an uncontrollable dance in that they were sort of spinning as if powered or driven by some unseen force. Richard our secondary French speaking guide started to dance, we found out that he was a professional Voodoo dancer that our host the French man had taken to Brazil and other places to dance the dance of Elegba.

Then from the outskirts of the village came the masqueraders, men I suppose dressed in Raffiq, in a sort of moving hut with eyes and ornaments on the top of its head with men chasing them, hitting the ground with sticks, seemingly chasing them around the village square. There were four or five of these masqueraders, or voodoo dieties that were being chased and that were chasing the children in the village. All the while the drummers had increased in their numbers and many people and children had gathered around them dancing and chanting and seemingly possessed by the hypnotic rhythm of the drums.

> Dance to The Beat of the drums
> Dum Dum Dum
> Dance to the beat of the drums
> The drums that beat
> That beat
> That beat
> The Drums that beat out the rhythm

The rhythm of Mother Africa
Listen to the beat of the drums
Feel the beat of the drums
The universal language
The thumping of our souls
Of our souls
Of our souls
The drums
Boom boom boom, dum dum dum
Feel the centuries of Black emotion
Feel Black sons and daughters
Of the universe
The history
The passion
The booming of our anger
Feel the sensuous rhythms
Feel
Feel
Feel
Feel
Um ah chiki boom
Chiki boom ah
Um ah chiki boom
Chiki boom ah
Um ah chiki boom
Chiki boom ah
Um ah

It seemed as if the whole village was immersed in these hypnotic rhythms, there was an intensity that permeated the air, an energy field had gathered and settled itself in our midst. Some of the people had reached a level that took them on another plane, one man came before us with two long steel spike like needles that were many times thicker than an average needle and so much longer. He allowed us to touch the needles and its sharp tips, he then proceeded to push one of these spikes into his face, through his cheek and into his mouth.

He opened his mouth to let us see that the spike had come through. He then began to insert the other spike through the other cheek, forcefully pushing it through until it came out of the other side into his mouth, where you could see that both points of the spikes were touching each other. This was no doubt an awesome, incredible feat that he was able to do under the power and influence of Elegba. A little later I found him among the crowd of drummers and people swaying to the drums and asked him to let me see his face.

He showed me the holes where drops of blood, somewhat dried had caked up around the wounds from the spikes that went through his cheeks, into the inside of his mouth. I had seen it with my own eyes but I had to check to see if perhaps I was being tricked, if this was an illusion. I did not know the answer for this, perhaps it was such a belief that it defied pain.

Voodoo ceremony (Man with needle through cheeks)

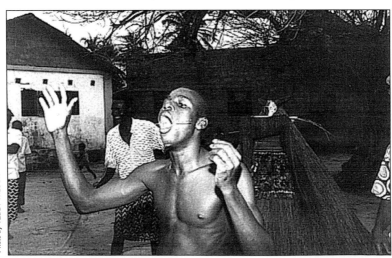

The next incredible thing to happen during the ceremony was a feat that defied the laws of gravity. Some of the men or priests took some beer that they had heated in a pot and poured the contents into a larger broad mouth container, took some sort of mesh and wrapped that around the opening of the smaller pot that they had heated the beer in. They then turned the pot upside down, doing so to show that there was nothing in the pot. They placed the smaller pot with the mesh over the opening of the larger pot with the beer. Then began to chant some words, and began to rub the mesh on the smaller pot, and lo and behold the liquid began to disappear from the larger pot on the ground, until it was all gone. Then he turned the smaller pot over with the mesh on top and poured the beer on the ground!

We looked for the trick, reasoned with our senses that there must be some unseen explanation for what we had just witnessed. Before we could close our gaping mouths the men or voodoo priests brought to us two empty beer bottles. They wanted us to feel the bottles, which we did, then they proceed to smash the bottles in a pot, they continued to smash them until the glass was grounded into fine powder. Then they poured beer into the pot and stirred up the contents of ground glass and beer, they then danced to the moving spirits in the rafiq, which also began to dance around them, and then they drank the mixture!, ground glass and beer!

Before they swallowed the mixture they held out their tongue and showed us the ground glass on their tongue and swallowed the glass, after they had finished they showed us their tongue and mouth to see that it was all gone. This was explained that under the influence of Voodoo many things are possible that are not so to the average person. The final presentation of the power of Voodoom was presented to us when the men in the group, which were just five of us including the Frenchman and our African co-guide. Was asked to pull with all our might on a rope that was attached to one of the Voodoo Rafiq in masquerade. The Rafiq in masquerade was in the center of the square, the other end attached to something inside.

We pulled and pulled and was not able to budge the Rafiq, in fact we were pulled closer, our efforts in vain. We had to eventually give up the effort for we had clearly lost this challenge of strength. When we looked at our hands we saw that the rope had cut into our skin, somewhat deeply, because it had caused severe imprints and had broken the skin in some areas. The French man's hands had turned red and blood was seeping from the deep cuts that the rope had made. Then they asked the women to line up behind each other and grab the rope with both hands like the men had done and pull as hard as they could. There were five women, they pulled and pulled and the masquerader or the person was pulled off of its base towards the women. Everyone in the village was laughing to see that the women were much stronger than the men. Of course the men wanted to investigate the source of this trickery, and looked behind the Rafiq masquerade to see if there was a rope tied to a tree or a rock, and we had the voodoo priests move the Rafiq to see if it had the rope tied to a root in the ground or something, but when it moved there was nothing there but the solid ground.

We left the village amidst the intensity of the drums that probably would go on for many hours after our departure, we said our good-byes, gave some gifts to the children and left for our boat, amazed, somewhat confused, and certainly questioning the experience that we were just a part of. I suppose belief is a very powerful thing, and I think that we had just experienced a people in their belief of the African spirits, which neither you or I can say it is not so. We boarded our boat and returned to the area where our vehicle was parked and returned to Grand Popo for another night of delicious food, powerful ocean waves, cool breezes and exotic mosquito nets.

The next morning after breakfast we started out for our tour to the magical and historic city of Quidah, road of the slaves, temple of the serpents. We reached the museum in Quidah late in the morning, led by our French host who the group was beginning to tire of his shallow jokes and braggadocios manner.

The museum was a treasure house on the history of the slave trade and the ancient kingdoms and traditional beliefs of the people of this region of West Africa. It is always interesting to note the nature of the artifacts and how they relate to the lifestyles of the indigenous people of the particular country. The museum housed an impressive collection of the culture, customs and history of the people, the kingdoms of Abomey, and the infamous Atlantic slave trade that I knew little about coming out of this area. After leaving the museum we went to the Temple of the Pythons, where we found in the Voodom of Benin, that the Python snake played a part in the mythology. After entering the gates of the compound we were led to a small round domed building where drawings of Python snakes were on the walls. Entering the building in front of us was a snake pit with steps that led down to a circular area, where on the floor were dozens of snakes of all sizes, slithering, raising their heads in slow, some might say majestic motions. We were captivated, some of us were fascinated, others repulsed and began looking back behind us for the door. That is when we noticed that behind us, in fact all around us on ledges that circled the round temple were Pythons, some laying flat, others moving slowly, and some in a raised position as if being commanded by a snake charmers flute. We were told to act casual, do not panic that it was okay, but you should see us as we slowly and carefully eased out of the rotunda. Keeping our eyes on the snakes on the ledges now before us, we turned around and faced them, the snakes in the pit now at our backs. We breathed a sigh of relief when the sunlight hit us, as in an escape for freedom.

The guide came out of the temple with a huge Python around his neck and asked if anyone would like to put one around their necks, we looked at each other as if to say "Man are you crazy?". However the leader in me said "hey I'll try it" and the temple guide placed this big snake around my neck and shoulders. Its skin had a cool, smooth unpleasant feel to it, and when it began to slowly tighten its body around my neck I quickly called to the guide to please remove this thing from around my neck.

At the Temple of Pythons

A few of the others in their daring mood also decided to try it, I suppose we figured 'what the heck this was a part of the adventure of this journey to The Motherland'.

We continued on to the area in Quidah called 'The Road of the Slaves', and we began on this short but historic and fascinating trek to the waters of the Atlantic Ocean. 'The Road' was perhaps half a mile to three quarters of a mile before you finally reached the ocean. 'The Road' had several stations and symbols along the way, we stopped at one big monument that was a big

202

mural depicting the scenes of slavery, the Africans being chained and marched down the road, the slave ship and the points where they were taken in the West. You had to enter a gate, somewhat like an outdoor temple, where there were interesting steel and stone sculptures that depicted the breaking of the chains of slavery. We entered another temple like courtyard along the route where we saw a large carved temple with various sculpture from the different ethnic groups that were captured during the

Slave Trade jutting out of the monument, Yoruba and ancient Dahomey heads, and artifact indications of cultural origins. We continued along the road and reached a tree with carvings and monuments, that had become a place of ritual for some of the local people. They would circle the tree three times in a backwards motion in order to indicate to the gods, the return of love ones who were sold, and taken into slavery. All along the route there were symbols, stone and woodcarvings indicating the path and symbols that reminded and warned the people of what had happened.

Photo by TEDDY WILSON

Tree along "Road of the Slaves"

Finally we reached the ocean and the 'Door of No Return' and what a door it was, this was one of the most magnificent structures that I had seen that told the story of this long and horrible episode in the history of humankind. I think that most of the slave dungeons and forts are left to reflect the horrible conditions that these African people lived in, and I think that it is rightfully so.

This 'Door of No Return' however was a recent venture by the government of Benin and the government of Brazil to connect their cultures and their people. Even though this connection has a horrendous history, it is never the less a connection that the people of both countries feel positive about, it is a connection of the family. Finding the missing link and putting it back together, making the family whole again, completing the circle, the cycle of life. There is no speculation on the connection, no broad based assumption of the origin of most of the people of Brazil. There was a connection based on culture and customs, on what some might call religion, Voodoo or Voodoom, movement, dance, and many of the cultural manifestations that make up the way of life and ethnicity of a people.

The 'Door of No Return' in Quidah is an arch with figures and carvings that symbolized the various cultures that left through this port and into slavery.

As you approach from the road, you walk on a sort of a bridge until you reach some steps and then you climb the steps and find yourself on a platform facing this huge and colorful archway that looks out on the Atlantic Ocean.

We found out that the joint governments of Brazil and Benin had erected this archway, this monument to the history and memory of the Slave Trade a few years earlier to mark the beginning of a celebration in recognition of the fact that the people of Benin, the old kingdom of Dahomey, the land of the Voodoo left this place and was sent to South America, to Palmares, Brazil, present day Baiha, Haiti and other points in the Caribbean. They had come together to celebrate this reunion and to keep a continual recognition of this history. Ever since that time for a few years now they have been involved in a cultural exchange celebration, where activities would sometimes be in Benin, and also in Biahia.

The 'Road of The Slaves' for us was a very emotional realization of this system that was called the Atlantic Slave Trade, we who had come to witness this place in the awful history of slavery. But it must have been one thousand times more horrible for those Africans who had to walk that road in chains. Probably at night, not knowing where they were going, smelling and hearing the powerful waves of the vast Atlantic Ocean, and perhaps finally realizing that they were saying bye bye to Africa.

Quidah is indeed an historical treasure that moves to the rhythm of Elegba, and to the spirit and soul of Africa.

'Door of no return'

Before we left Quidah we paid a visit to the king of Voodoo, the one who holds the most JuJu, or spiritual power in all of Benin. This was a most important visit that allowed us an audience with this person who comes from a long line of kings of Dahomey, as was depicted in his palace in drawings of the succession of the kings for three or four centuries right up until his reign. We listened to his representative as he gave us some history as to the importance and significance of his throne, and we took pictures with him as he sat there on the throne.

As we departed Quidah it was like leaving a part of ourselves, a part of what we discovered about ourselves, a culture that has been ongoing and consistent, as we once again confirmed the reality of our beginnings.

Abomey

Our visit to Abomey was to one of the largest and most important collections of the history and kingship of this country that is presently called Benin. Abomey, referred to as the "Royal City", it is the capital of Dan-Home (called Dahomey by the French), the ancient kingdom. It has one of the most impressive museums in Africa. Its artists and craftsmen, its weavers, jewelers, woodcarvers, iron and brass workers, are famous throughout West Africa, a city of approximately 80,000 inhabitants.

We reached the museum amidst the drumming and dancing of a large group of students, their teachers and parents who were engaged in a celebration of some sort.

After enjoying the dances, and talking with the teachers and students, we started on our tour of the museum, which told the story of the great kings of Abomey. Here you saw their thrones and staffs, their shields, and other items and remnants of their important stations in life. It was an impressive array of an organized and successive long line of royal kingship that went back hundreds of years in West African history.

These collections are extremely important in the ongoing discussion with African people today in contemporary times that question the importance of their history and legacy, and it is also important to the equally ongoing debates with so called European and European American scholars that will continue to argue that Africa had contributed nothing of importance to world civilization, and that it had a primitive history of underdevelopment and disorder.

Of course a casual reader of broad based world history will find quite the opposite, examining the kingly succession of Kemit (ancient Egypt), Ghana and numerous other African empires you will find information that will describe such kingly successions.

One of the important points about visiting these ancient places in Africa is to connect with that which you have studied to the actual physical place, for verification of the information that you have read and to complete the cycle from which Africans in the West came.

Abomey is a treasure house of such historical documentation, a monument to the past and a bridge to the future.

After our very rewarding visit to Abomey we returned to Grand Popo for a relaxing evening of good food and the majestic roaring of the waves of the mighty Atlantic Ocean.

Our French host told me that night that he felt the group was unhappy with his presence and perhaps we would like a change.

That he had located an English speaking African guide who was very good and if we wanted he could be our guide for the remainder of the trip. I did not argue with him concerning the group being unhappy with him, that was the case from day one. I did however tell him that I would speak with them and see how they felt and would get back to him. I discussed this with the group and they expressed while he turned out to be not so bad that they would prefer an African to guide them the rest of the trip. I returned to inform him of the groups' decision, not knowing at that time that our host was again perpetrating a fraud. When we inquired about whether the accommodations would be like where we were staying now, since we understood that he also owned the place where we were going, he expressed to us that it would be even better. To our dismay we found quite the opposite.

The next morning we met our new guide who's name was Paul, and who turned out to be a fairly interesting guide. We also continued with Richard, our French speaking guide who would assist Paul.

We were quite happy with this new arrangement for the time being, of course we found out later that Paul although being a good guide, did not make important decisions concerning the itinerary, that was closely instructed by the Frenchman.

We were finally joined that morning by the tour member who was left at JFK in New York. She had missed the three days that we had spent in Grand Popo. We welcomed her and the lively and jovial air that she brought to the group.

The Journey To Dessau

Paul told us that we would have to travel a good distance, several hours as Dessau was in the center of the country, but that we would benefit from the sites that we would see as we traveled. We did have a very interesting and learning experience as we traveled through Benin until we reached the center. Finally we reached the hotel in which we were thoroughly disappointed to find the place in a very sorry state, first of all it was in a mountainous area, not near the cool ocean area of Grand Popo, very hot and dry, and the place was not very clean. We were told that they did not have enough rooms with air conditioning, that some of the rooms had ceiling fans. Of course this caused a problem for me as tour leader to try to distribute the rooms that had air conditioning, and in addition to that the rooms with air conditioning some were single rooms and we had need for doubles. The rooms were extremely basic, poorly maintained and the out-door corridors were full of mosquitoes.

I told Paul that we were not going to stay here and that we needed to find another place to stay. He responded that there was no other place to stay in the area, that this was the best place that Dessau had to offer. I told him that well we had better return to Cotonou the capital, and that he need-ed to call the Frenchman and let him know the situation, in which he replied that it was difficult to reach him from here. I told him that we should just head back to Cotonou anyway and check into a decent hotel, that this was a run down fleabag. The group however said that it was just too long a drive for this time of day, which was by then five or six in the afternoon.

So reluctantly I went along with them and went through the difficult machinations of distributing the rooms. One of the members, a brother, after moving his bags into his room, came back to the reception area and told me that while he did not want to complain but that his bathroom did not have a toilet seat, it just had the bear porcelain. This had me totally upset that we had to spend two nights here under these terrible conditions, but the group of veterans that they were told me not to worry that they would manage.

After everyone was settled I moved my things into the room that I took for myself which was at the end of the corridor that was open with a con-crete railing. A few feet from my door was a light, around which looked like thousands of mosquitoes, I took this room because I did not want any-one else to stay so close to all these mosquitoes. However when I realized the number of mosquitoes, I asked one of the ladies to please give me back the heavy sanded door blockage that I had given her to keep the bugs out of her room, and gave her something else. Because after seeing all the bugs and mosquitoes in the corner near my room I then realized that was why the door plug was under my door. After we settled our things in our rooms, some of us went to check out the local scene while there was still a couple of hours of sunlight left. We crossed the road in front of the flea bag hotel where we were staying and engaged in conversation with several young men on motor bikes. We negotiated with them a price and several of us climbed on the back of their bikes for a very exciting and exhilarating ride through the villages, up and down the roads and pot holes and hills of the area of Dessau. It was wild! thrilling! and lends to the excitement and adventure that Africa offers. Later that night, after an interesting and tasty dinner, enduring a couple of power shortages that lent less than a romantic air to the dinner on the terrace, I was attacked by the parasitic Queen mother of African mosquitoes.

I did not realize that I had been bitten until I woke up the next morning rubbing three small irritating bumps that I found on my legs and arm. This may not seem like a big deal to most people, a few mosquito bites in the Summer, especially in Africa, but for me it was a matter of some concern as I explained earlier that I had never been bitten by a mosquito before this day. Yes I was concerned, and I had every reason to be so. As I would get sick when we went to Mali, and after having returned to the States and then coming back to Senegal a week later is when I got violently sick with Malaria. According to my sister who was on the tour to Senegal and The Gambia with me that summer of 1997, I was almost out of here. I must admit I was very sick, I do not think that I have ever been in such a state of deterioration before. My sister Yvette was instrumental in my surviving this case of Malaria, she was right by my side for three nights cooling this raging fever in me with cold towels, and having the doctor come in each night to administer medication. This was in The Gambia as we had left Senegal with me stretched out on the seat of the bus, too weak to sit up and suffering from the lack of strength and the bumpy road to The Gambia. Other reasons for my survival was that I had seen a doctor in Senegal before coming to The Gambia, who had said that I might be dehydrated and had given me some medication that helped in keeping the fever down for a day or two. In addition to that I was taking several herbal supplements daily for a few years. Of course the fever became so bad and I had become so weak that I had to take the next available flight back to the States. Let me tell you I crawled back to New York, fortunately my business associates in Senegal arranged for a first class seat for me where I was able to stretch out and sleep the entire flight back. I arrived at JFK airport in New York that morning and caught hell trying to retrieve my baggage as I could not even stand up I was so weak from the Malaria.

Later that day I went to my doctor's office and took tests that confirmed that I had Malaria, and had become an instant anemic, my blood count was so low. My doctor panicked and wanted to admit me into the hospital, and give me blood transfusions. He told me that he never had a case of malaria before and this was most evident in his state of excitement about my condition. I was treated that day by a doctor from India who had experience with Malaria, and within nine days the Malaria had left my blood.

It took almost two months however to build my blood count up to normal.

This is one of the experiences with the Motherland that occasionally happens, yet one that you thank God for pulling you through. As I mentioned earlier I had every reason at that time in Benin after having discovered these mosquito bites to be concerned. However at that time I felt fine as it takes in some cases weeks before the debilitating effects take hold as there is an incubation period, and then the problems start.

That morning in Dessau, in the center of Benin, we started out after breakfast to hippopotamus country, or so we thought. It was a long drive into the interior of the country, or as it is commonly called 'the bush', and bush it was, the vegetation and growth on the sides of the road that we were traveling on were seven feet high.

The road was rough and bumpy, it had rained the night before and there were mud puddles every where, trying to navigate these puddles put the vehicle in danger of getting stuck in the soft, muddy shoulders off the road. At certain points it was difficult to get around the puddles of which some were deep, and still avoid getting stuck in the soft shoulders. When we came to situations like this, and there were several, we all got out of the mini bus and broke off the tall blades of the bush, and laid them across the mud hole. Then the vehicle would back up and accelerate fast in order to cross the mud hole, using the blades of the bush as a sort of bridge.

Photo by TEDDY WILSON

We would repeat this several times until we got to a better portion of the road, then we would continue on until we finally reached a village and began to see some people. This was really the bush, the women were scantily dressed, some were bare breasted, and some of the children were naked. They were busy with their chores and responsibilities, but were delighted to see some visitors. The children stopped with some of their games and curiously came to see these strangers. We gave them gifts and candy, and nail polish and lipstick to the women, they handled them curiously as they obviously had little need for them. Although they loved my oils, I always carried around little valves of body oils, musk, Opium, Somali Rose, sweet essences from Arabia. I was known in a few countries as the man with the sweet smells, and these bush ladies just kept putting the vial to their noses and giggling, and expressing thanks for this small delight in their lives.

Village in Dessau

Photo by TEDDY WILSON

After visiting some of the people in their houses we walked down the hill towards the river to see the Hippos. It was a fascinating scene that we met when we reached the bottom of the hill, we were able to see the river and the trees, and the skies, vast and blue with the thick vegetation of Africa, meshing with the rippling waters. We enjoyed this exotic view of the African bush, but no Hippos. We were told after approximately forty five minutes that the Hippo herd had moved down to another point because the sun had become too hot in that spot. We began to wonder whether or not there were in fact any hippos here at all. I had become skeptical about the whole organization of this trip and dealing with this tricky, maverick white man. In fact the manager of the hotel, a Frenchman, and associate of our French guide had led us to this place, and funny thing is, he did not get stuck in the mud as our vehicle did. We finally left not seeing anything that remotely resembled a hippopotamus, we continued on until we reached what was called crocodile country, determined to see some of the species that was promised.

Reaching this destination was also a journey, but somewhat different, even though it was a long distance we saw a lot of people as we passed through various towns and villages. The road was a little better, there were potholes but it was not wet and muddy. We finally reached our destination and got out of the vehicle, leaving it and the driver as we made our way onto the path into the interior of this village, led by our guide. We stopped to witness a class of students and their teacher, we talked with the children who were very curious when they found out that we came from America. That magical place in their eyes that spoke of money, fame, excitement and Rap music. Everywhere you go in Africa, the visions of America looms large in the minds of the young, and Rap music is known and heard in every quarter. Although you did not hear it at this time, they asked about it, mentioned it, but with the seriousness and kindness of their teacher, you would not be hearing it. We then moved on to the crocodile pond, picking up a large entourage of children, teenagers and adults, snaking our way through the narrow pathways to reach the pond. There was a lot of excitement and expectations around the pond that was located in a very densely vegetated area. Our French speaking African escort, Francis had purchased a chicken in the village, and they were going to use the chicken as bait to bring the crocodiles into sight. They tied a long rope to the feet of the chicken and tossed it into the pond, holding on to the other end.

The idea was that the chicken floating in the water would attract the crocodiles, who would raise up out of the water to try to eat the chicken and we would see it. At the same time the man holding the rope would pull it back so that the crocodile would not eat the chicken. It did not work, the chicken just floated silently, in fact we all were silent so as not to scare off the crocodiles, silent and watching, waiting for that sudden moment when the crocodile would spring out of the water to devour the chicken. Nothing happened, we waited until the men decided to try something more daring, more challenging to the crocodiles, and that was to tie a rope to the legs of a dog! The tourist gasped, one or two said that they could not and would not watch this, and left. They tied the legs of the barking and fiercely resisting dog and threw him in the water. We all watched intently and quietly as the dog floated around the pond, expecting at any moment to witness a very gory site. But nothing happened, again as we waited for the crocodiles to make its move on the chicken, and there was no move on the dog, who just kept floating around the pond. We all finally gave up and started back to the road. Two women in the group said that it was a hoax, this whole thing about crocodiles in the pond, they felt we were once again being duped. We continued back to Dessau and to spend another night in the flea bag hotel.

The next morning after breakfast we would start our journey back towards Cotonou, with a half day visit to the fascinating village built on stilts above the water called Ganvie. You've seen the city of Venice in Italy and Shanghai in China, with people in little canoes paddling to and fro, a means of transportation. We got on a long motorized boat to come out to the area of Ganvie, a city of 26,000 people who get around like walking through the village on small boats, it was an incredible experience.

When we reached the village in the river, we climbed up a ladder and found ourselves in the hospitality lounge where we had cold drinks. After our welcome drink we got on a boat and began to visit places in the village. Little children waved to us from porches high above, where in order to visit them you had to tie your boat and climb up a ladder to the platform or porch.

Photo by TEDDY WILSON

Ganvie

This was the way the entire village functioned every day, an incredible situation. We moved slowly through the narrow waterways at some points, at other points the river widened. The boats used paddles to move through the village, they did not use motor boats within the village itself, which kept the rhythm of the village at a nice pace. Motor boats were mostly used to travel back and forth to the mainland.

We stopped at a craft shop, and climbed up the ladder one by one, until we reached the platform and entered the shop. In fact there were several shops built on this large platform on stilts above the water. In the shops there were many craft items that totally captivated our attention and time. Here we purchased voodoo masks, canes, headgear and other exotic and ritualistic items from the people of Benin.

We did some serious bartering and bargaining, and we both came away pleased with the purchases, buyers and sellers. We climbed down the ladder and once again entered our boat to continue our "city tour" of Ganvie. Then we saw a slightly larger boat then the one we were in, glide around the water lane filled with drummers and 'dancers' Yes dancers who gyrated to the rhythm of the drums, who moved their bodies and not their feet to the rhythm, to the beat, and provided the entertainment that makes the African marketplace the exciting place that it is.

We moved on, passing boats with individuals, some with families and groups of people as we waved to each other in the traffic of the river. We came upon one of the large mouth openings in the village. Here we saw the real Ganvie marketplace, what seemed like hundreds of small boats with women and their wares for sale. Boats piled high with merchandise, foodstuffs, clothing, cosmetics and many items and consumables. They were organized so that there was enough space for the shoppers in their boats to maneuver their way in and between the boats of the sellers. It made me

think about the ingenuity of the African, to have the ability to adopt to the ways of nature and deal with it as it is, whether to build where there is no earth or to use the earth to build civilizations.

Ganvie

214

We finished our tour and returned to the hospitality house to board the bigger boat with the motor that would take us back to the mainland. As our motor boat picked up speed, looking back the unbelievable city of Ganvie became smaller and smaller as visions of her inner life loomed large in our minds.

We reached the mainland amidst scores of boats moored to the harbor, pulling against the strong force of the afternoon tide. Boats filled with the citizens of Ganvie who were trying to get back to the village on stilts with purchased and bartered items for their families and for doing business in the community.

We boarded our bus and relished the experience of Ganvie with its hustle and bustle, and the excitement that permeated the air. I sat back in my seat as the bus began to move swiftly on the road heading towards Cotonou the capital of Benin, I began to think of Ganvie and how it might be when the sun descended and darkness fell on the community. When we speak of different cultural experiences, this certainly is very different then most people living in the United States have ever experienced.

The river becomes the center of the people's lives, as if almost a deity, it becomes the major consideration in the calculated movements of their day. It is another example that culture is diverse, and that it can not be viewed and measured from different cultural perspectives, in fact it is that people's way of life and if it works for them then so be it. Tooling along the road we heard a car horn blowing at us from the other side of the road going in the opposite direction, we all looked over and saw that it was the brother who met us at the airport, who was a friend of the Frenchman.

The driver pulled over to the side of the road and the other car did a U-turn and pulled up behind us. He got out of the car and told us that the Frenchman wanted us to go straight to the airport because our flight was leaving at 4:45pm and not 8:45 as thought.

We all were very confused and upset at this news, it was our understanding that we would come back to Cotonou and eat at the house of the Frenchman our host. He and his wife had invited us when she left us in the city of Quidah. After the time spent in Ganvie we were looking forward to a nice Benin meal and relaxing a bit before having to deal with the hectic ordeal of the airport and customs formalities. We drove back towards the capital pretty angry about this sudden change of plans, Paul our guide said that we would have to stop in town to pick up our tickets at the office, so we continued into town. The time was pretty close to departure, in fact we had only about an hour to make the flight. Here it is this major change and on top of that we had to rush in order not to miss the flight, which would really mess up our plans, as our hosts in Bamako, Mali would be waiting for us to arrive on this flight. I was thinking and was asked by the group how could such a thing have happened, I of course was trying to wrack my brain for an answer.

We drove into Cotonou and really saw the city for the first time, when we first arrived in the country it was at night and we went straight from the airport into the bush. We had no time to shop, which we were planning to spend an hour to visit the marketplace. To add insult to injury as we were driving through the city to reach the Frenchman's office, which was next to the restaurant that he owned, our guide Paul decided to do a little city tour and pointed out certain building that we passed, which angered the group even more because they missed an opportunity to really see the city. But what threw them into a state of shock and a murderous attitude towards me was when Paul pointed out the beautiful and expansive grounds and buildings of the Novotel and Sheraton hotels. After the trying experience of spending a week in the bush in very run down no star 'hotels' seeing these beautiful facilities made them see red. I was embarrassed because I had no idea of the sorry state of accommodations that we would find on our trip. I did not know that such nice accommodations were available in the capital, as I had not previously visited the country, as is my usual custom, to know the place before I bring people there. However I thought that I could wing it because the group consisted of veterans of African travel, as all of them had traveled with me on previous trips. Of course I had been had and this was mentioned to me by a couple of vocal members of the group. We pulled up to the restaurant and Paul and I quickly went inside to find the Frenchman to get the tickets.

He was full of apologies and could not understand how he could have made such a mistake, to plan the itinerary, the brief tour of the city and the meal on an itinerary that did not exist. I of course felt responsible because I should have realized it and figured it out as this is not the way I usually handle these plans and arrangements.

After getting the tickets we made a mad dash to the airport amidst the typical confusion of trying to depart an African country with lots of baggage, and rushing to get our boarding passes in the fifteen or twenty minutes that we had left before departure. Finally we all made it through to the departure area, my group with tight jaws, not speaking to me and one of my most vocal travelers criticizing me for allowing the white man to rip me off, and rip me off he did.

When we were having dinner in Bamako that night, which I wisely treated the group to, I asked them not to evaluate the entire trip to Benin based upon the experience at the end. But to relish the whole experience that was very unique compared to the other countries we had visited on previous trips. They agreed that it was a great experience in spite of the very poor accommodations, but that I had better revert back to my usual practice of scouting out the territory before I take people there. I readily agreed and we enjoyed a delicious dinner with the exotic experience of Benin in our minds while gentle waves splashed against the wooden supports of the restaurant of the hotel Mande above the Niger River.

Part 10
South Africa/Azania

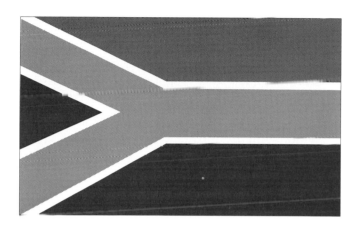

White settlers from Holland first came to South Africa in 1652, many bitter struggles were fought over land and cattle. Although the African kingdoms lost land and cattle they were still independent some 200 years later. But in the 1860's Britain brought large armies with horses, modern rifles and cannons to take control of South Africa. The Xhosa who had fought nine wars of resistance against the colonizers, were finally defeated in 1878, after more than 100 years of warfare. Led by Cetshwayo, the Zulu brought a crushing defeat on the British army at Isandhlwana in 1878, but were finally defeated at Ulundi by British reinforcements. Soon afterwards the British attacked and defeated the Pedi who had remained independent for many years.

Leaders like Sukhukhune, Sandile and Cetshwayo were captured and imprisoned or killed. By 1900 Britain had broken the power of the African kingdoms and they then fell under the control of the colonial government. In 1910, Britain handed over this control to the Boer and British settlers themselves, when it gave them independence. The Union of South Africa was formed with a government that recognized only the rights of White people and denied rights to Blacks.

On January 8, 1912, chiefs, representatives of people's and church organizations, and other prominent individuals gathered in Bloemfontein and formed the African National Congress.

The ANC declared its aim to bring all Africans together as one people to defend their rights and freedoms.The ANC was formed at a time when South Africa was changing very fast. Diamonds had been discovered in 1867 and gold in 1886. Mine bosses wanted large numbers of people to work for them in the mines. Laws and taxes were designed to force African people to leave their land. The most severe law was the 1913 Land Act, which prevented Africans from buying, renting or using land, except in the reserves. Many communities or families immediately lost their land because of the Land Act. For millions of other Black people it became very difficult to live off the land. The Land Act caused overcrowding, land hunger, poverty and starvation.

In 1944 the ANC Youth League was formed, the young leaders of the Youth League, among them Nelson Mandela, Walter Sisulu and Oliver Tambo, based their ideas on African Nationalism. They believed Africans would be free only by their own efforts.

In 1955 the Freedom Charter was drawn up and adopted, which included the Congress Alliance that declared that South Africa belonged to all that lived in it.

In the late 1950's a small group of members who called themselves Africanists and who opposed the Freedom Charter's policy of non-racialism. They objected to the ANC's growing co-operation with whites and Indians, who they described as foreigners. They were also suspicious of communists who, they felt, brought a foreign ideology into the struggle. The difference between the Africanists and those in the ANC who supported non-racialism could not be overcome.

In 1959 the Africanists broke away and formed the Pan Africanist Congress (PAC).

The Arm Struggle Begins - In 1961 the ANC took up arms against the South African government, went underground and formed "U"khonto we Sizwe (MK) to "hit back by all means within our power in defense of our people, our future, and our freedom" The PAC and other resistance groups also took up arms against the government of South Africa.

(From "A History of the African National Congress" - Mzabalazo, Internet)

Location : The Republic of South Africa lies between the Indian Ocean on the east and the Atlantic Ocean on the west, and bordered by Namibia, Botswana, Zimbabwe, Mozambique, Losotho and Swaziland.

Size: South Africa consists of nine provinces covering a total of 1,227,200 Km.

Climate: Generally sunny and temperate and the number of sunshine hours are the highest in the world. Winters are mild and clear, although in the high altitude areas of Eastern and Western Cape and KwaZulu/Natal, occasional snowfalls occur.

Population: 45,095,000 (1995 est.)

Peoples: The four major ethnic groups among Black people are the Nguni, Sotho, Shangaan-Tsonga and Venda. The Nguni language group consists of three sub-groups, which includes a large number of sub-ramifications. The Zulu people comprise a large part of the Nguni group. The Xhosa speaking groups are comprised of the Xhosa and several other groups, and the Ndebele, a smaller group. The Sotho group is comprised of three sub-groups (North Sotho, South Sotho, and the Tswana. The Tsonga are related to the Tsonga of Mozambique, and the Venda are largely a homogenous group that have a semitic origin. White people trace their origins to the Dutch east India Company settlement at the Cape in 1652 and the British settlement of the 1700's. The main language groups are English and Afrikaans. English speakers are descendents of English, Irish, Scot, Welsh, Australian, American and Canadians. Afrikaans language was developed locally, the Afrikaner community is unity conscious, and is tied to its culture, language, religion and organizations. This group also includes the Griquas, largely of the Khoi-Khoin European ancestry characterized linguistically by a broken form of Dutch-Afrikaans. The Cape Malays are descendants of the early Muslim people brought to the Cape by the Dutch East India Co. The first Indians came to South Africa in 1860 as indentured laborers of the Natal colonial government to work Natal's sugar plantations.

Languages: There are 11 official languages: English, Afrikaans, Ndebele, Northern Sotho, Southern Sotho, Swati, Tsonga, Tswana, Venda, Xhosa, and Zulu.

Religion: African Indigenous churches, Christian, Jewish, Muslim, Hindu.

Economy: GDP per capita (US$) 1993 $2,900 - Principal export: Gold. South Africa has a modern, well diversified economy in which agriculture, and mining play a major part.

Currency: Rand ($1 = 5.9 Rand)

(Internet sources)

Culture Clashes

U.S.A. (Union of South Africa)
Vibrations & Tonalities of Nordic/Nazi
Tribal utterings
Egos built on lies Fabrications and figments of distorted imaginations
Goose stepping on the souls of humanity
Condemning and denying the beginnings of a people
Born again supremacists rising from the ice
The rhythms and drums and rhythms and voices
And chants and beautiful organized harmony
And deep felt human tones
Songs of passion
Songs of determination and liberty and freedom
Songs of martial organization
Songs of resistance
Songs and rhythms of Xhosa, Zulu and Nbele
In the tail winds of nasal barks and commands

U.S.A. (Union of South Africa)
As it dances with Azania and the rhythms of Africa
Some say a dance of togetherness
Some say a dance of death

Free the land!

Free the Bantustands!
Free the land!

Free the Bantustands!

Free the land!

Free the Bantustands!

Power to the People! And Free South Africa!, have been popular slogans coming from political activists and the masses of African people from both sides of the Atlantic.

When freedom for Black people is discussed, argued, and passionately demanded, the struggle for self-determination in South Africa is always at the forefront.

When Nelson Mandela was released from prison in 1990, an immeasurable level of excitement reverberated around the world, echoes of Bob Marley's "Redemption Song" filled the hearts and minds of African/Black people from South Africa to South Central Los Angeles. Freedom loving people of other races were jubilant at the prospect of human equality. Well wishes came from around the world for the Africans of South Africa.

The icing on the cake came when Nelson Mandela and the ANC won the elections of April 1994 and formed the government of National Unity.

Bombs Will Not Stop Us Now

Bombs will not stop us now!
came the courageous cry
of the African masses
as they began the first and
final stage in eradicating white supremacy
the last bastion in Africa

Bombs will not stop us now!
as they began the initial stage
of restoring an African nation
as they moved steadily and straightforwardly
to the symbol of democracy
the ballot box
as they move towards official recognition

as human beings and citizens
of their own land
as they are fueled by tragic and
heart rendering visions of Sharpsville
and Soweto and Biko and Chris Hani and
thousands upon thousands upon thousands
upon thousands upon thousands upon thousands
of bloody and murdered African men, women and children
as they are angered and propelled
by visions of white induced
fracticide and division
pitting Zulu against Xhosa
against Ndebele against Pondo against Nguni
against Tswana (Bechuana)

Bombs will not stop us now!
as they move towards this political victory
this test of Kujichagulia
this test of African will power to be free
they move forward
seeking their taste of victory
with future visions of the next stage
total liberation for the African nation
the soil, the earth of our mother
the womb of the world must be restored
to its rightful owners
the Hue people

Bombs will not stop us now!
came the thunderous sounds
of the marching war boots
as the African masses push
the Neanderthals into the
Indian and Atlantic Oceans

Bombs will not stop us now!
Came the echo in the wind

Many people long to visit this country in the most southern part of the giant continent of Africa, to feel, see and experience a modern and developed country with a Black majority and Black president. As the big MD 11 jet of the now defunct US/Africa Airways neared the end of the second leg of its 17 hours of traveling from Washington, D.C., with a 1 hour stop over in the Canary Islands for refueling. As it neared this land of human suffering and struggle, this land of Shaka Zulu, this land of Sobukwe, Sisulu, Biko, Tambo and Mandela. There was a gratifying experience being a part of a group of predominately business people from the travel and tourism industry spread across the United States and Canada, members of ATA (Africa Travelers Association) whose goals and objectives are to develop tourism in Africa.

The organization's membership consists of government officials of African nations (ministers of tourism and culture), airline officials, hotel management, travel agents, tour operators and others who are a part of the tourist industry. An industry that for some countries are the number one money maker for that country. Certainly an industry that is more than flying people in, putting them in hotels and taking them on tours. This is an industry that supports restaurants, shops, entertainment outlets, taxi's, and feeds into the local craft business people of these countries. An industry that brings in much needed U.S. dollars and foreign currency into a continent that is many years behind much of the world, and certainly the West in its standard of living and developed infrastructure.

African centered scholars and thinkers often talk of Africa as the first world in terms of Africa being the cradle of civilization, the place where human kind was born, and its scientific, spiritual and intellectual contributions. However in terms of its standard of living it is definitely not in league with the United States, Britain, Germany, Japan, Russia, France and a few others that are classified as First World nations. It is also behind other European nations that are classified as Second World nations. Unfortunately the continent of Africa, (except for South Africa which might be considered Second World) along with Asia and Latin America are regarded as Third World, developing or underdeveloped nations.

So we can say that the Africa Travelers Association is a valuable concept in improving travel and business to Africa. However I feel that its conference on Eco Tourism that took place in South Africa, October 30 to November 4, 1994 was marred by the administration's failure to take into account the political and racial nature of South Africa when it was making plans and preparations and subsequent itinerary for its members. Four years later while attending another congress in East Africa, I came to a conclusion that the organization was not taking seriously its mandate, and that many who were regular congress attendees were there only for the high level of social activity that is associated with the ATA congresses.

There were approximately 300 people who attended the congress with more than half of them African Americans delegates and many from the African continent in South Africa in 1994. This is a very important point to consider if you understand the various reasons why African Americans visit Africa. The fact that these members who were on this trip, that their clients are almost exclusively other African Americans, which is their main market. For the majority of African American travelers, Africa has not been the first stop in international travel, most have already visited the Caribbean Islands, South America, some to Europe and the Middle and Far East. The primary reason why they travel to Africa so to speak is a heritage connection, to visit the land of their ancestors. To visit the slave dungeons, the historical monuments (pyramids, temples and tombs of ancient Egypt), the villages and exciting marketplaces, in a nutshell to see and feel the people! On the other hand White tourists either from Europe or the U.S. (of course with exceptions) primary interest in Africa are the animals (Safaris') and the almost never ending sunshine, beautiful beaches and warm waters.

The primary mistake the ATA administration made in preparing for this conference in South Africa, is not understanding the impact a closed and racist society like South Africa would have on the African American delegates. And how it would affect the indigenous South Africans who have just started their struggle to bring an improved level of life for their people. This is not to say that the congress should not have happened, I am saying that it should have been done differently.

Following are my reasons:

Concerning the African American market, the setting and the itinerary (congress venues, mini tours, congress presenters, etc.) was designed to attract a European/White American market. The conference should have been centered in Johannesburg instead of Sun City, which was certainly very nice because we all could relate to Las Vegas or Atlantic City, however I think that Sun City could have been a side trip or a setting for the reception or some special event. The problem of being 3 hours away from anything, confined the members and limited their involvement with the local people. This complaint came from a large number of the African American delegates. They could not shop or spend their money with the local merchants, the Blacks. The huge hotel had shops that were not owned by the Black/African population.

The question arose in the minds of many was "Am I really in Africa?" In addition SATOUR (South African Tourism Board) with an all white composition (except for a recent employee hired as the Executive Director in October of 1994. Walter Msimang, who is Black and a former anti Apartheid activist) and with an agenda left over from the recent days of Apartheid, compounded the problem. Satour was responsible for setting up everything, this was a mistake which we will go into detail later.

Satour put together presentations that was geared for as was mentioned before for a Euro-American market, not for an African American market, that had representatives in the majority at the Congress. In fact SATOUR is incapable of doing so for that would mean making video and oral presentations that would present the type of focus that Black people visiting Africa expect to see. i.e. The history of the struggle for freedom and liberation, heroes and heroines from the African masses, cultural places and faces, indigenous ethnic peoples, their life and customs, in addition to the animals and nature focus

Given the dual focus of the symposium Eco Tourism (That is to preserve the environment), the people and their living conditions must take priority in this focus, even before the animals, the rivers and the forests, etc.

ANC Minister of Tourism in Hotel/Casino

Hotel dining room

Myself, ATA member, Minister of Tourism for Zambia, ATA member

The White people of South Africa (Boers, English, etc.), who for 350 years have practiced White Supremacy over the African masses, cannot make an internal about face in a few years and be fair partners with the very people that they have oppressed. People that they have restricted to areas of work and industry, and relegated to living quarters that are far less in quality than their own!

The Whites of South Africa have built a very proficient, highly developed technical infrastructure, a leisure, entertainment and commodity center. I observed several large stores, one Woolworth store in particular in Capetown that was a magnificent modern glass structure that sold expensive items, compared to Macys', A & S, etc., no five and dime operation here, these commodity centers compare with the U.S.

For the average White person the standard of living probably surpasses those in the U.S., certainly because of the wealth of the natural resources and precious minerals (diamonds, gold, etc.) that the land possessed, and the structured nature of Apartheid that was the previous racial order. An order that still exist today, unwritten but unless the wealth is redistributed will continue for many years to come.

Many of us in the African American delegation were disappointed with the presentations and their focus, the insensitivity of the organizers and most of the presenters.

In one instance US/Africa Airways presented a video they produced to encourage travel to South Africa. David Gibson of US/Africa Airways introduced the video with comments concerning the music in the video, saying that because of sitting so long that if you wanted to get up and shake a leg, it was fine because the music in the video was quite lively.

The video splashed on the screen a number of images showing animals, Black people dancing, white folks frolicking on the beaches and hotels, etc. Fine it would seem but a Black woman that was seated next to me, a member of the ANC was incensed because she said that the song playing was "Senze Ni Ma" Who's English translation was "What have we done", one of the several anti-Apartheid songs. This is a freedom fighters song that is a serious part of the history of the anti Apartheid struggle! It is similar say to playing "Lift Every Voice and Sing" to images of Las Vegas, Coney Island and the Bronx Zoo!

I urged her to raise the issue during the question and answer period, which she did to acknowledgements of ignorance, but no mention of changing the video. In fact returning to the U.S. on US/Africa Airways the same video was played again with an extended announcement on the excellence of this video by a crew member.

For ATA to put SATOUR with its current structure in charge of hosting this conference of predominately African American travel industry people, was in the final analysis an insult and a bad business decision. The second and most important point, it was a slap in the face to the majority led government of President Nelson Mandela. As I mentioned earlier, SATOUR had hired an African, Walter Msimang as Executive Director we felt as a token of change. Mr. Msimang met with a group of some 20 African American travel agencies and tour operators in a private meeting to discuss our concerns.

He said that he would take seriously our suggestions and work to change the conditions in the travel business in South Africa that we found fault with.

We later discovered that day that SATOUR failed to invite the entire new tourist structure that President Mandela had recently put in place, inviting only two of the nine commissioners, one for each of the nine provinces that Mandela had designated. The invitation came by fax the day before the congress convened, even though SATOUR was involved in several months of planning.

The two commissioners represented the Northwest region (which includes Sun City, where we convened the Congress) and Johannesburg. It appears that in spite of President Mandela's new commissioners of tourism, SATOUR with its lily white board (except for Walter Msimang) was still in charge of all tourist activity in the country. At this point in the Congress I caucused with some of the African American delegates, and the two commissioners to inform them of the problem.

There were some who were concerned and upset about the whole order of the Congress, most of the African Americans unfortunately were not that concerned and were happy to just be there with important dignitaries and to socialize.

The next day one of the commissioners Patrick Moseki, and two other ANC members were finally urged to raise the issue, which they did. They announced a mandate issued by President Mandela that as of February 1995, SATOUR would no longer be exclusively in charge of tourism, and that the new structure would be put in place. The issue even though raised at the session lacked the strong oral support that we had hoped for, because the vast majority of the African American members were absent. Due to meeting burn out and wanting to get out of the fancy prison that they were in (the actual words of some) and see the people.

Some went to Botswana for a day trip, some to Soweto, and some to Johannesburg. However the issue was effectively raised even though we could not get much direct response from the responsible parties (SATOUR and Mira Berman, executive director of ATA), and because of the continued buffer interceptions of Lt. General Christian Tembo, Minister of Tourism of Zambia, and President of A.T.A.at that time. Sharifa Burnett of

Alken Tours in Brooklyn, N.Y. was part of one panel and delivered a paper on the types of tours that should be organized for the African American market, which was received with lukewarm enthusiasm. What all of this pointed out to us at that time was that the Mandela and ANC majority led government has a long way to go to control the systems of government in South Africa. In fact it appeared that the struggle on that level had just begun.

There was of course a sense of increasing impatience from the masses and the young lions in the ANC that I was sure would increase over the next 5 to 10 years that could bring this simmering crisis to a head

Certain important questions arose, will the White settlers of South Africa move over and share the resources and the land? Will their attitude of White supremacy change? These questions are yet to be answered.

As mentioned earlier we observed a high quality of life for the White settlers, modest and better than modest for the Indians and the coloreds, and for a few Blacks more than modest, but for the masses less than modest and a miserable life for the shanty town dwellers. To be honest the Black townships have a diversity of quality of life, much like any city in the U.S. with a major Black population, where some Blacks have very nice homes, most mainly modest working class homes and some very depressed areas.

The Homelands on the other hand are shacks without plumbing, and where misery has taken its toll on the people. A small group of us hired our own bus and guide and visited a couple of townships that our guide was familiar with. Our guide's name was Jimmy who was the owner of a small tour operation called 'Face To Face' that fed off of the spill over in the lucrative tourism business in South Africa. In spite of the sanctions many Europeans and some White Americans traveled to South Africa to enjoy areas such as Sun City, and the beautiful tourist area of Cape Town. Jimmy with small buses or vans would offer the tourists side tours for much less than the big tour operators. Jimmy shared with us his friends and the families of two townships that we found very interesting. We were quite surprised to find in the first township that we visited, a community of well kept one family brick homes, with small gardens and backyards evenly laid out on treeless streets.

This caught our attention because the houses were so well kept and if there were trees it could be any community in the suburbs of the United States. Thanks to Jimmy our guide we were able to visit a few families, engage in conversation and have a few cold drinks.

The homes we visited had the regular layout of one family homes, a living room or saloon with conventional furniture, carpeted with stereo components, televisions, etc.

The bedrooms were well furnished, kitchens with large refrigerators and custom designed cabinets. These were typical middle class homes in the townships of the Black majority. We wondered what the inside of the white homes looked like, for what was considered the White middle class? Jimmy pointed out to us some of these homes, which outside of these homes were extremely nice and much more elaborate than the Black homes.

Township near Johanesburg

City of Pretoria

After visiting another such township we continued on the road to Pretoria, the administrative capital of South Africa. This is where President Mandela's office is, his home, the home of the former president which is right across the street from his and the home of many prominent South Africans, Black, White, Indian, and Colored.

I understand that Bishop Tutu has a home there also. Pretoria is a beautiful city, resembling an old line European city as opposed to Johannesburg with its superhighways and overpasses which is more like an American city.

City of Pretoria

Pretoria is a very clean city filled with Jackorandem Trees which produces beautiful pink and lavender petals that when shed, its leaves appears like a lavender carpet on the streets and sidewalks. This is a city that used to be reserved exclusively for White people, neither Blacks, Coloreds or Indians were allowed to reside in Pretoria.

On the way we came upon one of the homelands and noticed that a large group of people was having some type of celebration, we asked Jimmy if we could see what was going on.

We discovered that they were celebrating a baby christening, they invited us to join them in their celebration, which we did and had a great time dancing and talking with them. We took pictures and shared in their newborn joy among the squalor of their shacks.

One observation of their misery was the fact that many were drunk! Beer bottles everywhere! The young adults, the old folks, most were drunk! Old ladies were literally laid out on the ground, in the dirt, exhaust-

ed! drunk! An obvious sign of misery and oppression when you see people in their 60's and 70's, especially women so immersed in alcohol, among the barren dirt grounds, no electricity and plumbing in these shanty towns.
I asked some of them about the new government and what it meant to them, and they were very pessimistic in their reply.

Shanty town celebration

Shanty town

Shanty town

These shantytowns are a stark contrast to the beauty of the land and the development in South Africa for the privileged race. Cape Town is a lovely area and the Cape of Good Hope is magnificent in its natural beauty, the most southerly point of Africa, either its beginning or its end. The beautiful view from Table Mountain, the powerful serene majestic Cape Point, that seems to put you closer to the heavens. A sort of Miami Beach for the wealthy White settlers with incredible houses and condominiums jutting out of the cliffs with powerful waves crashing against majestic rocks. We flew from Johannesburg to Cape Town where we were met by several large buses and transported to a reception area where we met the Minister of Tourism for the Cape Town area and other government dignitaries. We of course were once again treated to a feast of delicious food and exotic South African wines. We were also met with a marching band of one of the most despicable displays of racism that we had not witnessed in some decades in the United States. They presented to us for entertainment an old vaudeville type band of colored's (mix raced people/mulattos) in these striped suits with straw hats, banjos and other instruments doing a real 'mammy' type of performance from turn of the century America! It was insulting! And some of us let the White Minister of Tourism know our feelings. He and other White officials expressed their surprise at our anger over this and then began to engage us in discussion around our concerns of the African

American tourist market, as if they were genuinely concerned with making changes to appease and attract this market to South Africa.

The next morning after checking into our hotel we would began to see the attitudes of Klu Klux Klan, Skinhead mentalities, which began in the restaurant where we were having breakfast. In walked a group of young White men screaming out loud and disturbing the calm atmosphere of utensils striking softly against china coffee cups and plates. We immediately understood that this loud and boisterous behavior was due to the large number of African Americans that were present in the room having breakfast. To our amazement no one from the management said anything to reprimand this rowdy bunch. My feelings were that they should have thrown them out, certainly if it was a Black group they probably would have physically tossed them out, which is what I wanted to do.

After breakfast we boarded the buses and proceeded to do a full day tour of the Cape Town area. We almost had a revolution on the bus, we had a mix of Black folks, tour operators and travel agents, most of us from New York and Washington, D.C., the rest were Whites from various cities in the U.S. We had a woman guide who started out pretty good with her description of the landscape, etc., but when she came to discussing the history of South Africa all hell broke out. First of all she began by giving a history of Cape Town and the Cape of Good Hope, saying that her ancestors the Boers discovered the area. She was immediately stopped by a few sisters from Harlem that asked her well who was here when they arrived, weren't the Africans already here? She replied by saying that there were no Black people here that there were a group of Brown people here called the Hottentots who no longer exist, and that the Blacks came later from the interior to the coast. The sisters and others replied that who were the Hottentots?

Didn't she know that they were Black people, Africans? Which she replied that they could not tell her about the history of 'her country' that she would not attempt to tell them about the history of America. Well that caused the air to get real hot with attacks on her and the Whites of South Africa. Some of the White Americans tried to smooth out the arguments, and some really uncle tom Negroes tried to appease her by telling those of us who objected to her slant on history to not argue with her, that this was her country! Well we were about to almost throw one such Negro gentleman off the bus, with a sister telling him to shut his mouth and sit down.

After that heated exchange, the bus settled down some until we were passing by a large township. Some of us said that we wanted to stop at the township, as the people along the road began to wave at us when they saw a lot of Black people on this modern tour bus. We were told by the guide that it was not on our itinerary and it would not be possible to stop. We firmly insisted that this is what we wanted to do, and she told us that it was not a policy of their company to stop at Black townships because it was too hostile. We wanted to know what she meant and she said that they often stoned the tour buses, to which we replied that since we were on the bus that we were sure that this would not happen, seeing that they were excited about our presence. She adamantly refused and in fact the driver who up to this point was silent said that he definitely was not driving into the township, that he would get off the bus rather than drive there. After some more heated words we conceded and continued on, very upset about this entire situation.

The bus was silent for some time as we traveled along the highway to Cape Point, after which our guide started again to point out the geography and breathtaking scenic areas along the southern tip of Africa. We all took turns loading into the monorail type trolleys that lifted the people to the top of the mountain, where you could see for miles the powerful Ocean, and the beautiful natural coastline of southern Africa.

This is a place made by God for poets, writers and painters. Some of us decided to walk down the mountain, stopping at enclaves to absorb and enjoy the view at various points. This land, this cream of Africa that lay before me in all its majesty, reinforced my feelings that these white folks, these Boers and British will never voluntarily leave this place just because Black folks are now supposed to be free and are in charge of the government. This struggle for control of the land will continue for some time to come.

After our visit to Cape Point at the Cape of Good Hope we continued on to visit a vineyard where we would have lunch. They had prepared a picnic basket for each of us that had delicious sandwiches, cheeses, a bottle of wine and various other delicacies. We all sprawled out in a very cool and grassy area to have our lunch and engage in interesting conversation. Later we visited a vineyard processing plant where we participated in a most enjoyable wine tasting session.

We sampled some of the most delicious wines that I have ever tasted. The French seem to have a monopoly on quality wine, Italian wine is also quite good, but the South African wines are without a doubt the finest in the world. This wine has been kept somewhat of a secret due to I suppose the sanctions and the ban on various South African commodities. Everyone

Cape Point, Cape of Good Hope

purchased a few bottles each, I myself purchased two bottles but I wished that I had bought many more because the wine was a big hit with guests that visited my home. Later that evening we returned to our hotel for dinner and some relaxation.

A few brothers in the group decided that we would like to see what the nightlife of Cape Town was like, and went out to check out some of the clubs. We went to an area that was like the South Seaport area in New York City, or perhaps like City Island, where there are boats moored to the pier, seafood restaurants, bars and shops and just quite a lively area. We ventured into a couple of bars or clubs, not liking some and moving on to others. The reason we did not like a few of them because they were kind of wild, with drunk white boys and loud music. We did check out a few until we got bored watching drunk white boys and left the final club. As we walked out we observed a drunk and disorderly group of white guys beating and stomping into the ground what appeared to be another white youth. But as we drew nearer and as the police/guards picked up the assaulted person, he turned out to be a colored (mixed race, White and Black), the police/guards of course did nothing.

There are many other stories to tell, however it relates to the question of whether South Africa will be a major market for African Americans in regards to the environment and control that whites still have over the systems. This was the main contradiction that arose during the conference from the indigenous South Africans and many of the African American delegates. These contradictions again raised their heads on our return to Sun City and some final closing programs. We were being treated to a closing performance and banquet and filled one of the performances spaces in Sun City, our cultural sensibilities were again assaulted when we were presented with a real girlie girlie burlesque show. After some time some of us left, not enjoying what we felt was a cheap shot at entertaining us. Why couldn't they have had an African Ballet performance or a South African chorus group, which represented the culture of the country, rather than a cheap burlesque show? But I suppose this is the kind of entertainment that white tourists that visit South Africa appreciate.

In conclusion my first and only visit at this writing to South Africa was to participate in this ATA Congress, which I feel such congresses are extremely important in developing the tourist trade in Africa. The incoming foreign currency is most needed, however the manner in which they organize the conferences or approaches to developing tourism determines how it will operate, and it must operate in the best interest of African people. It must actively include African people in its operations (travel agents, tour operators, craft vendors, restaurants and social/cultural establishments, etc.).

Finally to ATA, which I am a member, and its future conferences in Africa, my advise is to be cognizant of the politics in the country you are convening (politics of government, culture, race, economics, etc.) and make sure that local involvement is broad based.

I do encourage African Americans to visit South Africa, but only with travel agents and tour operators who are going to make proper preparations and put together itineraries that will consider these issues that were raised here.

We must insist, (certainly I will) that any money we spend in South Africa is more than shared with the Black people of that country.

Freedom Song #1

After the smoke clears
freedom will come
after the appeals
and the marches
the arrests and strikes
and boycotts
and sanctions
freedom will come
after the soul searching
the religious and spiritual values
and intellectual reasoning
the solution process
the threats
the internal conflict
the ballot
the decision
freedom will come
freedom will come
like a mighty Black whirlwind
and destroy the enemies
of African respect and life
freedom will come
and bring sunshine and light
to a world of darkness
despair and death
for African people
freedom will come
and bless our ancestors
our children
and make us dance
with the joy of life
after the smoke clears
freedom will come

Part 11
Zimbabwe

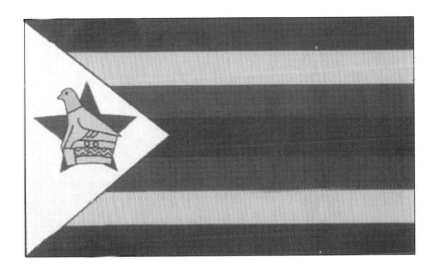

Zimbabwe, located in southeast Africa is bordered by the countries of Zambia, Botswana, Mozambique, and South Africa. Zimbabwe covers an area of 150,873 sq. miles. The Zambezi and Limpopo rivers flow through the country. The Victoria Falls named after Queen Victoria, is one of the main tourist attractions of Zimbabwe.

Population: 11,423,175, divided into two main groups, the Ndebele people in the Southwest, and the Shonas. There are several sub groups based on religion and dialect of each of the main groups.
The Ndebele consist mainly of two ethnic groups, the Ndebele and the Nguni. The Shonas are more varied with ethnic groups comprised of VaManyika, VaKaranga, VaZezuru, VaKorekore, VaNdau, VaTonga, VaRozwi and several others.

Capital: Harare

Language: Sindebele, Chishona and English as the commercial language

Religion: Christianity is the main religion, but traditional religions exist to a minimal degree. Islam and Hindu is also practiced by the Asian minority. Jewish and Greek Orthodox communities are found in the main urban areas.

Climate: Sub-tropical Winter (May to August) Spring/dry season (August to November) Summer/rainy season (November to April)

Currency: Zimbabwe dollar (Z$) Z$38.22 = US$1

Natural resources: Gold, asbestos, nickel are the main exports. Zimbabwe is the fifth largest supplier of chromium. Other products grown include: sugar, cotton, citrus fruits, tea, wheat, and peanuts, which are exported.

History:

a) Early history - Ancient paintings and tools found in the
country indicate that Africans lived in the region for thousands of years. Evidence of the earliest settlers, the Khoisan, date back before the common era. There followed a period of Bantu domination succeeded by the Shona people in the ninth century, who began their rule and built the great city of Zimbabwe. Early historical findings leave ruins of a tower 30 feet high. Part of a wall 800 feet round and up to 32 feet high also remains from this early period. These ruins were made of granite slabs fitted together mostly without mortar, much like the pyramids of ancient Egypt. Mining for minerals began in the seventh century.

b) Colonial history - The first British explorers, colonists,
missionaries arrived in the 1850's, starting a massive influx of mining interests, resulting in the territory being named Rhodesia in 1895, (after the notorious Cecil Rhodes) when the British mining interests seized control. These mining conglomerates ran the country until 1923 when it became a British colony. The Rhodesian government severed ties with Britain in 1965 proclaiming a Unilateral Declaration of Independence. Thus began in the late 1960's a war of liberation waged by the African masses until independence was won in 1980 by revolutionary African forces and a government was formed as a result of democratic elections won by ZANU under the leadership of Robert Mugabe.

(From: Zimbabwe home page and The House of SYNERGY - Internet)

My brief visit to Zimbabwe was in 1994, following my involvement in the Africa Travel Association (ATA) Congress in South Africa, it was less than a week and it was for two purposes.

First I am always interested in exploring other countries in Africa, as I was pretty much centered in West Africa for the past ten years prior to this visit to Southern Africa, mainly due to my tourist business in West Africa. (In 1998 I visited East Africa, Tanzania, Kenya and Uganda) Secondly, I had made arrangements with a family, friends of mine from New York, to stay with them for about four or five days. They had settled in Zimbabwe and were involved in the gold mining business.

The flight to Harare from Johannesburg on South African Airways was a short one, approximately one hour and twenty minutes, and a comfortable one aboard a South African aircraft. Arriving in Harare and going through customs I was finally met by Paulette and her son Rasean. They are a family from Jamaica, Queens that I had known and collaborated with for about four years. Paulette and her daughter had taken a trip with me to Senegal and The Gambia in 1990. Paulette like others fell in love with Africa, and I suppose this love, this calling led her to Zimbabwe, where she eventually moved and married a Zimbabwean businessman. A former investment banker, she invested money in a gold mining area that the government of Zimbabwe had set aside for development by small African companies. This was a deliberate attempt by the government to give these small companies an opportunity to become involved in the use of land for African inhabitants. The large mining concerns are owned by European multi-national corporations, that have monopolized the gold mining industry in Zimbabwe since they arrived in the territory in the nineteenth century.

The government of Zimbabwe since independence has been under heavy criticism for allowing the Europeans to keep the land (large farming concerns, mining operations, etc.) I suppose this was a small attempt to answer these criticisms and concerns of the African masses. All of the Europeans however did not stay, some felt that the revolutionary forces would confiscate their property and companies, and sold their concerns very cheaply, some felt that they might be killed and like wise got out, went back to Europe. This allowed some Zimbabwean business people to take advantage of the situation by acquiring property and businesses at very good prices. This was the situation with the man my friend Paulette had married, who was an educated man, a college professor who lived in the States for some time prior to the independence of Zimbabwe.

He like others, also a similar situation in South Africa, returned when the political situation allowed for African business people to realize their full potential. He showed me several of the properties and businesses that he had acquired. They lived in a very nice community and had a large house with a swimming pool and servant quarters.

Paulette's son Sean followed shortly after and together they began to vigorously develop the two claims that Paulette had staked, eventually laying claim to more than twenty plots that contained gold. I was on a mission to see these mines and their potential for investment.

Often we talk about Africa and the land, and most often it is just talk, no plan no action, just revolutionary dreams. I have been one that always tried to make my dreams come true, at least to put forward an effort. And I am not knocking dreams, because at first you must conceive it, we as African people must always dream, for one who does not dream and reach for the stars will forever be a slave to someone else. But we must plan and organize to make these dreams come true, we must really believe and have confidence in ourselves and in the ability of African people to once again be masters of ourselves.

I was quite excited about the possibility of African Americans with our few dollars, and some managerial experience to become involved in a production project in Africa. Not working for the white man, but actually organizing a company producing a major mineral for the world market. I was also excited about experiencing another African country, particularly in the Southern African region.

I stayed with Sean in his apartment, a very nice flat as apartments are called in Zimbabwe which was very comfortable in what might be considered a middle class community. Understanding that in Africa the middle class is very small, consisting of government officials, small and foreign business people. The wealthy class is also small and of course the masses are poor. This seems to be the case in Zimbabwe much like the situation in most African countries.

Harare from my brief observation did have some level of infrastructure that was somewhat impressive, its downtown streets and building, I even saw some parking meters. There were quite a number of Europeans moving comfortably around the city, and in fact when I was traveling to Victoria Falls, through a few cities on Zimbabwean Airways the vast majority of people getting on and off the many stops the plane made were white. It appeared that they felt that this was still 'their' country.

I was also impressed with the fact that the Mugabe government had changed the name of many streets in Harare to African names and personalities.

I visited some museums where famous Shona stone art and other artifacts were prominently on display. The marketplaces were typically African, wood, leather and straw made items for sale in stall type setups sold by Africans. Ivory was plentiful, but mostly sold in shops owned by white people.

My first visit to the minefields was a very educational experience. The business of gold mining seems to a lay person or one who is not familiar with the industry to be an exciting occupation. What I found out that it is a very hard job, the concept itself is very tedious, that is to extract very small amounts of gold from rocks. The basic idea is to crush the rock to get the gold out. Of course the big mining concerns have sophisticated machinery that make this process relatively easy, however the concept is still to get small amounts of gold out of hard rock.

First of all you have to find the whereabouts of the gold in the rocks by identifying where the concentrations are. These are called veins. The gold mining operation of my friends is a basic one, a manual operation, still at this writing. Where for the most part Alluvial mining took place, surface mining, panning, and sifting and getting the minerals (gold and silver) from the loose soil. Paulette and Sean told me as we walked over several acres, that we were actually walking on gold. That is to say that there were gold deposits in the soil underneath our feet, and using certain methods you could extract considerable amounts of gold using these methods.

It conjured up images of old western films of the gold rush days in the western United States in the late 1800's. Putting soil in a pan and dipping it into a river, sifting and shaking so that the heaviness of the minerals (gold and silver) would settle at the bottom of the pan.

This panning however has its drawbacks as it pollutes the water, and this was a concern of the people in the area that needed the water.

Another ingenious method that I observed that had the preservation of the river in mind I suppose was a very basic method that the workers on the land used, this was a form of sifting. The workers would devise a receptacle with a mesh cloth on the top and a sort of sliding board extending from the open bottom receptacle.

They would pour the soil in the bottomless receptacle with the mesh material on the top, then pour water into it and the soil would wash down the sliding board leaving the minerals caught in the mesh material. What they had created was a manual kind of sifter.

Of course there are mechanical sifters that do the same thing more effectively and much quicker, because the gold must still be extracted from the soil. Where most of the gold is however is not in the soil, but as mentioned earlier, is in the rock. In the more sophisticated large mines of Zimbabwe, South Africa, Ghana and other gold producing places, there are elevators, shafts, and trolleys that bring large chunks of rock from subterranean mine shafts where veins are detected by electronic equipment.

Electronic drills are then used to break large chunks of rocks from the earth and transported to the surface. There they are put into electronic crushers, then put into sifters where the gold and silver is separated from the rock and the soil, or sent to the mill for crushing and sifting.

This operation had no such equipment as elevators, trolleys, or shafts, there were two shallow type shafts on one of the two mines that were active, if only manually. These shafts were at one time deep productive shafts that German mining companies were operating just before World War II. When the war broke out these mines were closed and were never opened again until my friends gained title to the claims. Geological research on these two mines gave estimates of the possible life span of the mines that suggested that they had a productive life of from fifty to one hundred years that could produce gold of 22 carat quality. Chunks of rock were dislodged from the base with manual hammers and electric drills. From there the rocks and soil would be loaded into dump trucks and taken to an old mill that was nearby that the small African mining operations used. Old it was, it was what appeared to be a mill with equipment that looked like it was one hundred years old. It made incredible noise that one could hear for perhaps a half mile, churning and crushing the rock, and sending the soil and rock through a water supply that sifted and sorted the rock and soil leaving small amounts of gold. You had to literally crush tons of rock in order to get a few grams of gold. The small miners with their old trucks would line up for their turn which in some cases might take two or three days to reach your turn.

There were sheds with cots that the workers from the various mines would sleep until their turn came. You did not just leave your load and return to collect your gold, you had to be there to make sure that no one stole your gold once it had been crushed and sifted. There were other much slower and cruder methods of extracting the gold that was done at the minefield. This was an extremely tedious task that would involve taking pieces of rock and putting them into a round metal container, the worker would then take a round very heavy metal pole and began to manually crush the rocks until they turned into fine powder. The crushed rock would then be sifted with water to extract the gold, this was no joke this was heavy labor that produced small amounts of gold. This was definitely a manual grassroots type of mining operation, the workers were paid a percentage of the amount of gold they would mine, this was also a very difficult process to monitor for stealing. Who was to know if an employee took a few grams for him or herself? Of course they could not come up empty handed or considerably lower than the average amount of gold that they processed, but without the sophisticated methods to deter thievery, it was get what you can when you can. The large mining concerns use Geiger counters, metal detectors, etc. Some I understand use pocket less body suits, and of course during the days of the slave like labor of the Black workers of South Africa, the Africans mined naked. For this small mining operation this was a serious problem. The workers were further compensated for their labor by being allowed to erect houses on the land and live free of cost. In actuality this working relation with the African miners would be called a form of share mining/ cropping.

Some of the areas for development was that electricity was needed and a constant flow of water. In addition a dump truck, mechanical crusher and sifter were high on the priority list, also chemical tanks, etc. The family had put together a survey and business plan to raise $250,000 to purchase this equipment and to set up an effective administrative headquarters. I pledged my support for the project because I felt that here was an opportunity to become involved in a major business that would bring some real economics to the table for African American investors, and at the same time bring some jobs and decent wages to African workers. I pledged that I would take this package back to the U.S. and began to put some ideas together to encourage African Americans to invest in this enterprise.

I video taped the mines and the incredible process in which the workers mined the ore. I captured on video the methods of panning, crushing, sifting, the unbelievable roar of the ancient mill, discussions with the workers and the family, and brought to the United States a visual look at manual gold mining in Zimbabwe.

What happened, to bring this section of my Zimbabwe report to a close is that we failed to raise the necessary funds to put the plan into full action. We raised actually less than one third of the necessary funds, after giving several seminars, where Paulette and myself presented the plan to the public, and months later Sean would come to attempt to do the same thing. We had articles and features in the newspapers, appearances on radio talk shows, we made several serious attempts to build a broad base of investors in this project. More than forty people did invest a minimum of $1,125 each in the project though and I must commend them for having faith, practicing principles, and believing in the possibilities that African people can restore themselves to their traditional greatness. In spite of not meeting our quota we thought that we would go ahead with the plan and purchase some equipment, which we were able to bring the electricity, buy a truck and a used sifter. All the while we were vigorously trying to acquire some offshore banking loans and equity investments. Because we did not have any substantial assets in the United States we were not candidates for conventional loans. We met with so many people and groups that would promise, but could not deliver the money. We actually lost a few thousand dollars in pursuit of larger amounts dealing with some unscrupulous people. The project at this writing is not dead, but is struggling for dear life.

The highlight of my trip to Zimbabwe, other than the excitement of the mining operation at that time, would have to be the visit with Sean to Victoria Falls in the north of the country. The Falls are breathtaking, powerful, magnificent, awesome, and a natural wonder to behold. After traveling on one of the local air flight shuttles to Victoria Falls, stopping at several cities to discharge and pick up passengers, which much to my surprise were white people as I mentioned earlier. At some stops we had to get off and re-boarded where I became engaged in conversation with some, who thought that because of my dress in West African clothes that I was from West Africa. Much to their surprise and disappointment they discovered that I was from the States and became immediately disinterested. I guessed that given the reputation of African Americans as being militant and agitators they figured that they would leave this one alone.

However my being from the States caught the attention and interest of one individual, and that was the pilot of the plane who had one of the flight attendants summon me to the cabin. I wasn't sure what the reason for this request was but I was also curious and discovered that the pilot was a brother, an African American from Texas. He said that he picked up my accent as I boarded the plane and knew that it was an African American and wanted to meet me. He told me that he was flying for Zimbabwe Air and really liked the job and the country, he said that after trying for a lucrative commercial position in the States, this opportunity came up and he readily accepted it. I enjoyed my time in the cockpit, a most interesting place, and I really appreciated the skill of the pilots in manipulating these massive controls that held the life of so many people in their hands.

After landing in Victoria Falls, Sean and I caught a taxi to the Falls and began our visit. Entering the park I began to put my political cap on and the first thing that I thought about and analyzed was why had not the Park and the Falls been re-named as had a lot of the streets that I noticed in Harare? Also I objected to the statues of Cecil Rhodes and some of the other colonial figures that were erected in the park. But in spite of all of these concerns and objections I was thrilled with the magnificence and overwhelmed with the awesome power and majesty of the "Falls". The flow of the water crashing over the rocks create an incredible deafening sound, and the force of it hitting the sides of the rocks and the bottom creates huge splashes of water that has caused a sort of rain forest on the plateau, where vegetation and plant life is dense and has attracted small animals such as monkeys, baboons and other rain forest type animals. Walking through it you will certainly get wet, but it is so cooling in the hot and humid weather. Watching it is so fascinating, as some of the water cascades down parts of rocks that create smaller water falls, then collect at points to again create the massive forces of water that has the power as when it first feeds from the river. It then drops off the top creating this extraordinary crashing sound. It is a most incredible thing to watch, as is the power of the ocean and its mighty waves, only this time the sound is more magnified. This Victoria Falls is definitely one of the many wonders of nature, and projects again the natural beauty and majesty of Africa, the cradle of civilization.

As I prepared to leave Zimbabwe amid good-byes and well wishes from my friends and now new business partners. I thanked them for showing me a view of Zimbabwe, of the possibilities of doing business in Southern Africa, and the potential for resettlement in yet another part of the mother continent.

Part 12

East Africa/Tanzania, Kenya and Uganda

The final chapter in this sojourn, this love affair with Africa, was my brief but impressive visit to East Africa in May of 1998.

I was there to once again participate in an ATA (Africa Travel Association) Congress. It was being convened in Arusha, Tanzania, and the main hotel was the Novotel. I was packed and off and running to experience yet another major part of this vast continent called Africa.

It was a long and arduous journey trying to reach East Africa, no direct flight like West Africa, in this case you have to fly to Europe, lay over for 10 hours then continue on to East Africa. I flew to London on American Airlines, spent the day in Piccadilly Circus, then took a scheduled flight on Alliance Airlines to Tanzania. I didn't mind so much the layover, however I was not very excited. I had been to London before, about 7 years earlier I spent a few days after leaving Ghana with my extended family brother Kwabena who was living in London and studying for his PhD.

I got an opportunity to see some of the tourist attractions and to see the changing of the guards, and their national monuments. British culture does not impress me at all, it is alien to me. I viewed it with much amusement.

At that time I spent a day in Brixton, the Black area in London, the plantation, where you will find Africans from various countries in Africa, and the English speaking countries of the Caribbean. I always enjoy riding through a Black neighborhood and seeing how we live, observing the quality of life. Later that day we attended a community event, where there was a panel on community issues, guest speakers, entertainment, vendors and good food. My brief stay this time was spent looking in shops and having a very nice lunch at an Italian restaurant that faced a busy crosswalk, watching people as they walked past. There were two ladies that were also attending the ATA Congress and we kind of latched on to each other to complete the second leg of our journey to East Africa.

Later that evening we returned to the airport to get our flight to Tanzania. After enduring about an hour of drama, trying to check my baggage in with much difficulty, we finally boarded the plane. It was a huge plane with upstairs seating, this Alliance Airlines wide body jet. Alliance Airlines is a South African company that service East Africa. I was especially impressed with the painting of a huge lion on the tail of the aircraft, bold and magnificent, in full color.

It was an 8 hour flight from London to Tanzania where we would be landing in Kilimanjaro. The conference was to be held in Arusha, a thirty minute drive from Kilimanjaro. The big Alliance aircraft landed very smoothly on the runway, and we descended to the tarmac with much excitement on entering this much talked about East African country, known for its Pan-African philosophy, and its experimentation with African socialism.

Tanzania

Location: East Africa, bordering the Indian Ocean, between Kenya and Mozambique

Area: 945,090 sq. km, slightly larger than twice the size of California. It is the highest point in Africa.

Climate: from tropical along the coast to temperate in the highlands.

Natural resources: Hydropower potential, tin, phosphates, iron ore, coal, diamonds, gemstones, gold, natural gas, nickel

Population: 29,460,753 (July 1997 est.)

Ethnic groups: (Mainland) African 99% (of which 95% are Bantu consisting of more than 130 tribes), other 1% (consisting of Asian, European, and Arab)
Zanzibar: (Arab, African, mixed Arab and African)

Religion: (Mainland) Christian 45%, Muslim 35%, indigenous beliefs 20%
Zanzibar: more than 99% Muslim

Languages: Kiswahili or Swahili is the official language, English is the primary language of commerce, administration, and higher education. Arabic (spoken widely in Zanzibar), and many local languages. Kiswahili (Swahili is the mother tongue of Bantu people living in Zanzibar and coastal Tanzania). Although Kiswahili is Bantu in structure and origin, its vocabulary draws on a variety of sources, including Arabic and English. Swahili has become the lingua franca of central and eastern Africa. However the first language of most people is one of the local languages.

Capital: Dar es Salaam

Independence: April 26, 1964

Head of State: President Benjamin William Mkapa

Tanzania is one of the poorest countries in the world, depending heavily on agriculture. Some agricultural products for export are: coffee, sisal, tea, cotton, cashews, tobacco, etc.

Currency: Tanzanian Shilling, approximately 600 shillings is equal to one ($1) US dollar.

(Gathered from Internet sources - gov. fact book)

As my feet hit the tarmac I looked up at the huge plane that brought us to the other side of Africa, and marveled at the larger than life lion that was painted on the tail of the plane.

There were quite a number of people that was scheduled to attend the Congress on the plane that came from London, others who would attend would come on other routes, on other airlines from the U.S. and Europe. We all began to move towards the arrivals building. Entering I am extremely disappointed to see the run down condition of the airport. It was dimly lit and shabby, the luggage belt was old, and creaked under the weight of the many suitcases and boxes of the conference delegates. I cleared my luggage and rode into Arusha with some tour operators from California. It was about a thirty minute ride from Kilimanjaro to Arusha, we began to notice the climate and asked our driver what the temperature and season it was. He explained to us that this was the cool period, I really thought that he could have said cold because we were beginning to feel what the temperature was really like as the wind whipped through the open windows of our land rover. He also explained that we were in the highlands of Tanzania, we had just left Kilimanjaro, where the great mountain is located and that this mountain is the highest point in Africa. Arusha was the next city, 30 minutes away, it was pleasant during the day, but cold in the evening. The first night I was shivering at an outdoor dinner reception due to the very serious chill in the air. The next day I took a taxi and went into town to find a jacket to wear in the evenings. It was difficult to find the kind of jacket that would look presentable with my Ibn Nur Ashanti suits, that I planned to wear at all of these luncheons and dinners that I was about to participate in. After checking several shops I was able to find something that I was halfway pleased with. It was a simulated black leather looking jacket, it wasn't real leather and it was light in weight, probably some man made fibers, but it sure came in handy that night, I was really comfortable. Some people thought I was overdoing it because it looked like a leather jacket, some said they realized it was much colder than anyone had expected but it looked like I had gotten carried away.

The ATA Congresses are fun, that's what I think many of the people come for, most are in the travel business, but some are not and come with friends who are. There are all these great luncheons, and elaborate dinners where you mingle with important people from various African countries. Ministers of culture and tourism, top officials of the host country, an address by the president, networking and socializing with interesting people in the same industry, and enjoying the cultural presentation's of the host country. But the social affairs are not all that happens at the congresses, there are symposiums each day where topics that are important to the tourist business in Africa are discussed, debated, and video presentations are given. There are also trade fairs and displays of information concerning the tourist business from various African countries that are geared towards selling those countries as tourist destinations.

Attending ATA Conference, ATA regional members and on the far right the Ambassador from Tanzania to the United States

International ATA representatives

ATA Mid-Eastern representatives and myself at Conference

At this Congress four African countries including the host country hosted an event that focused on the culture of their country.

Nigeria hosted a fashion show that reflected the fashions of several African countries, and a sumptuous lunch of delicious Nigerian food. It was a grand affair that involved the delegates as models, male and female, designers and announcers. The Benin night was a night to remember with the room decorated with symbols from Benin, food and cultural presentations that reflect the culture of that country.

We ate and drank and danced and enjoyed the festivities of this African culture.

The grand evening for me was the Ghana night, Ghana was in the house! The walls draped with rich Kente, highlife music filling the air, and the aroma of fried plantain caressing my nostrils. The host country Tanzania of course gave an elaborate affair where we were presented with some of the country's top cultural performers at a beautiful cultural center in their out door theatre. This was in the midst of a simulated Masai village with life sized replicas of colorfully dressed Masai girls, women and men in a village setting with huts, and cattle. The entire cultural center was very impressive with the thousands of African carvings, sculpture and artifacts that were on display for purchase in the various rooms and alcoves.

The performances were great, drummers and dancers and stilt walkers, all joyfully expressed their artistry and their culture.

Tanzania, the host country on one of the days organized a safari for all the delegates, it was a huge undertaking to organize three hundred people on a safari. (The word Safari, means "a journey" in Swahili) We all loaded up in approximately fifty land rovers, those four wheel drives that hold five to seven people, and that had a push up roof where you can stand and see

Masai maidens

256

the animals with a clear view which allowed you to take pictures without obstructing your view.

It was a long caravan that snaked through the bush in search of the large animals. Our first stop was the Snake Park, here we saw various types and sizes of snakes in their natural habitat. Huge snakes, long and thin snakes, round fat ones, many species and types were visible behind glass windows. We saw huge turtles, and various other reptiles. Then we came upon the crocodile pen and became fascinated with these creatures, the park hands had thrown large chunks of red meat into the crocodile pen and the crocodiles snapped out their huge jaws to grab the meat from each other. They were very fast as they snatched the meat in their strong and long jaws a second before another was about to grab it. It was fascinating to see them crush the meat with their long sharp teeth in their mighty jaws. All our eyes were fixed on their throat and stomach as you saw them flexing their muscles to pull the meat through their body into their stomach. You saw it moving, the contracting and squeezing of the meat until it finally reached the area to be digested.

When we left the snake park we went across the road and visited a Masai village, we had seen a few of them at the snake park, regal and decorated with jewelry and rings, and elaborate colorful beaded necklaces, with their traditional red blanket and spear. Here at the village we saw many Masai, with their elongated ears and many earrings. We took pictures of some of the Congress members as they climbed upon the backs of the camels that the Masai allowed the people to do. Some took a camel walk

Crocodile farm

through the village on the backs of the majestic animals

We then continued our long caravan to the Tarangeri national park to see the big ones. It was quite a winding train of white four wheeled drives, snaking through the dusty roads of the bush. I stood up in the roof of the vehicle and looked back and saw an incredible caravan of these vehicles, surely the animals will take flight with the noise of so many motors and the big dust clouds that the vehicles stirred up. Our driver had quite a sharp eye as he saw and identified several species of birds in the trees, I was happy that I had brought this new fold away set of binoculars which allowed me to see the birds very well.

As we drove along, our driver spotted a herd of water buffalo that were down in a valley in a pond or small river, we got busy with our cameras and zoom lenses to try to bring into focus these huge creatures. This was proving to be a little better than the safari that I went on in South Africa. We continued on and saw a small herd of zebra, then we spotted the big ones with the floppy ears, the elephants. They were in an open clearing and not very far from the road, we could see them clearly without the use of binoculars, or zoom lens. At one point one of the elephants broke from the small herd and started to gallop towards the road and our vehicle, its ears were flapping in the wind, it was a very majestic view of this huge animal in what almost appeared to be its galloping in slow motion.

I found this safari somewhat interesting, but far from exciting, it was however much more interesting than the first safari that I went on in South Africa. The best part that I liked about this one was that it was not too long. The safari in South Africa was very long, about four hours, and it was very cool on the road, in the bush. We did not stop at any five star lodges either, in fact we did not stop at all. We actually stayed out much longer than planned in South Africa because our guide said that the lions would come out when the sun was going down, at dusk. So we stayed and caught a few shadowy glimpses of the fierce ones.

This safari in Tanzania was short and in this park there were no lions. One unpleasant observation was the amount of dusk that the 4 wheel drive vehicles created, and it was not because it was such a large caravan that the dust was raised, even though it did create a huge dusk cloud, it was because the place had a lot of dust. In fact our vehicle was alone for awhile, the stopping and starting of the various vehicles to watch and take pictures of the animals created spaces between the vehicles of perhaps a kilometer apart. When the vehicles of the caravan reached the lodge one by one, we were greeted with welcome drinks amidst an authentic oasis in the bush.

I then went to find the restroom and discovered that I was covered with red dust when I wiped my face with a hand towel, the towel turned red from the thick red dust that covered my face. The dust was all over, everywhere, on my face and hands, on my clothes, in my hair, everywhere!

The lodge was huge and gorgeous, rustic and traditional, yet smoothed and polished. There were drummers and singers sending out Karibu (welcome) rhythms to us as delicious aromas of exotic foods caressed our nostrils and caused our stomachs to growl.

We literally had a feast at this beautiful lodge. After eating we all went outside and gathered around the pool sipping rich Tanzanian coffee and listening to the guest speakers and our hosts praise the event and the coming together of so many people from various places in Africa, the U.S., Canada, and Europe. I enjoyed the fellowship, the sharing and learning that took place. I talked to several Tanzanians and folks from other African countries, about the economic conditions and tourism, and drank coffee that Tanzania is known for.

These places were created for the safari, so that Europeans could have the comfort of the hotel here in the bush. Where one minute you can be enjoying five star quality and the next minute you can get in your land rover and be in the bush filming lions and elephants.

These are viewing safaris' not hunting ones, I don't think that there are many hunting Safaris' still being conducted today in Africa with many of the animals being put on the endangered species list.

The Safari I suppose would appeal to all visitors to East Africa, but I think that African Americans are not as excited about looking at animals as is the European and white American tourists that seek out East Africa in search of these animals, as we talked about in the chapters on West Africa. Black tourists are in search of their past, they want to meet people and make cultural connections. The tourist industry in Tanzania, Uganda and especially Kenya is built around the Europeans and safaris'. There is a

European/western influence in Tanzania, you can see it in the dress of the people, unlike West Africa where the colors and flow of the garments are dazzling and natural in view of the tropical climate of the region. For the men it is most definitely western dress, pants and shirt, suit and tie, the women are also mainly in western dress, but occasionally you can see some women in a bubba and lapa. It seems that in the countries that I have visited in West, South and East Africa you will always find the women wearing their national dress more often than the men.

With the younger generation of women and men you will find almost 100% dressed in Western casual and business clothes. Tanzania in spite of its western influence still has a Pan African, revolutionary air about it, a people united air, that is the impression that permeates the air, regardless of the economic and infrastructure problems. The Ujamaa African socialism of the first president Mwalimu Julius Nyerere had faltered and fell. The West didn't want to see his dream of a return to Africa of a humanist system of community and people. They did not want to see a system where bread was shared, where houses were built not by unscrupulous and money hungry contractors, but by the collective sweat of your neighbors 'brow. Mwalimu Nyerere was attempting to build an egalitarian society where there was food and shelter and a respect for every member of the community. African Socialism was a natural philosophy that preceded Marxism and the European analysis of an egalitarian society.

Tanzania unlike its East African neighbors took a strong Pan African/socialist, Uhuru (freedom) stance, and paid dearly for it in terms of the lack of support and down right sabotage that it received from the Western/European nations.

Arusha was not impressive in terms of its infrastructure, its roads were in a very serious state of disrepair. Its buses and transportation vehicles were old. Seriously, you had to carefully and slowly maneuver around massive potholes, ditches actually, which makes it take that much longer to reach your destination. I had seen some bad roads in Ghana, The Gambia and Mali, but the worst road that I have ever seen in Africa had to be the road that led to The Masai Lodge. A few of us had been invited by a Masai businessman, (understanding that all Masai men were not warriors in their traditional red checkered blanket, huge colorful necklaces and numerous earrings in their ears), he owned a very lovely lodge or guest house. He warned us that the road was a little rough getting to the lodge, but that it was not very far from the hotel. He was certainly correct that the distance from the hotel to his lodge was not very far in kilometers, but it took a very long time to reach there because the roads were terrible. I am not exaggerating, the holes were so deep it made you feel as if you were on a roller coaster, up and down, very slowly less you caused damage to your vehicle. However after reaching there we found a very equipped and comfortable lodge with modern bungalows and a main building that housed a lounge, bar, and restaurant. The place had a beautiful garden with benches and chairs and a vast expanse of grass that was covered over with huge trees, it seemed as if we were in paradise.

The Masai businessman explained to us that he was a retired Colonel in the Tanzanian army, and had opened up this lodge and some other businesses. As I just mentioned the picture one sees of the traditional looking African is typical of how we in the West tend to look at Africa and its people with a narrow view. We want to see a monolithic example of a particular ethnicity, a compact made for the screen version of various ethnic groups commonly called tribes. There are many people that live in the rural areas, or on the border areas that still maintain their traditional dress, but that is not how the majority of Masai look. They are not all cattle herders, some are business people like our host, some are doctors, and storeowners, and various other professions and vocations that one finds in the metropolitan areas of any country. The lodge was nice, the roads were bad, but the people were friendly and still held the promise of tomorrow.

One late afternoon several of us were invited to the home of a Tanzanian tour operator for dinner. Our group consisted of a few African American tour operators and the ministers of Tourism for Benin and Guinea, Conakry. We enjoyed a delicious dinner and the conversation that ensued. Our Tanzanian hosts and some of their friends and neighbors, expressed to us their feeling about the rein of President Nyerere and his Ujamaa program. They felt it was a failure and that it had set the nation back in its material development, but they said that they had to admit that it brought a great feeling of nationhood and a feeling of brotherly and sisterly cooperation and respect for each other and the nation.

I believe that they soberly weighed the options of what was best for the country. But why is it that there must be such drastic choices, in fact why does it have to be a choice between material prosperity and an African philosophy of life? To want for your brothers and sisters what you want for yourself, to be neighborly and civil, to share and build together, to unlock your door and keep your eyes in front of you, to be concerned and caring, to be human.

Tanzania might be a little withered and worn from the struggle against western imperialism and capitalism, but its people still have pride and strength and will eventually prevail.

My time in Tanzania was drawing to a close, the congress was over, we had our farewell diner, our last lavish affair, we clinked glasses and toasted the future, said our good-byes and packed our bags for early departures in the morning. Everyone was not going back to the States, some were

Masai Woman

Masai man

Masai village

Watusi & Masai warrior

going on to Dar es Salaam, some to Zanzibar, others to Ngoro Ngoro, the crater, and a few of us were going to Kenya.

Our group consisted of five people, two men, including myself and three women, all tour operators. One of the women made the arrangements for our visit to Kenya.

We entered Kenya by road, which was quite interesting as we traveled further away from the cities, seeing how the people worked the land, the Masai herding their cattle in colorful dress. We went directly to the airport in Nairobi to catch a flight to Mombassa where we would spend a couple of nights.

Kenya

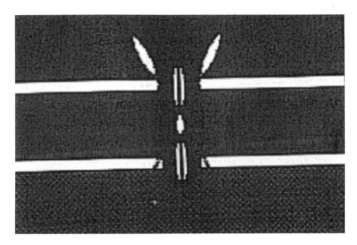

Kenya is a land of striking landscapes, ranging from snowcapped Mount Kenya to rich farmlands, barren deserts and tropical beaches. Kenya has eight provinces ranging in geographical size from the small Nairobi Province to the much larger Eastern and Rift Valley provinces. It borders Somalia, Ehtiopia and Sudan in the north, Uganda in the west, Tanzania in the south, and the Indian Ocean in the East. It covers an area of 583,000sq km (225,000sq. miles)

Location: On the East coast of Africa, right on the equator,

Population: 29.7 million

Kenya's capital is Nairobi with a population of approximately 1.4 million people, the other major towns are Mombassa on the Indian Ocean with an estimated population of 1 million and Kisumu on Lake Victoria with an estimated 400,000 people.

People: Bantus, who came to Kenya some 2,000 years ago, fused with the previous hunters and Southern Cushites. Bantus consist of Embu, Kamba, Kikuyu, Kisii, Kuria, Luhya, Mbere, Meru, Mijikenda, Pokomo, Taita, Taveta, Tharaka.

Climate: Hot and Wet, found in the coastal strip and in the lake basin regions of Kenya. Very hot and dry in the north eastern parts of Kenya.

Currency : Kenya Shilling approximately 60 to $1

Language: Kiswahili, which has a bantu grammar and Arabic vocabulary, it has become the lingua franca of many people in East and Central Africa. The word Swahili comes from the plural of the Arabic word Sahel which means coast. English is the language of commerce.

History: From the Great Rift Valley caused by volcanic eruptions that caused the formations which gave Kenya such beautiful landscapes, to the migrations of the Bantus, and the coming of the Europeans, many of whom believed that Kenya should be a white country as Australia or New Zealand. They believed that Africans would always be what they were, good natured, loyal labor.

Others believed that the country belonged to the Africans but should be run by their own people, so that the Africans could reach a higher social level than what they had. By the 1920's several Africans, mainly the Kikuyus started political associations, Jomo Kenyatta emerged as a leader of the Kikuyus. The first national organization the Kenya African Study Union was formed, and later renamed the Kenya African Union (KAU). In 1946 a group of ex-army Kikuyus formed the "Forty Group" and started organizing violent opposition to the white settlers, they called themselves the "Freedom Fighters". Kenyatta on his return to Kenya took over the KAU, he was seen by the Europeans as the brains behind the "Freedom Fighters" tactics, but he always denied being one of their leaders. From 1946 to 1952 the "Freedom Fighters" or Mau Mau were very successful in their guerrilla warfare against settlers farms, loyalists, and police stations. The British declared a state of emergency and in 1952 Kenyatta was arrested and sent to jail with 150 others. After several bitter years of fighting the might of the whole colonial and British army, and after more than 13,500 Africans were killed and another 100,000 had been herded into detention camps, and the capture and execution of "General" Dedan Kimathi in October 1956, the almost fatal blow came to the Mau Mau. The state of emergency was officially repealed in 1960.

In 1961 Kenyatta was released, in 1962 he was elected leader of KANU, in 1963 KANU won the majority of seats and formed an internal self government administration. The spirit of "Harambee" or pulling together permeated the air, the new country had a charismatic leader, who pledged to forget the ills of the past and bring together all races in a common task. Jomo Kenyatta, the first president of Kenya remained from 1963-1978.

The airport in Nairobi was large and well lit, modern and clean, it was

Jomo Kenyatta

a stark contrast to the airport in Kilimanjaro. The flight to Mombassa on Kenya Airways was not without the usual drama of African airports, the problems with baggage, always overweight, hands seeking money, the confusion.

We arrived in Mombassa and found a brand new airport terminal, it looked like some of the equipment had not even been removed from the containers. We were met by our guide and driver and taken to the beautiful White Sands hotel. This is a rich, sprawling, African paradise resort on the Indian Ocean, with a beautiful beach, and elegant town house type of rooms. It reminded me a lot of the resort area of Saly in Senegal.

It was interesting to see the various types of people that were vacationing here, Europeans, Arabs, Lebanese, and Africans from several countries. There were Muslim men and women and their families, on the beach and around the swimming pool, raising up their garments just a little and getting their feet and ankles wet.

I suppose the beach, the beautiful Indian Ocean, and the plushness of the grounds and pool was just too much for even the most religious fundamentalist to resist. That evening we had dinner in a very lovely, quaint atmosphere amidst plants, and trees and canals running underneath raised floors. Streams of moving water with tropical fish, lent an exotic air to the delicious food that we consumed.

There were chefs with grilled fish, steak, and Gazelle, with aromas rising in the air and tantalizing my taste buds. This would be the first night that I would become adventurous and try some of the exotic meats that are legend in Kenya. I am one while not a vegetarian, eat chicken and fish, and try to stay away from the red meats due to having diabetes. However occasionally I might try a piece of red meat, and this night I decided to give the Gazelle a try, being urged on by the African chefs to 'try it, it is very good'.

It was indeed very tasty, it had a sweet taste and was not very tough, I enjoyed it but not as much as I suppose I could have, feeling guilty about consuming red meat and one that I was not familiar with.

This would be just an introduction to a meat feast that I would have in Nairobi in a couple of days. The next morning our group started out for a tour of Mombassa. Away from the luxury of the White Sands Hotel and the serene beauty of the Indian Ocean,. Mombassa was a typical African city, those who have and those who have not. There is the new Mombassa, with its city center and shops, and market places, we visited a craft center, a somewhat village of wood carvers we were told that was the largest wood carving center in East Africa. It was huge, with many of the workers coming from other areas to work here. It was a hub of activity, creativity was at work here in Mombassa, carving intricate objects, animals of every kind, and images of the culture of East Africa.

If you wanted to purchase some items, you could not negotiate with the crafts people, their job was to produce not to sell, you had to make all your purchases at the gift shop, or perhaps you might say gift warehouse it was so big. In the building where you bought your items were thousands and thousands of carved items, tiny replicas of animals and warriors, to huge bigger than life sized statues of African warriors, elephants and Giraffes.

Each item had a number on it that indicated which artist or stall that the item came from, so that each artist could be compensated for if their crafts sold.

After we did our shopping we continued on to the old city of Mombassa, this is where the Swahili people live, a mixture of African, Arab and Indian. The old Mombassa is a poor section of the city, some might call it the ghetto, however I found it to be quite interesting with its narrow streets, and beautiful carved doors with polished brass studs and knockers.

In Mombassa

We visited several shops and got involved with some serious bartering for Tanzanite, a beautiful green stone that sparkled like a diamond and was quite expensive. We then went to the shoreline where workers were loading a cargo ship.

Given the unchanged atmosphere of the city, the old cargo ship, workers manually carrying heavy sacks of cement, rice and other items on their backs, it looked like a scene out of a 18th or 19th century book on slave labor. The ship was docked near the shore, long wooden planks connecting from the shore to the ship, with Africans navigating the narrow planks with heavy bags on their backs. It appeared to be a scene that was suspended in time.

The ancientness of the old city of Mombassa lent an appearance of yesteryear with its old buildings and a shameful chapter in its history. This was the Arab slave trade of Africans. One that was not as horrible as the Atlantic slave trade, but never the less the trade in human life that devastated the population of East Africa, which helped in the final decline of the great empires of the mighty continent of Africa. This Indian Ocean slave trade was started and controlled by Arab Muslims, a slave trade not spoken of very much, at least not the way that the Atlantic slave trade, or better yet "African Holocaust is discussed. Our guide, a Muslim took us on a tour of the slave castle called Fort Jesus, here we saw the dungeons, fortifications, and holding pens. Our guide was trying to explain to us about the dungeons and holding pens. At one such place he was saying that this was where the female prisoners were kept, we asked what were their crimes that they would be held in such dreadful places, which he fumbled with for an answer and finally said that the holy Quaran forbade the practice of slavery.

He said it was against slavery and those who were engaged in it were in direct violation of the principles of the holy book.

This slave dungeon is not spoken of as often as the dungeons in Senegal, Ghana, and to a lesser extent Benin, in the city of Quidah, however it like the others are an existing testimony to the horrors and genocide of the very people that gave humanity to the world.

Fort Jesus (Slave Dungeon)

City of Mombassa

We left Mombassa after another day or so and took a flight to the capital of Kenya, the Western influenced metropolis of Nairobi. We arrived and was met by our tour operator and transferred to our hotel in the center of town. We were booked at a very posh and conservative hotel that was as staid as British royalty. It was a hotel with suites, and a very beautiful and commanding view of Nairobi from the 25th floor. I wasn't complaining though as I was enjoying the luxury and the very quality service the hotel offered.

However it was quite different from the greenness and openness of the White Sands hotel in Mombassa, that had African artwork, paintings and batiks, and the roar and splash of the Indian Ocean.

Nairobi is a very busy and crowded city, with its massive traffic jams, shops and stores and numerous banks with fantastic skyscrapers and glass facades, commerce humming to the tune and rhythm of a modern metropolis. On our city tour we visited important and impressive government buildings, a huge statue sitting in the courtyard and entrance to one complex of 'Mzee' (the elder/wise old man) Jomo Kenyatta, the first president of Kenya. We drove through various commercial areas, residential communities, observing Kenyan life unfold, we walked at other times along boulevards, through various shopping areas that offered Western made and influenced commodities, through open air and housed African market-

Nairobi

places. Kenya was no different from other African countries that had foreigners (Indians, Arabs and Europeans) controlling the shops and stores and the original inhabitants of the land, the Africans operating the stalls and setups in these African marketplaces. In Kenya you will probably see more foreign involvement in the economy than most African countries.

Court house/ Kenyatta's statue

The cultural presence or should I say the lack of a cultural presence is very obvious in Nairobi, the color and flair of SeneGambia, Ghana, Nigeria, Mali, etc is absent from the streets of Nairobi. Western dress, suits and ties and European dresses is in abundance, and the shops and department stores reflect this. British influence is strong, just as dress in the business centers of America is influenced by Euro-American style and fashion, so is that of Nairobi influenced by British culture and style. In the banks and other such type places of business, the suit is always the norm as opposed to say Senegal where entering a bank, you will see many colorful Grand Bubba's on the backs of the people, customers and employees. To say the least Kenya has been culturally dominated by European views and values which will seriously continue to retard its own views and interests.

One of the doormen at the hotel that we were staying in midtown Nairobi asked me if I was from West Africa, obviously because I always wear clothes of West African prints, tailored West African 'nationalist/political' suits, and the ever present West African crown.

I explained to him that no I was from America, but visit West Africa often and that African culture has been my pursuit and my involvement for more than 30 years, and that I respect our culture and run a cultural center in New York that propagate this philosophy. He explained that unlike West Africa, in East Africa there was a lack of these cultural clothes and things, and that he was a race man but it was not encouraged in East Africa, and that in Kenya everyone wanted to be like White people. I found that many people respected this cultural presence, especially if it is in good taste.

Our last night in Nairobi our group of five persons were invited by our tour operator, a Kenyan African, who is co-owner with his British partner of a tour and travel agency to dinner at a place that was named "Carnivore", I later got to understand what the name represented. This restaurant was an exotic indoor/outdoor garden paradise, as we entered we saw chefs in high hats cooking and turning huge pieces of meat over large charcoal pits, thick aromas filled our nostrils as we passed by the pits going to our tables.

We started our evening of feasting with exotic drinks, various mixtures of alcoholic and non-alcoholic concoctions, then came the food and the meats and my experiment with the Kenyan wildlife, this time with a more broader menu than what was offered in Mombassa where I had a taste of Gazelle. After our vegetables were brought then came the meats, each chef came by with a big piece of meat on a large metal rod asking us which meat did we want to have and slicing pieces from our selection. These were meats that I had never eaten before, as was the Gazelle in Mombassa. As I mentioned earlier I am not a vegetarian but I do not usually eat red meat due to my diabetes and a sense of health concerns, however as was the case with the Gazelle I wanted to be adventurous, so I decided to try some of this meat.

The first chef that came with his offering brought a slab of Giraffe, another brought Zebra, and still another brought Crocodile, which I initially refused, but after tasting the others I asked that he return and slice me some of the 'croc'. The British fellow told us to apply some of the colorful sauces that the waiters brought on small Lazy Susans, these sauces were white, red, green and brown, each was used to put on a particular meat. Let me say the meats were delicious, and the sauce really added a unique seasoning to its taste. When I told of this experience to friends and colleagues at The Afrikan Poetry Theatre they could not believe that I had eaten all of these animals. Abiodun Oyewole of "The Last Poets" who was doing a series of workshops at the theatre just cracked up over my revelation and said "Watusi ate the whole jungle". It was an interesting and tasty experience.

The next morning we gathered our bags and prepared to head for the airport where we would begin our long journey back to the U.S. Our schedule was that we would take Uganda Airways and fly into Kampala, where we would spend the entire day and evening and catch a 1:00am flight on Alliance Air to London, and from there we would take a flight back to JFK on American Airlines. The airport was business as usual, overweight bags, hassle and hustle, and greasing palms, such is the life at African airports.

It seems that each country and airport have their own version of how much luggage and weight is allowed, never the less we paid some money and eventually boarded the plane for Kampala, the capital of Uganda. On the plane I met an interesting brother who was born in America, he said that he saw me a few times in Arusha, Tanzania at the ATA Congress, but did not get an opportunity to talk with me. Originally from Compton, California, he had been living in Tanzania for 24 years! He has been a citizen of Tanzania for 14 years when he gave up his U.S. citizenship. He worked for an NGO (Non governmental Organization) that provide assistance of various types to African countries and especially to people in rural areas.

He had a Ph.d and was obviously making out fairly well. He was married to a Tanzanian woman and had a family. His job was quite interesting and allowed him to travel to several countries in Europe and East Africa. In fact he was on his way to another conference in Uganda, after having attended the one in Arusha in his country.

I asked him did he miss the U.S.? he replied that at times there are various things that he missed but he does visit the U.S. now and then, he told me that he would be visiting California soon for a couple of weeks, and would stop in New York where he would spend perhaps another week or so before returning to Tanzania. As we talked I discovered that he knew many of the activists and cultural workers that I also knew from New York and the West Coast. This was great to meet someone who had given up America and made Africa his home, and with no regrets. Talking with him you could tell that he was comfortable, talking about his traveling, and the coffee farm that he used to operate. One important thing about living in Africa is that you have to bring enough skills and business acumen along with some cash and then you can be quite comfortable, without it the struggle to survive is multiplied many times over in Africa as compared to the United States.

He wanted us to try to get together in Uganda that day, but he said he would be in a meeting most of the day in an area far from the capital of

Kampala. I would only be there for the one day, so we parted with well wishes and hopes that we would see each other again soon either in New York or in East Africa in the near future.

By this time our group had dwindled down to 3 persons, the other two ladies left Kenya the night before in order to connect with their flight back to the United States. They were traveling on Air Aitalia and would have to stop in Rome before continuing on to the States.

The three of us had to connect with Alliance Air which would take us to London and then we would take a flight back to the U.S., however I was on a different airline from the other two who were traveling directly to Washington, D.C. We wound up in Kampala, Uganda because that was where we had to connect with Alliance Air.

We had a 12 or 13 hour layover until our flight left so we gathered our carryon bags, made our way through customs, and found a very nice air-port with very friendly and pleasant employees, I thought to myself that I was going to like this place. One of my traveling companions made her way to a telephone to call some people in the travel business that she met on a previous visit to East Africa. Unfortunately she could not reach her party and we began to wonder how we were going to spend our day. We decided to get a taxi and go into town and perhaps visit a man our col-league had been referred to.

It was quite a good distance into the city from the airport, but it allowed us to see a lot of the Ugandan landscape. Uganda is a very beautiful coun-try, for some reason I had in mind a not so developed country, one with a weak infrastructure. I suppose this might have been developed in my sub-conscious mind due to the negative reporting about Uganda, and its much talked about former President Idi Amin Dada. This perception would soon change as I enjoyed not only the greenness of the land, but also the infra-structure and a developed city center. We were headed towards a hotel that one my colleagues had suggested we go directly to meet the manager who was an associate of the tour operator in Kenya, who had referred her to. We arrived in Kampala to find a very clean organized city, and a classy hotel complex. We left some of our carry on things in the storage room and asked to see the manager.

My colleague used her finesse and charm to impress upon the manag-er the importance of our visit in regards to the tourist business and to request of him a tour of his facility. This was important because we did not have any concrete plans to spend this day and evening in Kampala. He called for someone to give us a thorough tour to see some of the rooms, the conference rooms, restaurants and offices of his staff. He said after we finished the tour to be his guest in the restaurant for lunch. We had really struck it rich and enjoyed a sumptuous lunch and interesting discussion.

The manager mentioned to us in our world wind discussion, of the active business involvement of Americans in Uganda, that there was a very strong American business presence in Kampala. I now began to see some of the reasons why President Bill Clinton visited this country during his visit to Africa in 1997. There appeared to be a concerted American involvement in a country that had become an enemy of the United States during the regime of Idi Amin Dada.

It appeared that the adversarial attitude towards Uganda was no longer there, and probably had not been there for many years.

There obviously were some things happening that were very quietly going on in Africa involving some U.S. interests. I am not sure whether these activities were clandestine or urged on by Black political figures and lobbies. In either case African Americans need to take careful notice of this and began to bring our business expertise and dollars to Africa to insure that real development takes place, development not only for foreign and domestic business interests, but development for the people of Africa themselves.

The rest of our very brief time in Uganda was spent seeing a bit of Kampala, we hired a car, a Lincoln Continental at that to tour the city, visit market places and the offices of two travel agents and tour operators. Everyone we met was so friendly and warm, I really liked the vibe in Uganda. I was sorry that our visit was so short, but we all agreed that Uganda would make for a very interesting tour. Perhaps we would take a journey into the mountain areas where the gorillas are, and to visit the national parks.

We returned to the hotel to collect our things and to bid farewell to our new friends at the hotel. We arrived at the airport and fell into the usual hassle and hustle of African airport departures and began our long journey back to 'the land of the free and home of the brave' as colorful rhythmic visions danced in our heads and drumbeats bid us farewell ❖

In Conclusion

Afriquest

Afriquest is a four week program designed to introduce inner-city youth to African life and culture. It is a program that was conceived by myself and Emmanuel Annan, director of I.E.P. (Intercultural Exchange Program) a non-profit organization located in Accra, Ghana, West Africa. I.E.P.'s primary focus is to promote peace and understanding through cultural exchange. The program is approximately 30 years old and offers an immersion into the culture of Ghana that mere tourism cannot provide. There are three facets of cultural exchange that IEP offers:

❖ **Ghana Short Stay Program** - The four week program of which Afriquest is a participant, we created out of a larger program to accommodate African American High School and College Students. Afriquest is the first youth program to participate in IEP's Ghana Short Stay Program. The itinerary in Ghana is varied and comprehensive. Courses are given that allow participants to interact, compare, and exchange ideas and information with other students and young people. Lectures are given and discussed on the following topics: History & Geography of Ghana; Ghanaian Family & Kinship Systems; Greetings and Etiquette in Ghanaian Society; Rites of Passage; Marriage Institutions; African Traditional Religion; Religious Ideas & Ethics; Chieftaincy in Ghana; Festivals of Ghana; Music in Community Life; Proverbs, Wise Sayings & Folk Philosophy.

Interspersed with the courses and lectures are hands on workshops and excursions to various museums, historical sites, villages, and contemporary and ancient cultural sites. The stay also includes visiting important chiefs and Queen Mothers in the cultural structure of Ghana, living with families part of the time, and workshops in traditional drumming, dancing, singing, cloth and cane weaving, pottery and wood working. The youth become more culturally astute and are better able to look at and understand their own culture. Bridges and ties are built that can last a lifetime.

❖ **Teachers's Program** - Teachers from various countries come to Ghana and teach in several regions to foster the exchange of pedagogical methods and ideas.

❖ Student Program - Individual students of high school and college age study for a year in Ghana while staying with host families.

Participants from all over the world, Ireland, Switzerland, Germany, England, Iceland, just to name a few countries, participate in the above programs.

Through our Afriquest program the students and adults (parents and teachers) who have been able to participate in this exciting experience since 1991, have been able to broaden their view of the world and the diversity of culture. For the youth in particular it has given them options in social cultural views and practice.

Special thanks to Emmanuel Annan, the administration and staff of IEP in Ghana; and to the hard working coordinating committee of Afriquest at The Center For Culture, The Afrikan Poetry Theatre, Inc. In Jamaica, New York (Joann Johnson, Carol Allen, Leroy Johnson, Kathleen Cole, Tehira Zambeha, Sis. Yaa Peace, Eileen Edwards, and many others) who have served the youth in this program, either as chaperones or program organizers.

I started writing about Africa long before I ever set foot on her soil. From studying and reading about the history and culture, watching films and speaking with historians and natives of this continent, I was able to gain a certain perspective and view in my minds eye.

In 1971 I wrote a poem titled "African Dream" which talked about beautiful gods and goddesses, green hills and drums playing in the villages. However it would be another twelve years before I would get the opportunity to really experience the true essence of the 'Motherland' I found that my visions and dreams were correct, but there was much more detail, more flavor after having been bitten by the African bug. Following is a poem called 'African Dream 11'

African Dream II

Sometimes I think of my Africa
of BlueBlack women stepping regally
with multi colors
gele wrapped, intricate braids
of short cropped hair and jerri curls
with big behinds and swaying to the
Fromtomfrom rhythm of Adowa
and stacato sharp beats of Jembe and Bata
and swift leg bending knee opening movements
of SeneGambia
Sometimes I think of my Africa
of the ability to manage and keep and struggle with
the remnants of a raped and colonized people
Sometimes I think of rhythmic movement
of the Teranga, Akwaba welcoming of the people
of the light and glow of the always present
beautiful and disciplined children of Africa
Sometimes I think of my Africa
of Baba Maal, Youssou Ndour, Pozo Hayes,
Kojo Minta, Pat Thomas, the Ramblers, Fela,
Sunny Ade and the exciting music of Africa
Sometimes I thin of Tiep au dieng, Bena Chin,
Yassa, Maffet, FuFu, Kenke, Wongo juice cous cous, Jolof
rice and peanut soup and palm wine and Schnapps and
Apathusi and mango and yam chips and Flagg/Club/Julbrew
and Bissop
Sometimes I think of my Africa
of green serene Akuapem mountains
of bush green Gambia, of still Senegalese plains
of intricate Dogon cliffs
of Malian mud culture, of Ivorian architecture
of dashing palms and corruption

of exciting and aggressive marketplaces
of Kermel and Soumbedioune
Banjul tourist, Bonwire and Jufferre
Sometimes I think
of Anglicized Africanized Christian hymns
of powder faces and talking in tongues
of drums and organ heart dragging sounds
Gyenyame and praises to the lord
of Humduallah and voodo heads and Akan shrines
Yoruba chants and Cheikh Ahmadou Bamba and
his spiritual African powers
Sometimes I think of my Africa
of safe Black women on dark lonely roads of
Akuapem
of extreme patience in traffic and long lines
of the structured obedient nature of the family
of them old ways like down south days
but really back home
no French ideals of humanity for me
no Anglicized models for me
Sometimes I think
of mirrored images of Blackness
reflected in the manifestation of our gods,
our spiritual icons, our religious leaders
who set the tone, gives inspiration and direction
for our growth and development
not glow in the dark Michelangelo's cousin image
Sometimes I think of my Africa
of being the economic and commercial center of the
world of standing strong on the foundation of
centuries of leadership in human development
of service to the creator
Sometimes I think of my Africa

Dakar, Senegal Skyline

Arial view of Dakar and Presidential Palace

Independence Square, Dakar

280

Approaching Goree Island

Houses on Goree Island

Tie dye Print

View from the mountain of Goree Island

Entrance to Slave House

Curator Joseph Njie, Slave Chains

Goree Island Slave House

Door of no return

Pink Lake

Senegal Independence

Cheikh Anta Diop University

Holy City of Touba, Grand Mosque

Tomb of Cheikh Ahmadou Bamba

284

Main entrance to Grand Mosque, Touba

Inside Grand Mosque, Touba

Gold Chandelier, Grand Mosque, Touba

Tomb of one of Bamba's Sons

Holy Water Monument, Touba

Library, Touba

Library, Touba

John Watusi Branch (Khadim Mbacke) in Grand Buba

Randy Weston & Jazz & African Musicians & Artists

African Dancers

Senegalese Ballet

Boabab Tree

Watusi and Baay Fall   *Watusi and Young Baay Fall*

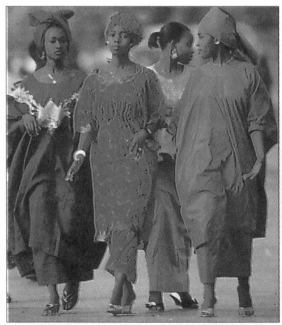

Women of Senegal

New Revolutionary Archway in Banjul,
The Gambia

Mama Tie-dye

Women of The Gambia

Family Celebration (Garba's House)

*Otumfou Osei Tutu II
New Asantehene*

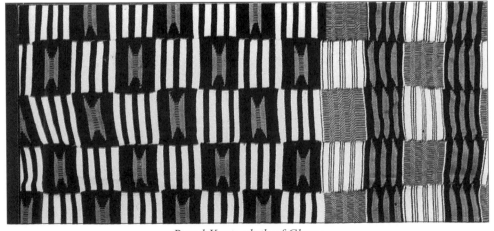

Royal Kente cloth of Ghana

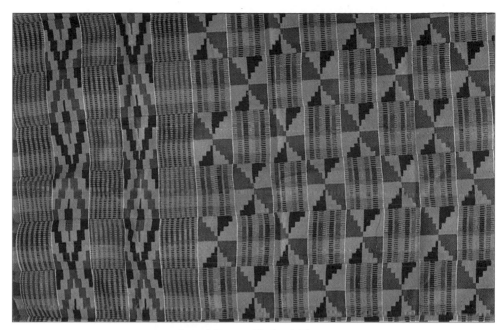

Royal Kente Cloth of Ghana

The Late Asantehene Otumfou Opoku Ware II

Oseadeeyo Addo Dankwa III

Nana Boakyewa Yiadom II (As Queen Mother)   Nana Osei Boakyewe Yiadom I

Dr. Kwame Nkrumah   Nana Osei Kwabena II

Aburi Botanical Garden, Akuapem, Ghana

Sacrifice in Adamorobe

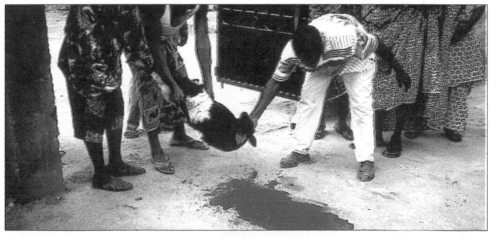

Sacrifice in Village of Adamorobe

294

Residents of the Village of Adamorobe

Bill Dyer and myself in Chief's Council

Asantehene in Royal Durbar

W.E.B. Dubois Center

Tomb of Dr. Dubois and the ashes of his wife

Nana Dankwa during book promotion with Nana Boakyewa, Gary Byrd of WLIB and myself

Black Star Square, Accra, Ghana

Kwame Nkrumah Memorial Park, Accra, Ghana

Cape Coast Castle

Cape Coast Dungeon

Fetu Afahyse

Fetu Afahyse (Annual Festival)

WOMEN OF GHANA

Abijan, Ivory Coast

Public Laundry

National Theatre, Lagos, Nigeria

Woman and Child in Ilé Ife, Nigeria

Woman and Children in Bozo Village, Mali

Camel ride, Mali

Mosque of Mud, Djenne', Mali

Dogon house in the cliffs

5th Day Market, Dogonland

Ganvie, Benin

Dogon Temple

Dogon Cliffs

Dogon Dwellings

Dogon Temple

Myself and guide on Rocks, Dogonland

Village in Dessau, Benin

Woman on cliffs, Dogon

Council House, Dogonland

Mud Cloth Artist
Djene' Mali

Watusi & Son
at Goree Island

Holy Water Fountain
inside Grand Mosque
in Touba

Tomb of
Kwame Nkrumah

Granaries, Dogon Land

Myself, ATA Member, Min. of Tourism for Zambia, ATA Member

ANC Minister of Tourism in Hotel/Casino

307

City of Pretoria, South Africa

City of Pretoria, South Africa

Cape Point, Cape of Good Hope, South Africa

Office of the President of South Africa

In the gold mines, Zimbabwe

ATA Regional Members and the Ambassador from Tanzania to the U.S. on the far right, attending a conference in Arusha, Tanzania

Masai Woman, Tanzania

Crocodile having lunch, Tanzania

Masai Man, Tanzania

*Masai
Village,*

*Decorated
door in
Mombassa,
Kenaya*

Court House/Kenyatta's Statue, Nairobi, Kenya

Nairobi, Kenya

Masai maidens, Tanzania